The State of Working Britain

MANCHESTER
UNIVERSITY PRESS

The State of Working Britain

edited by
Paul Gregg and Jonathan Wadsworth

Manchester University Press
Manchester and New York

distributed exclusively in the USA by St. Martin's Press

Published by Manchester University Press
Oxford Road, Manchester M13 9NR, UK
and Room 400, 175 Fifth Avenue, New York, NY 10010, USA
http://www.man.ac.uk/mup

Distributed exclusively in the USA by
St. Martin's Press, Inc., 175 Fifth Avenue, New York,
NY 10010, USA

Distributed exclusively in Canada by
UBC Press, University of British Columbia, 6344 Memorial Road,
Vancouver, BC, Canada V6T 1Z2

British Library Cataloguing-in-Publication Data
A catalogue record for this book is available from the British Library

Library of Congress Cataloging-in-Publication Data applied for

ISBN 0 7190 5646 2 *hardback*
     0 7190 5647 0 *paperback*

First published 1999

06 05 04 03 02 01 00 99   10 9 8 7 6 5 4 3 2 1

Typeset in Sabon with Gill Sans
by Northern Phototypesetting Co. Ltd, Bolton
Printed in Great Britain
by Biddles Ltd, Guildford and King's Lynn

Contents

Figures

Tables

Foreword

The lack of inquisitiveness about the condition of working Britain is extra-ordinary. Wages, job insecurity and economic opportunity are now urgently debated, but against a background of widespread ignorance. We still know very little, for example, about the experience of the low paid, women, or male over-50s in the labour market – so that politicians, pundits and policy advisers develop their views informed by little more than scraps of statistics, anecdote and prejudice. This book, bringing together the best of the available research and launching more of its own, sets out to close the gap. It is long overdue. Indeed it is remarkable that it has taken until the last year of the twentieth century to produce such a collection of informed economic analysis and research on the labour market.

It is also timely. We are now two years into the New Labour Government with its belief in the social and moral value of work. New Labour's view is that individuals should be helped, given incentives and at the limit compelled to help themselves find work, rather than stay at home living on Income Support; and there are to be no exceptions, including the disabled and single parents, from this general injunction. Hence the New Deal. Hence Working Family Tax Credits, so that virtuous working families get an income top-up if a parent works. Hence the interviews for single mothers and social security recipients alike to 'help them' in their search for paid employment, and upon which their social security cheques will be increasingly contingent. Work is seen as the new social glue, remoralising a culture that was drifting towards amoral dependency upon the welfare state, cutting the social security budget and re-energising otherwise static and decaying communities.

There is an obvious link with this view and the old post-war consensus's commitment to full employment. After the 1930s there was a cross-party agreement that unemployment, economic inactivity and involuntary idleness for able-bodied men and women were desperately enervating experiences and should be avoided if at all possible. But if the Butskellites in the 1950s were prepared to use the tools of Keynesian demand management to secure full employment, New Labour hopes to secure the same ends less by the state ensuring that there is a buoyant labour market, but more by structuring the pattern of individual incentives so that individuals are persuaded and com-pelled to find work.

Demand management is felt to be inflationary and in any case constrained by the veto of international bond markets; the demand for labour is increas-ingly seen as an exogenous variable over which the state can have little influence – at least if it is concerned to run the economy with sustained low inflation. Thus the only means to promote employment is on the supply side, ensuring that there are few disincentives to job hire and job search, encour-aging firms to provide training and workers to train, and making sure that those who do work are better off than if they were living on benefit.

This has been accompanied by a new ideology in which it is seen as good for workers to take individual responsibility for their lives, and to understand that benefit payments are not a citizen's right but come with reciprocal oblig-ations. This 'third way' thus seeks to reconcile the left's commitment to work, decent conditions and pay, with the right's commitment to minimalist eco-nomic management and individual responsibility. It is a proposition that seems to be widely supported in the country, and is regarded as an advance on the excesses of Keynesian demand management or Thatcherite self-help.

But policy must be developed with reference to what is actually going on in the labour market. This book may start to make a difference. For example, the book paints a sober picture of how the underlying economic structure in many parts of Britain means that the demand for male labour, especially for unskilled men in their 50s, is virtually non-existent. New Labour can devise New Deals, Working Family Tax Credits, aggressive interviews and with-draw social security benefit from those claiming they are incapable in some way from working – but they will achieve little if there is no work for this siz-able category of the labour force. The book also indicates that firms have used apparently generous pension settlements to persuade men to opt for early retirement, even though for many men with pension schemes this has been a bad 'investment' decision. Every year they continued working would have increased their final pension, and they face a longer retirement on a lower income than if they had worked nearer to their formal retirement age. Yet this issue is inadequately debated, and the policy response so far has been niggardly and mean.

What is also revealed in these pages is the increasing polarisation of work. Thus income inequality is taking on a new complexion. It is becoming increasingly important to be born and live in one of the rich urban environ-ments rather than in one of the poor cities. Again policy has made little dif-ferentiation between cities, but it is evident that the problems of, for example, Liverpool, Strathclyde, Middlesbrough and the West Midlands are qualitatively different from cities like Leeds, Edinburgh or Bristol. Virtuous and vicious circles in urban development are becoming more marked, and require a considered and activist policy response.

Moreover, the evidence here is that the economy is generating greater numbers of low-paid jobs, and that it is hard for individuals in those jobs to climb up the income distribution ladder. Low-paid jobs also tend to be insecure jobs. For those at the bottom the picture is of finding low-paid work, losing it and then being re-employed at low pay again – a disheartening and depressing way of living a life: the chance of upward progression is less than in earlier periods of history. Britain is becoming a more ossified, stratified society in which early advantages in education, family and location are increasingly fundamental to any individual's life chances. The 'low pay – no pay' cycle described in the book is, I suspect, more likely to be experienced if you live in the 'wrong' geographic parts of the country. If you want to prosper in contemporary Britain, make sure you are born to a work-rich family, committed to education and living in one of the more prosperous conurbations. To an extent it was ever thus, but this book underlines that the trends are becoming more entrenched and more marked.

An intriguing bright spot is the improvement in the lot of women, and a sharp rebuttal to the conservative New Right and their allies in New Labour who regard all forms of regulation of the labour market as necessarily counter-productive. The granting and extension of Maternity Rights along with equal pay legislation has been sometimes bitterly opposed as obstructing 'natural' economic forces, and thus inevitably limiting the growth of female employment opportunities by making women's work more expensive relative to what it should be. In fact the opposite has been the case. Women's employment has risen strongly, helped by Maternity Rights that allow women to return to the same employer after child-birth, while women's wages have begun to approach men's – one in five women now earn more than their working partners. There is a long way to go, but the trends are encouraging.

Whatever your politics and your prejudices, *The State of Working Britain* will give you food for thought. Its authors and editors should be congratulated. They have produced an important book that may deliver that rare result; a change in the way we think, analyse and talk about the world of work.

Will Hutton, 14 February 1999

Contributors

Simon Burgess is Professor of Economics at the University of Bristol and the Centre for Analysis of Social Exclusion, London School of Economics.

Tanvi Desai is Data Manager at the Centre for Economic Performance, London School of Economics.

Richard Dickens is a Research Fellow at the Centre for Economic Performance, London School of Economics.

Richard Disney is Professor of Economics at the University of Nottingham and Research Fellow at the Institute for Fiscal Studies.

Francis Green is Professor of Economics at the University of Kent at Canterbury and Associate Member at the Centre for Economic Performance, London School of Economics.

Paul Gregg is a Senior Research Fellow at the Centre for Economic Performance, London School of Economics and a member of the Council of Economic Advisers at HM Treasury.

Kirstine Hansen is a Researcher at the Centre for Economic Performance, London School of Economics.

Susan Harkness is a Lecturer at the Department of Economics, Sussex University.

Richard Jackman is Professor of Economics at the London School of Economics and Director of the Human Resources Programme at the Centre for Economic Performance.

Genevieve Knight is a Researcher at the Policy Studies Institute, London.

Stephen Machin is Professor of Economics at the University College London and Joint Group Leader of the Labour Markets Programme at the Centre for Economic Performance, London School of Economics.

Stephen Nickell is Professor of Economics at the London School of Economics.

Carol Propper is Professor of Economics of Public Policy at the University of

Bristol and the Centre for Analysis of Social Exclusion, London School of Economics.

Peter Robinson is a Senior Research Fellow at the Institute of Public Policy Research, London.

Savvas Savouri is a Quantative Strategist at Credit Lyonnais.

Julian Steer is an Economist at British Steel.

Mark B. Stewart is Professor of Economics at Warwick University.

Jonathan Wadsworth is a Researcher at the Centre for Economic Performance, London School of Economics and a Lecturer in Economics at Royal Holloway College, London.

Acknowledgments

Stephen Nickell is most grateful to Tanvi Desai and Joanna Swaffield for their valuable assistance. Richard Disney would like to thank Ylva Heden for research assistance and participants at a workshop at the Centre for Economic Performance for comments on an earlier draft. Francis Green's chapter is based, in part, upon research financed by the Economic and Social Research Council (ESRC) under grants L123251032 and R000235924. Stephen Machin's work draws on some Department for Education and Employment-funded work (jointly with Susan Harkness) on 'Graduate Earnings in Britain, 1974–95', and on some recent work published individually and with John Van Reenen. He would also like to thank Richard Dickens, Paul Gregg, Susan Harkness and Julian Steer for their help with some of the data and Alan Manning for comments. Mark B. Stewart is grateful to Richard Dickens and Paul Gregg for comments on an earlier draft and to Abigail McKnight for advice on use of the Labour Force Survey (LFS) data files. Simon Burgess and Carol Propper are very grateful to John Hills of the Centre for Analysis of Social Exclusion and to Hugh Davies of Birkbeck College for help. Their work on poverty in the United States was supported by ESRC grant R000235144.

The editors would also like to thank Tanvi Desai, without whose tireless efforts at co-ordination this book would not have appeared.

Material from the BHPS, LFS, GHS, NES, FES and RS is Crown Copyright; it has been made available by the Office for National Statistics through the Data Archive and has been used by permission. Neither the ONS nor the Data Archive bear any responsibility for the analysis or the interpretation of the data reported here.

Introduction

Asked thirty years ago to predict what the major features of the labour market of the 1990s would be, it is unlikely that even the most prescient of economists would have foreseen a tripling of unemployment, a degree of wage inequality without precedent in the last hundred years, one in five children growing up in poverty, one in two less skilled men out of work and one in five households without access to earned income. Yet, incredibly, all these events have come to pass within the last decade. Why this has occurred is the subject of this book.

Yet, it should be said that, despite these adverse developments, there have been some positive events over the same period. Women have made major advancements in the workplace. The gender earnings gap has narrowed and more women than ever are in work and staying in the workforce longer. Real wages, for those in employment, have risen. The numbers staying on in further and higher education are higher than they have ever been. The government is now pursuing an agenda to address many of the problems that have developed. The national minimum wage has arrived. Britain has agreed on the package of measures contained in the Social Charter. The unemployed are being given help to get back into work. Substantial tax and benefit reforms aim to increase the take-home value of low-paid work.

This book is an attempt to assess why all this has happened, to make the connections between events and to offer some comment on whether these developments have been good or bad for the labour market and the individuals affected. In doing so we draw on writings from a range of labour market specialists, who each contribute chapters on their own area of expertise, using a wealth of data on incomes, wages, employment and unemployment. There is more information about the labour market available than ever before and this book is intended to be, not just a reference source of events and figures, but an aid to encourage practitioners and policy makers alike to make better use of available information. Many of the chapters draw on the findings from the large and growing longitudinal or panel databases, which follow the same individual over a period of time. This makes it easier to reveal the connections between events and labour market outcomes, such as the link between low pay and unemployment. The result, we hope, is a reasonably comprehensive analysis of the British labour market over the past thirty years and an insight into possible future developments.

In undertaking this effort we were partly inspired by *The State of Working America* published by the Economic Policy Institute in Washington. Although the style is very different, their pulling together a large literature and array of statistics into a single coherent text was a powerful motivating force. Many of the issues we explore here are covered by them for the United States and have also appeared in Britain's Employment Policy Institute's *Employment Audit*, an attempt to offer a broader range of inquiry into current British labour market issues. As the labour market is exceedingly complex, diverse and dynamic, it is hoped that *The State of Working Britain* will become a regular feature, passing judgement and offering insight into labour market developments at regular intervals. The book has a number of holes which we hope to address in the future: those that come to mind immediately are issues of race, the demise of unions, inter-generational links and small firms. In some way this will go towards mitigating the current, unacceptable, practice of condensing everything we know about the labour market into a few summary statistics. Work is more important than that.

The book is divided into three parts. The first deals with the lack of jobs. The second looks at the characteristics of jobs, such as hours, tenure and youth or gender composition. The final section looks at various aspects of earnings.

At the time of writing, the economy is slowing down and rising unemployment is once again upon us. In some quarters, there is hope that the much vaunted, but little proved, flexible labour market will be able to cope better with recession than before. Certainly there is a belief that the level of unemployment should not reach the three million endured during the last two recessions. Stephen Nickell's chapter on unemployment suggests that the level of unemployment consistent with stable inflation is lower now than it has been in the past. Measures coming into play in the labour market, such as the assorted New Deals, could mean that the economy can be expanded further than before without the Central Bank or Treasury having to resort to deflationary measures that are likely to raise unemployment. Moreover, the unemployment rate need not rise as far as in the past before the threat of inflation has subsided. Richard Jackman and Savvas Savouri's chapter on regional unemployment suggests that the traditional North–South unemployment divide has substantially receded and that there is now less chance of large regional differences emerging. There is a downside to all this since the reason that Britain's regions are more balanced in terms of industrial structure is because many of the traditional employers of labour in the North

– steel, mining, shipbuilding and manufacturing – have disappeared, or been allowed to disappear.

The consequences of these actions have left lasting legacies. There are now fewer men in work than ever before and, as the chapter by Paul Gregg and Jonathan Wadsworth shows, there are more men than ever before that have given up looking for work, becoming economically inactive. The authors show that there is a direct link between an area's recent economic perform-ance and the level of economic inactivity. Areas that have done badly have more men out of work, and also more men out of work who are not mea-sured by the conventional unemployment count. This indicates that the unemployment rate is no longer a good measure of the true extent of labour market slack. Richard Disney's chapter on older men highlights how early retirement is an option increasingly used by employers in order to save on pension contributions. This then exacerbates the problem of joblessness amongst older men who in most cases no longer appear as unemployed but appear instead amongst the ranks of the long-term sick.

Indeed the problems facing older men are a recurrent theme in other chap-ters. Older men comprise a substantial fraction of the rapidly growing num-bers of workless households in Britain documented by Gregg, Kirstine Hansen and Wadsworth. Despite Britain's adequate job creation record – the number of jobs relative to the population is the same now as in the 1970s – the distribution of work has polarised with simultaneous rises in the number of households that have everyone in work and in the number of households where no one has access to earned income, currently just under one in five of all households. Even more alarming is that one in five children are growing up in a household where no one works and in 60 per cent of these households none of the adults present has worked in the last three years. Recent analysis by the Organisation for Economic Co-operation and Development (OECD) suggests that the UK has the worst record of any developed nation in this regard.

Jobs

Susan Harkness' chapter shows that, contrary to popular myth, the 24-hour economy is still not with us. But the 9-to-5 job is a thing of the past. The growth of part-time work and long hours amongst managerial and profes-sional staff means that there now really is no such thing as a standard work-ing week. While nearly 60 per cent of men have basic hours between 30 and 39, only 15 per cent work these hours when paid and unpaid overtime is included. Paul Gregg and Jonathan Wadsworth also deal with the changing patterns of job tenure. Job tenure has declined in the 1990s, but for most workers only marginally. Indeed women with dependent children are now staying with the same employer longer than ever before. The pace of new job creation has not changed much but there are now fewer long-term jobs in the economy for men. Much of this decline has fallen on workers over the age of 50. The later chapter by Paul Gregg and Jonathan Wadsworth on displacement and the cost of job loss also shows that while, on average, older workers are less likely to be made redundant, if they are unlucky enough to be laid off, the earnings loss will be much greater. Older workers face pay cuts upwards of one-third of previous earnings compared with a 10 per cent average for all displaced workers. Part of this pay gap is caused by the changing nature of jobs on offer. There are more low-paid, part-time and temporary jobs around and these feature disproportionately in the stock of vacancies so that many features of jobs on offer do not resemble the features of jobs lost. These two chapters have a large bearing on the debate over job insecurity in the United Kingdom.

Francis Green explores the subjects of skills and training. He explodes the popular conception that vocational training is an alternative to education undertaken for teenagers. Rather training appears to be a supplement to education with the bulk of training going to those with advanced educational qualifications. It is thus a driving force behind wage gaps between the well- and the less-educated, not an equalising force. This is reflected in growing numbers of young people staying on in education rather than entering work at 16. Peter Robinson highlights how the majority of young adults now stay in school or college until the age of 18. A third of each youth cohort now goes on to study for a degree or the equivalent. Together with increased returns to education, youth unemployment and, especially, the lowering of exam hurdles at 16 appear to lie behind this profound shift in behaviour.

While participation of older men has fallen, women have continued to advance into the labour market (see the chapter by Tanvi Desai, Paul Gregg, Julian Steer and Jonathan Wadsworth). Most of the rise has come primarily from women with young children in households where the partner was already in work, contributing to the rise in workless households. Maternity Rights provision has clearly helped women with young children to remain attached to the labour market and maintain job status and tenure after child birth. This in part lies behind the convergence in pay of women in full-time work towards rates achieved by men. In one out of five couples where both partners work, the woman now has the higher hourly rate of pay. Women in part-time jobs, however, are doing no better than twenty years ago. If anything the pay gap for these women has widened relative to men. Pay in part-time jobs does not reward age and experience.

Wages

One of the defining features of the last twenty years for the British labour market is the unprecedented rise in wage inequality, outlined by Stephen

Machin. Machin argues that while most attention is focused on low pay, exaggerated pay rises for those at the top of the earnings distribution are at least as important. The primary driving factor behind wage inequality appears to be that technological advancement is raising demand for skilled workers and that the supply of those skilled workers is lagging behind. Firms can only obtain skilled workers by trying to offer higher wages. The idea that wages of low-skilled workers in the West have been held back by increased competition from the developing world for goods can in no way account for most of what has gone on. Moreover there is still a substantial residual rise in inequality that cannot be explained by the simple idea that demand has exceeded supply. A steady erosion of institutions that could have protected the interests of the low paid, like trade unions or wages councils, is an important extra explanatory factor.

Low pay is sometimes thought of as a transitory state mainly applying to the young and thus may be less of a concern. If workers are able to move easily out of low-paid work, then rising wage inequality is less of an issue. The chapters by Richard Dickens and Mark Stewart show that this line of reasoning is unfounded. Dickens shows that mobility up the pay distribution is lower in the 1990s than in earlier, more equal times. Stewart shows that rather than move up the distribution, there is a growing danger that many low-paid workers are instead moving between low pay and no work. The labour market is throwing up more relatively low-paid jobs and fewer individuals in these jobs are able to advance out of them. Indeed many low-pay jobs end in an exit to unemployment and even lower wages on return to the labour market. There is a danger that Britain has managed to generate a 'Low Pay – No Pay' cycle.

Involuntary job loss results in substantial decline in wages on return; including forgone wage growth, the difference is of the order of 15 per cent. This is substantially higher for more experienced workers. These wage declines diminish with continuous subsequent employment but about half of the loss is still apparent after two years. But, as has been noted, the replacement jobs are very unstable – over 20 per cent of post-unemployment jobs (entry jobs) are temporary. Over the last twenty years, wages for entry jobs have been declining relative to other jobs and have barely risen in real terms. Simon Burgess and Carol Propper look at how all these patterns affect poverty. They conclude that widening inequality in access to work and wages underlies the massive rise in poverty in Britain over the period. In the 1980s, rampaging wage increases for the better off only, ended the conventional belief that economic growth would benefit all and so reduce poverty. Only in the 1990s, when the pace of rising pay inequality slowed down, has the incidence of poverty stabilised. Women are still likely to dominate the stock of poor. This is mainly because lone parents are some of the most likely to be poor and women are far more likely to be lone parents.

What can be done?

Can anything be done to make things better? That government can intervene for the good is seen in the improvement in women's pay and employment, where policies outlawing discrimination and the provision of maternity leave have helped narrow the earnings gap and helped keep women attached to work longer. Policies aimed at upskilling the workforce, while laudatory, will do nothing in the short run to improve the lot of the vast army of dispossessed men. Something else has to be on offer. The minimum wage, the New Deal and the Working Families Tax Credit are all to be welcomed and should help prevent the worst excesses from recurring. All the evidence suggests that problems worsen the longer individuals are out of work. Intervention at an early stage would help avoid problems building up.

This book is, in part, a description of the legacy left to the present Labour government. There are many worrying aspects of the state of working Britain which must be addressed soon if the situation is to improve. The present government is faced with a hard task. We hope that we will be able to assess the new agenda in the future.

1 Stephen Nickell

Unemployment in Britain

Keypoints

- The immediate post-war period in Britain, until the late 1960s, saw the lowest unemployment rates in the last 150 years, averaging around 2.5 per cent. During no other era have average unemployment rates fallen below around 5 per cent.

- The dramatic rise in unemployment after the mid-1970s was not due to any substantial rise in turnover. The average employee is only slightly (20 per cent) more likely to become unemployed now than thirty years ago. However, once they enter unemployment, they remain without a job for nearly three times as long.

- It is easy to understand why unemployment rose substantially in the 1970s and early 1980s. The period started with an enormous jump in commodity prices, which rose by around three times relative to output prices, putting upward pressure on wages and downward pressure on jobs.

- It is hard to understand why unemployment did not fall back to early-1970s levels in the late 1980s and 1990s, since the factor described in the previous point had been reversed. Possible explanations include the fact that certain aspects of the benefit system still encourage unemployment and that the substantial shift in demand in favour of the skilled has outpaced supply, leading to inflationary pressure in the labour market even at quite high levels of unemployment.

- Men without qualifications have a very high unemployment rate. It does not fall below 15 per cent even during a boom. By contrast, women in the same position suffer much lower levels of joblessness, with their unemployment rate barely reaching double digit levels even in the depths of slump.

- Unemployment in Britain can be reduced by a long-term strategy. This would include programmes targeted on the long-term unemployed (of the New Deal type) and on the unskilled, improved education and training for the bottom half of the ability range and reforming the benefit system.

Unemployment has probably been the most talked about economic indicator in Britain for the last fifty years. And rightly so. The work of Andrew Oswald and others (see Clark and Oswald, 1994, for example) indicates that becoming unemployed is one of the most important single causes of unhappiness. So the fact that unemployment has been so much higher for the last two decades than it was in the 1950s and 1960s is an economic problem of the first order. The extent of the problem is illustrated in Figure 1.1, where we see the dramatic rise during the 1970s and early 1980s, a rise which has been mostly sustained ever since.

In this chapter, an attempt is made to describe and explain what is going on. Unfortunately we are a long way from having a complete understanding but we do know something and what follows is an interpretation of what we know. First, we discuss how unemployment is defined. This is important because at least two definitions have been widely used for many years and unless these things are sorted out, confusion reigns. Then, we provide a brief

Figure 1.1   Unemployment rate

Source: Labour Market Trends, various issues.
Note: The unemployment rate in the United Kingdom on the ILO definition, although prior to the late 1970s, the ILO data have been spliced onto the official UK series for registered unemployment.

description of who the unemployed are, focusing on the enormous variations in the incidence of unemployment across different groups in the working population. Despite these variations, however, when overall unemployment goes up a lot, everyone's situation tends to worsen whichever group they belong to. So, next we try and understand why the unemployment rate has risen so much in the last twenty years. Finally, we set out a few ideas on how to reduce unemployment and end with some final thoughts.

What is unemployment?

The ILO rate

'Individuals are unemployed if they are currently without a job but would like one'– there are two aspects of this statement which require precise definition. The International Labour Organisation (ILO) suggests that being without a job means not working more than one hour per week. A person who works more than one hour is deemed to be employed. The ILO also suggests that in order to be considered as wanting a job, individuals must have used at least one active method to find work in the previous four weeks or be waiting to take up a job and they must be able to start work within two weeks. The unemployment rate under this definition is known as the ILO rate and is typically obtained from a sample survey such as the UK Labour Force Survey (LFS). It has the great advantage that it is based on an internationally agreed definition and is not *directly* affected by changes in the regulations governing unemployment benefit, for example.

Other definitions of unemployment

To see how the ILO rate is affected by changes in the precise details of the definition, we present in Table 1.1 a comparison of the ILO rate with the unemployment rate obtained if we include people who are seeking work but are unable to start within two weeks[1] (column 3) and if all those who want jobs are included[2] (column 4). The inclusion of those who cannot guarantee to start within two weeks adds only around one percentage point to the rate, but if we add those who say they want a job but have not actively sought work in the last four weeks, the rate goes up by a substantial 6 or 7 percentage points. This illustrates how important details of the definition are, in partic-

---

[1] For example, a woman may be unable to guarantee that she can arrange child-care within two weeks if she were able to obtain a job. This column also includes a small number of so-called 'discouraged' workers who would actively seek work except they feel there are no jobs available.

[2] These are individuals who say they want a job but have not actively sought work within the last four weeks.

Table 1.1 Various measures of unemployment

	ILO unemployed		Plus discouraged workers and those seeking work and unable to start in two weeks		Plus all those who want jobs
1977	6.1*				
1979	5.6*				
1981	9.6*				
1983	11.0*		12.3		
1984	11.7		13.1		18.3
1985	11.2		12.7		18.0
1986	11.2		12.6		18.0
1987	10.7		12.0		17.3
1988	8.7		10.6		15.4
1989	7.2		8.5		14.0
1990	6.8		8.0		13.3
1991	8.4		9.8		15.3
1992	9.8	10.6	11.4	16.4	16.3
1993	10.4	11.3		16.9	
1994	9.7	10.5		16.7	
1995	8.7	9.4		15.8	
1996	8.3	8.9		15.5	
1997	7.1	8.5		14.4	
1998	6.1	7.1		12.8	

Source: Numbers on the left are from the LFS quarterly bulletin (seasonally adjusted). Those on the right are generated from LFS data by the Employment Policy Institute.
Note: * Based on a one-week job search period rather than the four-week period in the standard ILO definition.

ular because this particular gap is considerably larger in Britain than in the major European countries.

For example, in France in 1996 the ILO unemployment rate was 12.1 per cent, considerably more than the UK rate. However, if we add in all those who are unable to start in two weeks and all those who want jobs, the French rate rises only to 13.4 per cent which is smaller than the corresponding UK rate (Table 1.1, column 4). So is this latter measure a 'better' measure of unemployment? One possible way of shedding light on this question is to look at the chances of the 'extra' individuals (those in Table 1.1, column 4 but not in column 2) gaining employment relative to the ILO unemployed. In 1996, 22.5 per cent of the ILO unemployed in the UK were employed within three months. Of the 'extra' individuals, only 6.7 per cent were employed within three months. So while some of those who are in the 'extra' category gain employment, their probability of doing so is less than one-third that of the ILO unemployed (see Gregg and Wadsworth, 1998, for a comprehensive treatment). In the light of this, the standard (ILO) definition, which requires some evidence of the desire for a job in the form of active search, is the one upon which we shall focus.

The Claimant Count

For many years, the most familiar measure of unemployment in Britain has been the Claimant Count, that is the number of individuals who are out of work and claiming benefit. Until recently, it is this measure which has been widely accepted by the general public and the government alike as *the* measure of UK unemployment. In Figure 1.2, we show the Claimant Count alongside the ILO rate. Both series show a similar pattern. After the mid-1980s, the rates have been almost identical in slumps, when unemployment is high, with the Claimant Count being somewhat lower than the ILO rate in booms.

Figure 1.2   ILO and Claimant Count unemployment rates

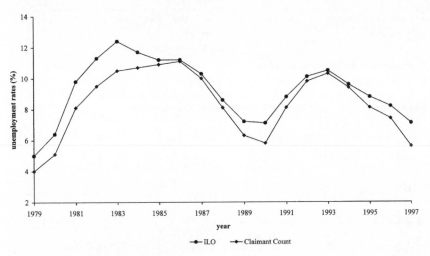

Source: *Labour Market Trends*, various issues.

Despite the fact that the two measures give a rather similar impression, the overlap of individuals in the two groups of unemployed is by no means complete. In the Spring of 1995, some 18 per cent of men who were ILO unemployed were not claimants and around 24 per cent of male claimants were not ILO unemployed. The corresponding numbers for women were 59 per cent and 37 per cent respectively (see Ghidoni, 1998: Table 2.2). It is easy to understand why some claimants are not ILO unemployed. Around two-thirds of this group are economically inactive on the ILO definition, because they do not fulfil the search or availability criteria. The remaining one-third are working on the ILO definition but work a small enough number of hours to remain eligible for benefit.

Figure 1.3a   ILO and Claimant Count unemployment: men

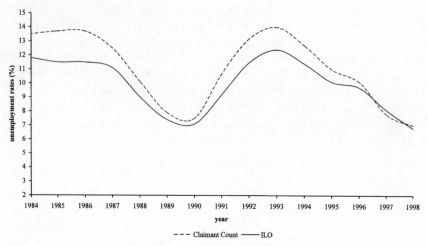

Source: Employment Trends, various issues.

Figure 1.3b   ILO and Claimant Count unemployment: women

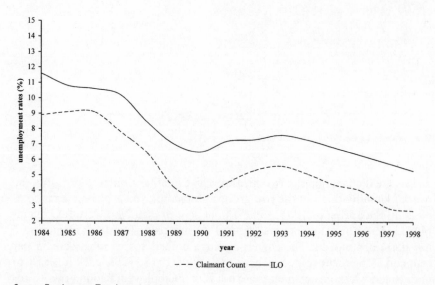

Source: Employment Trends, various issues.

The ILO unemployed who are not claimants fall foul of the eligibility criteria. To understand this, some grasp of the system is required. The unemployed who have paid or been credited with enough National Insurance Contributions in the previous two financial years were eligible for (contribution-based) employment benefits for up to twelve months. This duration was reduced to six months in October 1996. These benefits are *not* means tested. Those unemployed who do not qualify for these benefits because they have not paid enough contributions or because the twelve-month time limit has passed are eligible for a means-tested benefit, known as Income Based Job Seekers Allowance. In addition, by far the majority of 16 and 17-year-olds do not qualify for any of the above benefits.

As a consequence of these rules, the groups of ILO unemployed who are most likely to be non-claimants are: married women because they are liable to fail the means test if their husbands are working, lone parents who are placed on other benefits (Income Support) and young people who, even if they are over 17, are less likely to have an adequate contribution record. In Figure 1.3, we show the ILO rate and the Claimant Count for men and women separately and these series bring home how few ILO unemployed women are now eligible for unemployment-related benefit. It was this fact more than any other which finally discredited the Claimant Count as a measure of unemployment and led the government to choose the ILO rate as its preferred official measure.

Summary

An unemployed individual is someone who is currently without a job but wants one. The definition of unemployment we prefer is that used by the ILO. This asserts that having a job means working in excess of one hour per week and wanting a job means having actively searched within the previous four weeks and being ready to start work within the next two weeks. The main alternative measure of unemployment used in Britain is the Claimant Count, that is all those who are eligible for unemployment-related benefits. Since around half of ILO unemployed women are not eligible for benefit under the present rules, the Claimant Count measure has rightly become discredited and is no longer treated as the 'official' unemployment rate.

Who are the unemployed?

Unemployment is very far from being equally distributed across the UK labour force. Indeed there are many groups, such as professional workers, amongst whom unemployment is very rare indeed and others, such as young men without qualifications, amongst whom unemployment is commonplace.

In this section we shall provide a brief picture of the distribution of unemployment across various groups.

As we can see from Figure 1.3 in the previous section, unemployment amongst women is now consistently lower than it is amongst men, the gap being particularly noticeable during the recession of the early 1990s. This is most unusual in the European context, for in nearly all the countries of Continental Europe, men are less likely to be unemployed than women with the difference in Southern Europe being substantial. Only in Sweden does male unemployment exceed that of women by as large an amount as in the United Kingdom.

In Table 1.2, we see that this gap is consistent across age groups and that it has grown since the 1970s. In unemployment terms, women have certainly done better than men over the last two decades despite their increasing rates of participation in the labour force over the same period. Comparing the different age groups, younger workers have substantially higher unemployment rates than their elders, a feature which is common to nearly all OECD countries with the notable exception of Germany. Furthermore, in the United Kingdom, we can see that the relative position of the young has worsened since the 1970s, particularly in comparison to the over-fifties, although the non-employment rates of this latter group have risen substantially as more workers retire early for one reason or another.

Table 1.2 Unemployment rates by age

	All			Men			Women		
	16–24	25–49	50–59/64	16–24	25–49	50–64	16–24	25–49	50–59
1975	7.8	4.9	6.0	7.9	4.1	6.1	7.8	6.2	5.7
1985	17.2	9.4	7.7	18.5	9.4	8.5	15.5	9.2	6.1
1990	10.5	6.2	6.9	11.5	6.0	7.8	9.3	6.5	5.3
1991	14.6	7.6	7.6	16.7	8.0	8.8	11.9	7.0	5.4
1992	16.4	8.6	8.4	19.8	10.0	10.2	12.2	6.7	5.0
1993	18.4	8.9	9.7	21.9	10.5	11.9	13.9	6.8	5.8
1994	17.1	8.4	9.1	20.2	9.8	11.0	13.2	6.6	5.8
1995	15.7	7.6	7.5	18.5	8.6	9.1	12.0	6.3	4.8
1996	15.3	7.2	6.9	18.4	8.2	8.5	11.3	5.9	4.4
1997	13.7	6.1	6.0	15.9	6.8	7.0	11.0	5.1	4.4
1998	12.4	5.2	4.9	14.0	5.6	5.8	10.4	4.8	3.5

Source: Spring LFS, ILO definition.
Note: Unemployment rates are a percentage of the working age population.

Turning now to the unemployment differences by qualifications. Table 1.3 shows the importance of education in determining joblessness. Those without any educational qualifications are much more likely to be unemployed than any other educational group in the labour force, with the differential being particularly marked amongst men. Furthermore, the situation of those without qualifications has worsened considerably since the late 1970s, both absolutely (in terms of percentage point increases) and even relatively (in terms of the ratios of unemployment rates). This, of course, reflects the worsening position of this group in terms of earnings over the same period (see Chapter 11) and is, at least in part, due to the significant fall in demand for unskilled workers. This shift seems to have influenced men more than women on the unemployment front, so that even in the recent boom the unemployment rate of men without qualifications has not managed to fall below 15 per cent.

Table 1.3 Unemployment rates by level of qualification

	1979	1985	1990	1991	1992	1993	1994	1995	1996	1997	1998
All											
degree	2.1	4.1	2.9	4.2	4.7	5.4	5.2	4.5	4.1	3.3	3.0
higher intermediate	3.2	8.2	5.5	7.3	8.8	8.8	8.3	7.9	6.4	6.0	4.2
lower intermediate	4.0	11.4	6.9	8.8	9.4	10.2	10.0	9.0	8.4	7.6	7.1
none	7.1	16.5	11.6	13.4	14.5	16.2	15.7	14.6	13.4	13.1	12.2
Men											
degree	1.5	3.4	2.2	3.9	5.0	6.0	5.9	4.8	4.5	3.5	3.0
higher intermediate	2.4	8.2	5.5	7.7	10.3	10.7	9.8	8.7	7.4	6.6	4.5
lower intermediate	3.3	12.4	7.3	10.1	10.8	11.7	11.2	11.1	9.8	8.8	8.3
none	7.0	19.1	13.6	16.3	17.6	19.6	19.2	19.0	18.1	17.4	15.6
Women											
degree	3.4	5.7	4.2	4.7	4.2	4.6	4.2	3.9	3.5	3.1	2.9
higher intermediate	4.2	8.2	5.7	6.2	6.6	6.1	6.1	6.2	4.5	5.0	3.8
lower intermediate	5.3	10.6	6.6	7.7	7.7	8.4	8.5	7.1	7.0	6.3	5.9
none	7.2	13.0	9.2	10.0	9.9	11.3	10.6	9.8	8.7	8.5	8.4

Source: Spring LFS, ILO definition.

These features of the distribution of unemployment are equally reflected in the unemployment differentials by social class reported in Table 1.4. As we might expect, the unemployment rates among semi-skilled and unskilled men are much higher than those of any other group and the social class differences in unemployment for women are very modest by comparison.

Table 1.4 Unemployment rates by social class

	1985	1990	1991	1992	1993	1994	1995	1996	1997	1998
All										
professional	1.5	1.2	2.4	3.1	4.2	3.5	3.0	2.6	2.2	1.4
intermediate	3.6	2.8	3.4	4.4	4.7	4.4	3.8	3.6	3.2	2.3
skilled non-manual	6.0	4.5	5.8	6.8	7.5	6.9	6.7	5.9	5.4	4.6
skilled manual	7.8	5.7	8.8	11.6	12.6	11.4	9.4	8.5	7.4	5.8
semi-skilled	10.4	8.0	10.6	14.3	14.4	13.7	11.9	11.4	10.8	8.7
unskilled	14.4	11.6	12.9	16.2	17.4	16.9	15.8	16.3	15.2	11.5
Men										
professional	1.3	1.1	2.3	3.1	4.3	3.6	3.3	2.9	2.3	1.2
intermediate	3.4	2.8	3.7	5.3	5.4	5.3	4.3	4.3	3.7	2.4
skilled non-manual	5.3	4.5	7.0	8.2	10.3	8.4	8.9	7.6	6.8	5.7
skilled manual	7.8	5.6	8.9	12.3	13.4	12.1	9.8	8.8	7.6	5.9
semi-skilled	12.3	8.8	12.3	17.3	17.7	16.7	14.6	14.6	13.5	10.4
unskilled	21.1	16.4	21.2	26.8	27.0	26.2	24.0	25.0	23.0	17.1
Women										
professional	3.0	1.7	2.8	3.2	3.7	3.3	2.0	1.2	1.9	2.1
intermediate	3.9	2.7	3.0	3.1	3.7	3.3	3.1	2.8	2.6	2.2
skilled non-manual	6.3	4.4	5.3	6.2	6.4	6.3	5.8	5.2	4.9	4.1
skilled manual	7.8	6.5	8.4	7.9	8.3	7.7	7.1	6.9	5.9	5.4
semi-skilled	8.3	7.2	8.6	10.6	10.5	10.1	8.8	7.8	7.8	6.8
unskilled	7.3	6.6	6.0	6.7	8.2	8.1	7.2	7.7	7.2	5.2

Source: Spring LFS, ILO definition.

Finally, it is worth looking at the distribution of unemployment across ethnic groups, not least because the differences are so startling. In Table 1.5, we report unemployment rates across five ethnic groups. As might be expected whites have by far the lowest unemployment rates with Indians having somewhat higher rates and the other groups suffering massively higher unemployment. Amongst all ethnic groups, the relative position of men has worsened since the late 1970s and another noticeable feature is how badly black men did in the last recession, with their unemployment rate nearly trebling between 1990 and 1993. This indicates that this group faces particularly high levels of job insecurity when times are bad.

This completes our brief picture of the composition of unemployment in Britain and we now turn to the question of why unemployment changes so much over time.

Table 1.5 Unemployment rates by ethnic origin

	1979	1985	1990	1991	1992	1993	1994	1995	1996	1997	1998
All											
white	5.0	10.3	6.8	8.4	9.4	9.9	9.2	8.2	7.8	6.6	5.7
black	9.6	20.4	12.5	16.7	21.9	28.4	26.8	24.1	20.4	18.9	14.6
Indian	6.1	17.2	9.8	12.5	12.7	12.7	13.4	11.5	12.4	7.9	9.1
Pakistani/											
Bangladeshi	11.0	30.3	20.0	26.6	25.3	31.9	28.3	26.7	25.2	22.8	20.4
mixed and other	3.0	15.1	11.6	12.2	13.6	17.8	19.1	15.9	14.2	13.5	12.7
Men											
white	4.4	10.5	6.9	9.2	11.1	11.9	10.7	9.5	9.1	7.6	6.3
black	7.6	22.4	12.7	18.9	28.1	34.7	33.6	26.6	21.5	20.3	15.4
Indian	4.5	18.2	8.9	13.2	13.3	13.7	14.4	12.3	12.8	7.4	9.1
Pakistani/											
Bangladeshi	8.1	28.1	17.5	26.7	25.6	31.9	29.4	27.5	25.1	22.4	19.7
mixed and other	2.1	16.2	13.5	11.4	15.9	16.9	21.8	17.3	19.0	15.7	14.8
Women											
white	5.8	9.9	6.6	7.4	7.1	7.3	7.1	6.4	6.0	5.3	4.9
black	11.9	18.2	12.4	14.4	15.1	20.8	18.5	21.5	19.3	17.4	13.7
Indian	9.2	15.5	11.4	11.5	11.9	11.3	11.9	10.2	11.7	8.8	9.0
Pakistani/											
Bangladeshi	32.4	43.5	28.0	26.4	24.3	32.1	25.0	24.4	25.7	24.0	22.3
mixed and other	5.0	13.4	9.1	13.3	10.3	19.1	15.4	14.0	8.1	10.6	10.1

Source: Spring LFS, ILO definition.

The history of unemployment

As we saw earlier (Figure 1.1), unemployment in Britain remained very low through the 1950s and 1960s, then rose rapidly, reaching a peak in the early 1980s. Subsequently it has fluctuated around a relatively high level although there is some evidence that there has been a decline in long-run average unemployment rates during the 1990s. In this section, we shall attempt to shed some light on these drastic fluctuations, starting with a brief discussion of the theoretical background.

Why does unemployment change?

Unemployment falls when aggregate real demand expands faster than the growth potential of the economy and rises when there is a relative contraction. Since unemployment is undesirable, why does the government simply not organise an expansion of real demand which is so large that it eventually eliminates unemployment? Such demand expansion is certainly possible if fiscal policy is expansionary and interest rates are reduced sufficiently,[3] so what is the problem? To see what might happen, we look at the history of unemployment policy since the mid-1980s.

In 1986, unemployment had been in excess of 11 per cent since 1982. By the Spring of 1990, it had fallen below 7 per cent. This dramatic fall was produced in part by expansionary fiscal and monetary policy, in part by an international boom and in part by a large fall in commodity prices in the mid-1980s. Why did the unemployment fall come to an end? Basically because inflation, as measured by the rise in the price of UK output (GDP deflator), rose from 2.5 per cent per annum in 1986 to 7.8 per cent per annum in 1990. Indeed during one month in 1990, the headline inflation rate (based on the Retail Price Index) reached double figures. Furthermore, in 1990, the trade balance had moved into deficit to the tune of 4 per cent of GDP. The government began to worry about the rise in inflation and the trade deficit in 1988, and the short-term interest rate (Treasury Bill Rate) rose from around 8 per cent in the Spring of 1988 to 15 per cent by the Winter of 1989. The policy contraction started to operate on inflation and unemployment after 1990 and by 1993, unemployment had risen to 10.5 per cent with GDP price inflation falling to 3.4 per cent along with a considerable improvement in the trade balance. By 1994, GDP inflation had sunk to 1.3 per cent.

Already by 1992, the government was anxious about the high level of unemployment and by the Winter of 1992, the short-term interest rate had fallen to 6.5 per cent from over 10 per cent at the beginning of that year.[4] Again, within two years unemployment started to fall again and as I write it has reached 6.2 per cent. However, it seems likely that it will begin increasing again fairly soon. As is well known, interest rate policy is now in the hands of the Bank of England's Monetary Policy Committee and they were already worrying about inflationary pressure and thus raising interest rates by early Summer of 1997. It is this policy shift which is likely to generate a turnround in the direction of unemployment rates.

So what we have is a clear picture (see Figure 1.4) of rising inflation and low unemployment in booms, and falling inflation and high unemployment in slumps. When unemployment gets too low, the rise in inflation tends to induce a policy shift in a contractionary direction. When unemployment gets too high with inflation falling, this tends to induce a policy shift towards

[3] If such a policy was felt by financial markets to be wholly irresponsible, there could be difficulties. Furthermore, the present situation in Japan reveals that there can be practical problems in generating a demand expansion. However, it would be perfectly possible, today, to organise a demand expansion in the United Kingdom which would reduce unemployment substantially.

[4] Britain had, of course, left the European Exchange Rate Mechanism in the intervening period.

Figure 1.4 Unemployment and the change in inflation

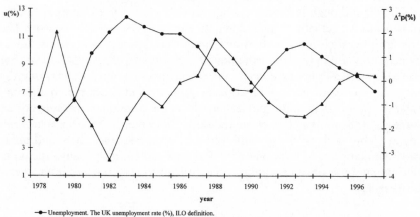

—●— Unemployment. The UK unemployment rate (%), ILO definition.

—▲— The change in inflation (% points p.a.). The annual change in the rate of inflation of the UK GDP deflator (3yr centred moving average).

Source: Economic Trends, Annual Supplement 1998, Office for National Statistics.

expansion. There is also a general tendency for the trade deficit to worsen when unemployment is low. To some extent, the institution of the Monetary Policy Committee is an attempt to try and reduce the size of these business cycle fluctuations. Whether it is successful in this regard remains to be seen.

This pattern of inflation rising and the trade balance worsening when unemployment gets too low and inflation falling and the trade balance improving when unemployment gets too high suggests the following. During any particular period, there is some baseline level of unemployment such that if actual unemployment moves too far below it, then inflation starts rising and the trade balance deteriorates. This continues until macroeconomic policy is reversed, unemployment moves above the baseline level, inflation then falls and the trade balance improves. This baseline level of unemployment is generally known as the 'equilibrium rate' or the 'natural rate' or the 'NAIRU' (non-accelerating inflation rate of unemployment). Only the first of these names seems sensible, so we shall use it in future. The natural rate is a misnomer, since there is nothing natural about it. As we shall see, it can be systematically changed by some types of policy (not monetary or fiscal policy). The NAIRU is a misnomer because it should actually be the *non-changing* inflation rate of unemployment. Non-accelerating is one derivative too many.

Despite its name, the equilibrium rate may change quite significantly from one decade to the next. How and why it might have changed in Britain we shall discuss below. What is important to understand here is that, broadly speaking, it cannot be changed by messing around with monetary, fiscal or exchange rate policy. What these policies can do is change the way in which actual unemployment fluctuates around the equilibrium rate – they cannot generally influence the equilibrium rate itself.

Finally, although it is easy enough to talk about the equilibrium unemployment rate, actually pinning down the number is less straightforward. The equilibrium rate is influenced by any factor that systematically changes inflationary pressure in the labour market *at a given level of unemployment*. For example, increases in payroll taxes or income taxes or value added tax (VAT) may all potentially increase inflationary pressure and hence the equilibrium rate. A rise in trade union power may increase inflationary pressure or an increase in the mismatch between the skill requirements of job vacancies and the available skills of the unemployed job searchers. Since these and many other similar factors, both observed and unobserved, may change the equilibrium rate, it is obviously going to be difficult to keep track of it on a year-on-year basis.

The history of actual and equilibrium unemployment

The key feature of the path of unemployment in the post-war period is the fact that it is much higher in the period after 1975 than in the period before. Before looking at this more closely, it is worth placing these changes in a broader historical context. Broadly speaking, when thinking about UK unemployment, we can divide the last 144 years into four periods, namely 1855–1914, 1920–39, 1945–75, 1975–98. During the first of these periods, unemployment probably fluctuated around a long-run average of around 5 per cent (or more), during the second it fluctuated around 9 per cent, during the third it fluctuated around 2.5 per cent and during the last it fluctuated around 7 per cent to 9 per cent.[5] It is clear from this that the third period is quite exceptional and is the one on which we can expect future economic historians to focus.

In order to understand what has happened in the post-war period, we must first attempt to make a rough estimate of the path of the equilibrium unemployment rate. In order to do this, we can make use of the fact that when actual unemployment is well above the equilibrium rate, we can expect to observe falling inflation and/or a large surplus on the balance of payments. Conversely, when actual employment is well below the equilibrium rate, we can expect rising inflation and/or a large deficit on the balance of payments. So when inflation is rising and the balance of payments is in deficit, equilibrium unemployment will be below the actual rate. And the gap will be larger, the faster inflation is rising and the bigger is the payments deficit. In work elsewhere, we have calibrated this relationship (see Layard *et al.*, 1991: 435–48) and this underlies the numbers reported in Table 1.6. The numbers in the final row are estimates of the so-called 'structural' unemployment rate

---

[5] The published data have been adjusted in an attempt to make these numbers comparable.

Table 1.6 Estimates of equilibrium unemployment

	1969–73	1974–81	1981–86	1986–90	1991–97	1994–98
Unemployment (%)	3.4	5.8	11.3	8.9	9.0	8.0
Change in inflation (% p.a.)	1.5	1.1	–1.2	0.5	–0.8	–0.1
Balance of payments deficit (% of potential GDP)	–0.7	0.9	–1.3	0.8	0.8	0.3
Equilibrium unemployment (%)	3.8	7.5	9.5	9.6	9.1	7.3
Equilibrium unemployment (%) (OECD measure)			9.1	9.2	7.9	7.5

Sources: unemployment, *Employment Trends*; inflation, balance of payments, *Economic Trends*; equilibrium unemployment, authors' calculations, exactly as described in Layard *et al.* (1991), pp. 442–5; equilibrium unemployment (OECD measure), provided by OECD. Calculation described in Elmeskov *et al.* (1998), Appendix, p. 29.

Notes: Prior to 1990, the values of inflation changes and the trade balance are lagged one year and two years respectively to take account of the time it takes for these factors to feed into unemployment. After 1990 we use current values because the reaction of unemployment to economic conditions appears to be more rapid in recent years. 1998 numbers are forecasts taken from *Economic Trends*, October 1998, and the *OECD Employment Outlook*, 1998.

provided by the OECD (see Elmeskov *et al.*, 1998). The overall pattern of the estimates of the equilibrium rate from the two sources gives the same impression, despite the difference in the underlying methods of calculation.

The notable features of this pattern begin in the late 1960s. Earlier, both actual and equilibrium unemployment were relatively stable at around 2.5 per cent. Until 1980 unemployment was sustained below the equilibrium rate at the cost of rising inflation and a balance of payments deficit in the latter part of the period. Then in the first half of the 1980s unemployment rose above the equilibrium rate with falling inflation and a large payments surplus. As unemployment fell relative to a stable equilibrium rate in the late 1980s, inflation began to rise and the balance of payments went into deficit again. More recently the equilibrium rate appears to have fallen and currently actual employment is probably a little below it, although it is unlikely to remain so for very long.

What explains the changes in the equilibrium rate?

The key features of the path of equilibrium unemployment which we must address are first, why did it rise so dramatically from the late 1960s to the early 1980s and second, why has it not fallen more rapidly after the mid-1980s? It is worth pointing out at the outset that we do not have a complete answer to these questions. In particular, we do not really know why equilibrium unemployment was so low in the 1950s and 1960s, not only in Britain but in almost every country in the OECD with the possible exception of the United States.

Turning to the first question, it is worth mentioning initially that unemployment has not risen dramatically because of any substantial increase in turnover. In Figure 1.5 we show the average probability of a person in work entering unemployment in any given month. This average probability in the 1980s and 1990s is around 20 per cent higher than in the late 1960s but given that unemployment has risen by around 300 per cent over the same period, the contribution of the increase in inflow rates to the overall rise in unemployment is very small. What this means is that the average employee is only slightly more likely to become unemployed now than thirty years ago. However, once a person enters unemployment, they remain without a job for nearly three times as long. So while job loss is only a bit more common than it was in the late 1960s, it is a much more serious event because it takes so much longer, on average, to get back into work.

In Figure 1.6, we show how this enormous rise in the average duration of unemployment spells has generated a substantial increase in the number of long-term unemployed (those without work for over twelve months). We see that in the late 1960s, only around 17 per cent of the unemployed could be deemed long term. By the mid-1980s, this proportion exceeded 40 per cent. While this is not close to the proportion in some European countries with

Figure 1.5 Monthly percentage probability of entering unemployment

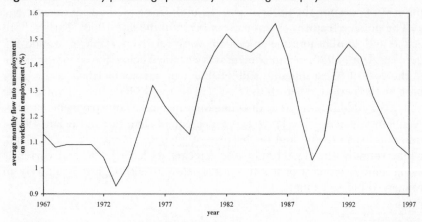

Notes: These data represent the standardised monthly inflow into unemployment excluding school-leavers, normalised on the workforce in employment. The former are currently published monthly in the *Employment Gazette* (Table 2.19) and were first published in the *Gazette* of September 1976 (Table 117) going back to 1967. Various revisions were made in 1980 (excluded self service), 1982 (move from registration to Claimant Count) and 1983 (GB to UK). The data have been adjusted to the most recent definition (i.e. UK Claimant Count).

Figure 1.6 Percentage of the unemployed with duration exceeding 12 months

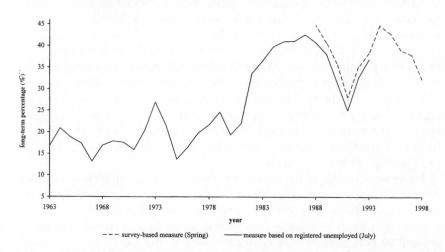

- - - survey-based measure (Spring)   ——— measure based on registered unemployed (July)

Sources: The survey-based measure is calculated from the Labour Force Survey and the registered unemployment measure is from *Labour Market Trends*.

Belgium, for example, having a proportion typically in excess of 60 per cent, the British long-term unemployed still form a substantial and important group. Aside from the personal costs of being without work for long periods, this has a significant macroeconomic impact because the long-term unemployed tend to lose skills and motivation as well as being discriminated against by prospective employers. This weakens their attachment to the labour force, making them far less likely to obtain work than the short-term unemployed. So they become ineffective at holding down wage inflation and this leads to the impact of adverse shocks to the economy persisting for very long periods.

Looking now at the specific factors underlying the rise in equilibrium unemployment, the increase from the mid-1960s and in the early 1970s is probably due to a marked increase in the generosity of the unemployment benefit system over this period allied to a sharp rise in trade union pressure on wages. This latter appears to have been part of an international shift which saw the number of industrial conflicts per employee in the OECD almost double in the period from 1967 to 1974. (Incidentally, this number has declined continuously since 1974 to less than half its 1967 level!)

The period from the early 1970s to the early 1980s saw an enormous rise in commodity prices (from 1972 to 1980, they rose by around three times relative to OECD output prices) and this was the major force behind the rise in equilibrium unemployment during this period despite the offset due to North Sea oil.

Other factors which have been discussed with reference to the rise in equilibrium unemployment include the rise in taxes on labour, particularly payroll taxes, the introduction of employment protection legislation and the sharp increase in real interest rates at the start of the 1980s. The impact of taxes on equilibrium unemployment is controversial. There is a general consensus that payroll taxes, *per se*, are of no special importance since they have more or less the same impact on the labour market as personal income taxes or VAT, for example. So there is no particular unemployment cost in switching taxes from VAT to employers' payrolls, say, since both taxes are shifted mainly onto workers.[6] This explains why, for example, Denmark and Australia do not appear to gain any special benefits on the unemployment front from having virtually no payroll taxes.

However, the role of the overall tax rate on labour, which is the sum of the payroll, income and consumption tax rates, is less clear-cut. There are numerous conflicting research results here (see Nickell and Layard, 1998 for a summary), but it is possible that the rise in the overall labour tax rate of around 10 percentage points from the 1960s to the 1980s may have contributed to the rise in equilibrium unemployment to the tune of a percentage point (see Nickell, 1998: 814–15 for more detail). On the other hand employment protection legislation and real interest rates have only a very minor role. There is little strong evidence that employment protection has any impact on the equilibrium unemployment rate although it does reduce adjustment speeds. As for real interest rates, the general consensus is that even very large changes in the real interest rate have only very small effects on equilibrium unemployment (see Nickell, 1998: 815 for details), so shifts in the real interest rate in Britain make essentially no contribution to understanding the long-run rise in unemployment.

The second issue we noted at the beginning of this section was the question as to why equilibrium unemployment has not fallen faster and further since the mid-1980s than it apparently has done (see Table 1.6). So why should we have expected it to fall far and fast? Basically because many of the original causes of the rise in the equilibrium rate have gone into reverse. First, commodity prices are, in real terms, back where they were at the end of the 1960s. Second, the unemployment benefit system appears to have been substantially toughened up over the last decade with lower replacement rates and stiffer work testing. Third, the power exercised by unions over wage determination has been weakened, although by how much it is hard to say. These crucial factors have all reverted back towards their levels in the 1960s. Has there been anything to offset this, for equilibrium unemployment is nowhere near the 1960s level?

[6] An important exception to this statement applies to workers who are paid the minimum wage. Since their wages cannot adjust downwards when there is a switch from VAT to payroll taxes, the increased tax burden is shifted to employers who will then reduce the employment of the relevant group of employees.

First, it is not clear that shifts in the benefit system are all one-way. In particular, it is worth noting that housing benefit (which pays the rent) represents a very substantial part of total benefits for single persons when they are unemployed and is withdrawn at a rapid rate (65p for every £1 of net income) when they are employed. In high rent areas (such as London), this substantially reduces the incentive to work. Second, after the very deep recession of the early 1980s and encouraged by the indefinite availability of benefits, the proportion of long-term unemployed was very high (more than 40 per cent over one year). This markedly increased the persistence of high unemployment because, for a variety of reasons, the long-term unemployed find it very difficult to get back into work. Third, the decline in the value of North Sea oil production since the mid-1980s has put pressure on the trade balance and this has, in turn, tended to raise equilibrium unemployment.

However, perhaps the most important factor has been the collapse in demand for unskilled workers over the last two decades caused both by technical change (e.g. IT and personal computers) and by competition from the Newly Industrialised Countries (NICs). There has also been a substantial fall in the supply of unskilled workers over the same period but in the 1980s this did not keep pace with the fall in demand. On the other side of the coin, of course, the rise in demand for *skilled* workers appears to have outpaced supply over the same period (see Nickell and Layard, 1998 for further details). This has a significant impact on the equilibrium unemployment rate because skill shortages can generate inflationary pressure in the labour market even at historically high levels of unemployment. Our best estimates indicate that this has been a significant factor in sustaining equilibrium unemployment in Britain into the 1990s (see Nickell and Bell, 1995) which will only fade away when the supply of skilled workers catches up with the demand.

To summarise, despite the supply-side changes induced by government policy and the significant decline in commodity prices during the 1980s, equilibrium unemployment in Britain remains relatively high for a number of reasons. First, certain aspects of the benefit system still encourage unemployment in general and long-term unemployment in particular (notably the housing benefit system, particularly its impact on single people, and indefinite benefit availability with no serious changes in regime). Second, the decline in the value of North Sea oil production has tended to raise equilibrium unemployment by putting pressure on the trade balance. Third, the substantial shift in demand against the unskilled and in favour of the skilled has outpaced the changes in relative supply. This means that even when unemployment is at a historically high level, inflationary pressure tends to appear in the labour market because of shortages of labour with the right kinds of skill. Finally, it must be emphasised that this is not an exhaustive list. There are undoubtedly other important causes of the persistence of high unemployment which remain to be identified.

What can we do about high unemployment?

It is most important to recognise that policies to combat high unemployment over the long term are unlikely to work rapidly. What is required is a consistent strategy.

Where *not* to look for the answer

Cunning demand-side policies   For example, instituting an independent Bank of England, joining the EMU, staying out of the EMU etc. These policies may be of value in their own right by helping to reduce economic fluctuations, but they will not have much impact on the average level of unemployment about which the economy fluctuates.

Reducing labour supply   For example, job sharing, *imposed* cuts in working hours, early retirement, persuading women that their place is in the home etc. Policies of this type increase inflationary pressure at any given level of labour demand unless they are precisely targeted on workers whom nobody wishes to employ. Since the rise in inflationary pressure must be combatted, labour demand is reduced and we typically end up with similar levels of unemployment, lower employment and lower output. So unemployment is the same and the country is poorer. Note that we refer to *imposed* cuts in working hours to distinguish them from cuts which are freely chosen or negotiated. The latter are simply part of the process of getting richer and taking some of the increased wealth in the form of leisure.

Cutting employment protection   There is no strong evidence that employment protection legislation has any impact on levels of unemployment although it slows down the speed at which the economy responds to shocks, thereby increasing the persistence of unemployment. Thus it may encourage the persistence of high unemployment after an adverse shock although the effect is not large.

Where to look for the answer

Programmes targeted on the long-term unemployed   A typical example would be job subsidies for the long-term unemployed of the type currently being instituted for young people in the New Deal programme. These may help because the long-term unemployed tend to become discouraged and are often discriminated against by employers. Consequently, they play little role in holding down inflation. Ultimately, it is worth constructing a scheme which prevents long-term unemployment completely by forcing individuals off unemployment after a certain period, with the government providing various alternative options. The proposed New Deal programme for those over 25 is precisely along these lines.

Programmes targeted on the unskilled   The general idea is to raise the returns to work for those with low skills as well as reducing the cost of employing them. Possibilities include cutting payroll taxes for the unskilled or extending the existing system of in-work benefits to families and single persons without children.[7] More generally it is worth bearing in mind that policies focused on getting the unskilled into reasonably paid work are of vital importance. As time goes on, the market rewards for unskilled work are likely to decline substantially, particularly relative to the market rewards for crime and other anti-social activities. Basic policies to counteract this involve either subsidising unskilled work or, in the longer term, reducing the supply of unskilled workers in order to raise their market rewards. This leads on to the next topic.

Education and training   As we have already seen, the shift in demand against the unskilled seems to have outpaced the shift in supply in the same direction with adverse consequences. Over the longer term, this suggests that we must focus on improving the quality and quantity of education and training for the bottom half of the ability range. Many ways of doing this have been proposed but any reasonable costing of such an activity will include the transfer of resources away from the top 30 per cent of the ability range. For example, it must be right to transfer resources from higher education to nursery or post-school vocational education and the obvious way to do this is to impose some form of graduate tax rather than go down a fee-based route.[8] In the long run, of course, the benefits in the form of reduced expenditure on crime prevention, prisons, unemployment benefit and so on will substantially offset the increased education and training costs.

Reform the benefit system   The overriding principle must always be to maintain the rewards of working relative to not working while sustaining the well-being of those without work. Thus, wherever possible, it is best to avoid providing benefits which depend solely upon an individual not working. Just as important is to avoid benefit structures which discourage spouses from working. This points in the direction of an insurance-based rather than a welfare-based system. Unfortunately, the Job Seekers Allowance introduced in 1996 was a move in the opposite direction, reducing the insurance element (from twelve months to six months) and raising the welfare element. I am

---

[7] We currently have in-work benefits for individuals with children. These take the form of Family Credit, shortly to be replaced by the tax-based Working Families Tax Credit.

[8] Arguably the present £1,000 fee with its attendant loan/payback rules is an attempt to create a graduate tax while calling it a fee, the word *tax* being taboo.

also in favour of raising the level of unemployment benefit for a limited period (say six months) from its current miserable level, since I feel there is little to be gained from plunging families into poverty the instant they become unemployed. Allied to this, there should be a time limit on benefits of the type described under the long-term unemployed heading.

Final thoughts

Unemployment in Britain is high by historical standards and can be reduced by the introduction of a long-term strategy. Some ideas on what should be included in such a strategy are programmes targeted on the long-term unemployed and on the unskilled, improving education and training for the bottom half of the ability range and reforming the benefit system. However, even with an effective strategy in place, it is hard to imagine that we could ever return to the exceptionally low rates of the immediate post-war period. Reducing the equilibrium unemployment rate to 5 per cent would be a very significant achievement.

References

Clark, A. E. and Oswald, A. J. (1994), 'Unhappiness and unemployment', *Economic Journal*, 104, 648–59.

Elmeskov, J., Martin, J. P. and Scarpetta, S. (1998), *Key Lessons for Labour Market Reforms: Evidence from OECD Countries' Experience*, Organisation for Economic Co-operation and Development (OECD), Paris.

Ghidoni, M. (1998), *Alternative Measures of Unemployment in the UK*, M. Phil. thesis, University of Oxford.

Gregg, P. and Wadsworth, J. (1998), 'Unemployment and non-employment: unpacking economic activity', *Economic Report*, 12:6, Employment Policy Institute.

Layard, R., Nickell, S. and Jackman, R. (1991), *Unemployment: Macroeconomic Performance and the Labour Market*, Oxford, Oxford University Press.

Nickell, S. (1998), 'Unemployment: Questions and some answers', *Economic Journal*, 108, 802–16.

Nickell, S. and Layard, R. (1998), 'Labour market institutions and economic performance', in O. Ashenfelter and D. Card (eds), *The Handbook of Labor Economics*, Amsterdam, North Holland, and Discussion Paper No. 407, Centre for Economic Performance, London School of Economics (LSE), London.

Nickell, S. and Bell, B. (1995), 'The collapse in demand for the unskilled and unemployment across the OECD', *The Oxford Review of Economic Policy*, 11:1, 40–62.

2 Richard Jackman and Savvas Savouri

Has Britain solved the 'regional problem'?

Keypoints

- The traditional 'North–South' unemployment divide has all but disappeared in the 1990s.

- This may prove to be a permanent development since the manufacturing and production sectors, the main source of regional imbalance in the past, no longer dominate shifts in the employment structure to the same extent. Future shocks will have a more balanced regional incidence than has been the case in the past.

- The changed cyclical pattern is also attributable to shocks hitting the economy, which in the 1990s were, for the first time, concentrated on the service sector rather than the manufacturing industry.

- The labour market is also becoming more flexible. Some of the factors discouraging migration in the past have been reduced or removed, so that the prospects are for a more rapid adjustment to regional imbalances.

- There is also some evidence that wages now respond more quickly to regional shocks than in the past, so that regional adjustment falls here as well as on employment.

By July 1998, the Claimant Count unemployment rate in Great Britain had fallen to 4.6 per cent. This rate of unemployment, the lowest for twenty years, was accompanied by an even more remarkable decline in unemployment in the less prosperous regions. In Wales, the unemployment rate was 5.5 per cent, in Scotland 5.6 per cent, in the West Midlands 4.7 per cent (Table 2.1) and even in the newly created North Eastern region, the unemployment rate of 7.3 per cent represented a sharp improvement on the 12.4

Table 2.1   Regional unemployment rates

Region	1974	1979	1984	1990	1993	1997
South East	1.3	2.8	8.1	4.0	10.3	5.1
East Anglia	1.5	3.4	8.2	3.7	8.3	4.5
South West	2.0	4.3	9.2	4.3	9.6	4.6
West Midlands	1.7	4.2	13.1	5.9	11.2	5.6
East Midlands	1.7	3.6	10.2	5.2	9.8	5.1
Yorkshire and Humberside	2.1	4.4	12.2	6.9	10.6	6.8
North West	2.8	5.4	14.1	7.9	11.0	6.3
North	3.8	6.8	15.7	9.0	12.5	8.2
Wales	2.9	5.8	13.6	6.9	10.6	6.7
Scotland	3.3	6.1	13.3	8.4	10.1	6.7
Great Britain	2.1	4.2	11.0	5.7	10.4	5.7

Source: Labour Market Trends.

per cent recorded only four years earlier. Figures 2.1a and 2.1b show the
unemployment rates of the Northern regions, the West Midlands (Britain's
most industrialised region), the South East (the most prosperous region) and
of Wales and Scotland as against the unemployment rate for Britain as a
whole. Whereas in the 1980s the Northern regions had unemployment rates
substantially above the national average, by the mid-1990s the differential
had all but disappeared. Clearly unemployment in Britain has generally been
dominated by medium-term economy-wide factors rather than regional differences, and the latter seem to have become even less important now than
in the past.

Figure 2.1a   Regional unemployment rates

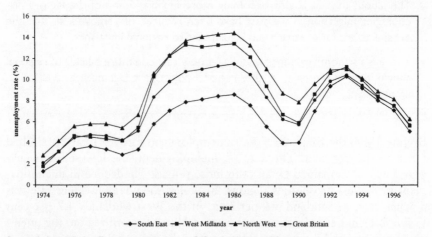

Source: Labour Market Trends, various issues, Office for National Statistics.

Figure 2.1b Regional unemployment rates

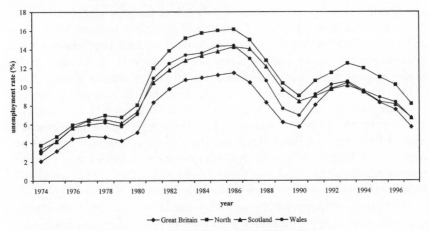

Source: *Labour Market Trends*, various issues, Office for National Statistics.

These recent observations have led some to argue that Britain has solved its century-old regional problem, possibly even that the much vaunted measures to improve labour market flexibility introduced during the past twenty years have borne fruit in at least this area. Others feel that the incipient (at the time of writing) recession will re-open the historic regional divide between the prospering South and the depressed North. This chapter asks whether Britain has in fact solved its regional problem. It looks at various characteristics of regional labour markets, and attempts to describe how labour markets work, both in the short run in response to the business cycle and in the long run in response to structural change. It examines whether the workings of labour markets have changed in recent years, and if so, how? Finally we comment on the prospects for regional imbalance over the coming years.

The regions

For more than thirty years, the regional map of Britain was drawn on the basis of 'standard statistical regions'. There were eight in England – the North, the North West, Yorkshire and Humberside, East Midlands, West Midlands, East Anglia, the South East and the South West – while Scotland, Wales and Northern Ireland each constituted a single region. We thus have 24 years of annual data (1974–97) for the ten standard statistical regions of Great Britain and these will form the basis of our statistical analysis. We exclude Northern Ireland from the study because of various special features, both political and geographic, which mean that its labour market experience cannot be regarded as equivalent to that of any other British region.

Economic characteristics

The regional problem is in essence a problem of unemployment. Of course, unemployment is not the only dimension of economic welfare, but it is the dimension within which there is most clearly a regional problem. For those in work, wages may differ between regions, but then so do living costs, in particular housing costs, travel-to-work times and other aspects of the 'quality of life'. It would be hard to argue, for example, that the standard of living of a teacher on basic pay rates in Warwick or Exeter was not higher than in London despite the London allowance amounting to a salary supplement of about 10 per cent. But the concern over the regional problem reflects the perception that there are (or were) clear-cut differences in labour market opportunities across regions and that these differences manifest themselves most importantly in differences in levels of unemployment.

The basic idea that regional unemployment differentials reflect differences in labour market opportunities is supported by the evidence of correlations between regional unemployment, vacancy and participation rates. (We take correlations for 1984, as 1984 is in the middle of the period we study, but other years show a very similar pattern.) There is a consistently negative correlation between unemployment and vacancies ($r=-0.48$), which supports the presumption that differences in unemployment reflect differences in labour market opportunities. Similarly the negative correlation between unemployment and the participation rate ($r=-0.58$) is indicative of a discouraged worker effect, of people dropping out of the labour force when opportunities are not good. The negative correlation between unemployment and wages ($r=-0.25$) might also be indicative of weaker labour markets in high unemployment regions, but is in fact somewhat ambiguous, because there are differences in the cost of living across regions and a lower wage may permit a higher standard of living in a depressed region. Regional cost of living indices are not immediately available, but there is a strong negative correlation ($r=-0.72$) between unemployment and house prices. This suggests that, taking all other things into account, high unemployment regions are less desirable places to live in.

All of these statistics are consistent with the idea that though wages do differ across regions they do not differ sufficiently to fully counteract other cost advantages or disadvantages of the regions, leaving a lower demand for labour (relative to the supply) in some regions than in others. The unemployment rate is the most serious manifestation of this labour market imbalance.

Just as the regional problem is in essence a problem of unemployment, so the belief that the regional problem has been solved reflects the belief that disparities in regional unemployment rates are much lower now than they were in the past. However, the convergence of regional unemployment rates is a feature of every cyclical upswing, and there is correspondingly an

Figure 2.2a   The variance of regional unemployment rates

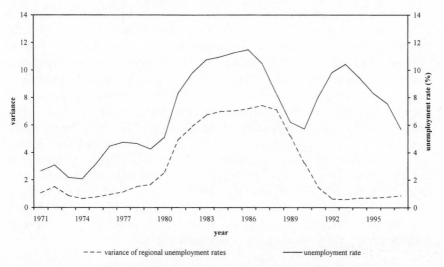

Source: Labour Market Trends, various issues, Office for National Statistics.

Figure 2.2b   The variance of relative regional unemployment rates

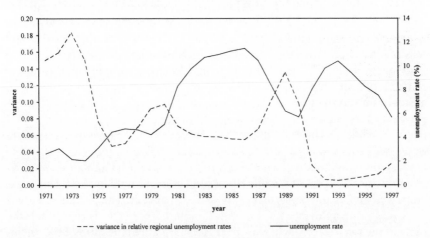

Source: Labour Market Trends, various issues, Office for National Statistics.

increased divergence of regional unemployment rates in every downturn, so that historically there tends to be a concern about 'the regional problem' in every recession, which fades away in the succeeding recovery. Thus, it is not surprising that in the recovery of the last few years, when there has been a substantial fall in unemployment overall, there has also been a marked narrowing of regional differentials.

However, the experience of recent years appears to be much more than a cyclical effect. Figure 2.2a shows the variation of unemployment rates in relation to the national average unemployment rate. In the 1980s, as unemployment increased so did the dispersion of unemployment rates and when unemployment declined so did its dispersion, but in the early 1990s the increase in unemployment was associated with a continuing decline in regional variation, which has remained low in the boom. In the past, it has been suggested that the cyclicality of the variance of unemployment means that it may be more appropriate to focus on the ratio of unemployment rates rather than absolute (percentage point) differences. In Figure 2.2b we plot the time series of the variance of relative unemployment rates. This series was more stable than the time series of the dispersion of the actual unemployment rates in the 1980s, but it also shows a sharp reduction in the early 1990s. On any measure, regional unemployment rates look more closely clustered together in the 1990s than in any comparable period.

The changing cyclical behaviour of regional unemployment

The observation that the ratio of unemployment rates has tended to be more stable over the cycle than the absolute (percentage point) differences calls for some explanation. If, in the first instance, one imagines a cyclical fall in demand being neutral in its effect on different sectors, so that if total demand falls by, say, 5 per cent, the demand for each product falls by 5 per cent, the consequence would be that all regions would experience an equal (proportionate) fall in employment. This would result in approximately equal absolute falls in the unemployment rate. For example, if one region had 95 per cent of its labour force employed and hence an unemployment rate of 5 per cent, while another had 90 per cent employed and an unemployment rate of 10 per cent, and both suffered a 5 per cent fall in employment, then the first region would end up with 90.25 per cent employed and an unemployment rate of 9.75 per cent, while the second region would have 85.5 per cent employed and an unemployment rate of 14.5 per cent. The percentage point increase in unemployment rates, of 4.75 and 4.5 per cent, is thus much the same in the two regions, whereas there is a sharp fall in the ratio of the unemployment rates (from 2 to just under 1.5).

Thus if fluctuations in demand were neutral across sectors, one would expect stability in absolute rather than relative unemployment rate differences. In this case, how can we explain the observations for the 1980s in Figures 2.2a and 2.2b? The standard 'mismatch model' explanation (Layard *et al.* (1991)) is perhaps given its clearest exposition in Nickell and Bell (1995). The model states that a given percentage point increase in unemployment can be expected to have a bigger impact in depressing wages where unemployment is low than where it is high. Both intuition and econometric evidence suggest that an increase in unemployment from say 2 per cent to 4 per cent will have a much sharper effect on wages than an increase from say 12 per cent to 14 per cent. A fall in relative wages in a low unemployment region will to some extent counteract the employment effect of the original fall in demand, and this offsetting effect will mean that, at the end of the process, unemployment will have fallen by less in percentage point terms in the low unemployment regions. Nickell and Bell suggest that as much as 80 per cent of the impact of a neutral demand shock on relative unemployment rates will be offset by induced wage effects. However, this process takes time and the Nickell–Bell model is intended to provide an explanation for the stability of relative unemployment rates in the long run rather than in a cyclical context.

An alternative explanation might start from the theory of labour market dynamics which points to differences in the cyclical pattern of job creation and job destruction. Davis and Haltiwanger (1992) have shown that there is a very systematic tendency for job destruction to be concentrated in cyclical downturns, whereas job creation proceeds continuously through boom and slump. The corollary is that employment in declining industries will be more sensitive to cyclical fluctuations than employment in growing industries. Hence regions 'specialising' in declining industries will be more vulnerable to demand shocks, which will therefore not be neutral in their regional impact. In Figure 2.3 we plot employment in manufacturing and in services: the former shows sharp declines in employment in economic downturns, with stability in between, the latter shows moderately steady growth throughout the

Figure 2.3 Employees in employment: manufacturing vs non-manufacturing

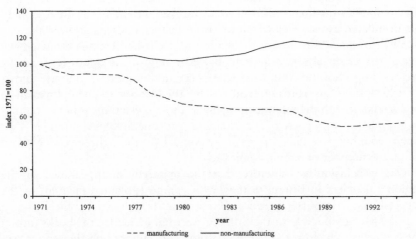

Source: *Labour Market Trends*, various issues, Office for National Statistics.

whole period. There is a close correspondence between periods of sharp decline in aggregate manufacturing employment and years in which regional unemployment differentials increased. The hypothesis that all sectors are affected equally by a demand shock does not seem the right starting point in relation to the British experience.

In Table 2.2, columns 2 and 3, we show the relationship between a region's employment share in manufacturing in 1979 and the rate of decline in total employment between 1979 and 1984. There is a clear inverse correlation ($r=-0.51$) with five of the six regions that had high shares in manufacturing losing more than 10 per cent of their total employment whereas those with the lowest shares in manufacturing, the South East and South West, had total employment losses of less than 5 per cent. Column 3 shows a close relationship between the total loss of employment and the increase in unemployment. The relationship is not one-for-one, but over this period just over half of the fall in employment showed up in higher unemployment in 1984. The remainder was reflected in changes in participation rates and in migration. Thus, it could be argued that in the 1980s the dispersion of regional unemployment rates increased because regions specialising in declining industries suffered bigger impact effects on employment. This concentration of impact effects on manufacturing in the early 1980s was driven by a sharp appreciation in the pound following the adoption of the Medium Term Financial Strategy.

Pursuing this approach, we now examine the position in the early 1990s. Columns 5 and 6 relate the fall in employment between 1989 and 1992 to the proportion of the workforce employed in manufacturing in 1989. There is essentially no correlation ($r=0.064$), and remarkably the sharpest fall in employment was in the most service-orientated of the regions, the South East. The immediate explanation is that the recession of the early 1990s was precipitated by the financial crash which marked the end of the financial bubble of inflated asset prices which followed financial deregulation in the second half of the 1980s. Just as the main stimulus from deregulation had been felt in the financial services-orientated economy of the South East, so the greatest impact of the crash was experienced in this region. Column 7 shows a fairly clear, if unsurprising, tendency for the increase in unemployment to be correlated with the fall in employment, though even this is not as tight as one might have expected. For example, the unemployment rate in East Anglia rose by more than 4 percentage points over these three years with no fall in the number of people employed.

Our conclusion is therefore that the apparent disappearance of the regional problem in Britain in the 1990s can be explained in terms of the atypical character of the recession of that time. The changed cyclical pattern is primarily attributable to the different sectoral incidence of shocks hitting the economy, which were for the first time concentrated on the service sector rather than on the manufacturing industry.

Table 2.2 The relationship between employment in manufacturing and total employment

Region	1979	1979–84		1989	1989–92	
	share of manufacturing in employment	change in total employment	change in unemployment	share of manufacturing in employment	change in total employment	change in unemployment
South East	23.2	–4.0	5.3	15.9	–6.7	5.4
East Anglia	27.3	0.3	4.9	21.0	–0.2	4.1
South West	25.4	–3.6	4.9	19.6	–2.8	4.9
West Midlands	40.3	–12.4	8.9	30.3	–2.5	3.9
East Midlands	36.5	–7.0	6.7	29.1	–2.6	3.4
Yorkshire and Humberside	33.1	–11.9	7.8	24.3	–0.9	2.4
North West	33.7	–14.5	8.7	25.3	–3.7	2.2
North	30.7	–15.0	9.0	23.5	–0.6	1.1
Wales	28.7	–14.1	7.8	22.5	–3.5	2.6
Scotland	26.8	–9.5	7.2	19.3	2.8	0.0
Great Britain	29.2	–8.4	6.8	21.3	–3.4	3.6

Source: Labour Market Trends.

In the future, while no business cycle is exactly like its predecessor, if Britain were an isolated economy with floating exchange rates relying on monetary policy to control inflation, we would expect stabilisation policy to work primarily through the exchange rate. An upsurge in domestic inflation would lead to a tightening of domestic monetary conditions leading to an appreciation of sterling and hence the traded goods sector would bear the brunt of policy, rather as it did in the early 1980s. The exchange rate was clearly overvalued in 1998, but the regional incidence of this overvaluation now seems much less pronounced. Were Britain to join the single European currency, domestic inflation would lead to loss of competitiveness relative to other European countries and hence to domestic recession with no scope for changes in interest rates. Again, however, the regional incidence of any such recession might be less unbalanced than has been the case in the past because of trade in services as well as goods.

The longer term

If unemployment is the measure of regional economic welfare, its most remarkable feature in the British context is its persistence. The depressed regions of the 1930s, the North, Wales and Scotland, were again the most depressed areas in the 1980s. Over the last twenty-five years, the correlation of unemployment rates over regions between 1997 and 1987 was 0.91, and more remarkably between 1997 and 1974 the correlation was 0.87. The problem in Britain, as in many European countries (though not the United States), is not simply that economic opportunities differ across regions but that these differences have persisted for decades.

During the nineteenth century, there was a rapid growth of employment in the manufacturing industry, and this was clustered around the sources of its raw materials, mainly coal and iron ore. Thus employment grew rapidly, in particular in the North East, in South Wales, Southern Scotland and in the Midlands. Since the early twentieth century these industries have been in decline. The Great Depression of the 1930s took a very heavy toll on employment in heavy manufacturing, in particular mining, mechanical engineering, metal manufacture, textiles and shipbuilding. The southern regions suffered much less due to their 'more flexible and diverse economic structures' (Aldcroft (1984: 14–16)).

During the past twenty-five years, the British economy has again suffered further large-scale de-industrialisation. As in the 1930s, employment has been growing in light, often science-based, industries, and in services, and these again tend to be located close to major national and international markets. In regional terms, the demand for labour has again shifted from industries located mainly in the North, in Wales and Scotland and in the Midlands, to those located, above all, in the South East.

The background to any analysis of regional labour markets is then the evolution of the industrial structure and its implications for the location of economic activity and hence for the demand for labour. Unemployment rates have been systematically higher in regions of declining employment and lower where employment has been growing. This then might set in train a number of reactions which restore the balance, to some extent. First of these is migration. Workers in high unemployment regions may seek jobs in the growing regions where they are more readily available, either by migrating and then looking for work, or by searching outside their region and moving if they find a job elsewhere.

Migration is not the only response. High unemployment rates in a region tend to depress wages, other things being equal. Lower wages in a region help local firms both to compete more effectively in national markets and to sustain local service employment in the face of weak local purchasing power. A sufficient decline in local wages could so improve the competitiveness of local businesses that there would be no need for job losses. But if wages were very flexible, workers might well move out of the region, preferring a higher wage job elsewhere in the country to a low-wage job at home.

To what extent do these adjustments operate in the British labour market? Do workers migrate in search of better economic opportunities? Do wages adjust in local labour markets? And if they do, does that create jobs to replace those that are lost? If these adjustments do operate, why has Britain for so long suffered great disparities in its unemployment rates across regions? And might these disparities decline over the longer term?

To summarise, the regional adjustment process works slowly in Britain. As a result, high rates of unemployment persist in regions of declining employment. These large and persistent unemployment differentials play a crucial role in driving migration, so that in the long run the movement of the population follows the movement of jobs. Wages are lower in relative terms in the declining regions but, because housing costs are also lower, real wages do not differ greatly across regions and do not play an important part in inducing migration. Lower wages do sustain employment but only a relatively small proportion of lost jobs are recovered through the effects of lower wages. We think there is some prospect of a diminution of the regional problem over the longer term, because the concentration of declining industrial sectors in particular regions seems to be a historical circumstance rather than an inevitable feature.

We look first at the relationship between the migration of people and the migration of jobs. Figure 2.4 shows changes in regional employment and in labour supply by region (that is, the employed plus the unemployed) over the past twenty-five years. There have been large changes in both, with employment growing by almost 20 per cent in the South West and East Anglia, but falling by over 10 per cent in the North and North West. What is remarkable is that in each region the growth or decline in employment is almost exactly equal to the growth or decline in the labour supply. This means that the economies of the regions have been growing larger or smaller with minimal changes in their relative unemployment rates. The flows of people and jobs are consistent with a stable pattern of regional unemployment rates.

The regional distribution of job losses in Figure 2.4 clearly reflects the historic pattern of changes in the industrial structure. But why is labour supply falling in the areas of industrial decline? Our argument is that this is largely attributable to the impact of unemployment on net migration flows, which is well established in the UK (Hughes and McCormick (1985), Jackman and Savouri (1992), Pissarides and Wadsworth (1989)). As shown in Figure 2.5, there has been a clear correlation between high rates of unemployment in a region and a reduction in its labour supply. Further, as shown in Figure 2.6, of the various factors that can contribute to a fall in the labour supply (a fall in the population of working age, for demographic reasons or through migration, or a fall in the participation (or activity) rate), the most important in the long run is migration. There is a systematic tendency for workers to migrate away from areas of high unemployment (see Figure 2.6), and a comparison of Figures 2.5 and 2.6 shows that the bulk of the changes in the labour force take the form of migration.

The magnitude of migration flows in relation to unemployment over this period is around 0.15, which is to say a region whose unemployment rate is 1 percentage point above the national average will experience a decline in its population at a rate of 0.15 per cent a year, equivalent at a given participation rate to about one-sixth of the unemployment differential. This has the

Figure 2.4 Changes in employment and labour supply: 1974–97

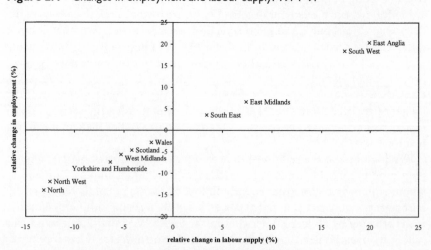

Source: *Labour Market Trends*, various issues, Office for National Statistics.

Figure 2.5 Unemployment rates and the change in labour supply: 1974–97

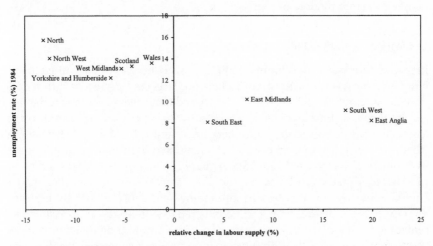

Source: Labour Market Trends, various issues, Office for National Statistics.

Figure 2.6 Unemployment rates and the change in population: 1974–97

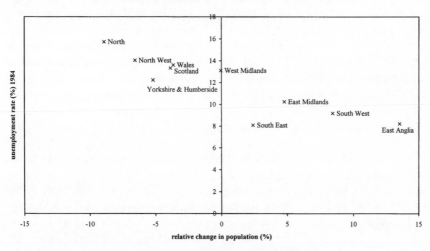

Source: Labour Market Trends, various issues, Office for National Statistics.

implication that if the number of jobs in each region were held constant, migration would halve any unemployment differentials across regions within about four years. Another way of thinking about the magnitude is that if employment in a particular region were falling at a rate of 1 per cent a year, the unemployment rate in that region would need to exceed the national

average unemployment rate by 6 percentage points to generate an outflow of
people to match the loss of jobs.

Comparison with the United States

In many respects, the development of regional economies in the United States
has much in common with Britain. There are large and persistent differences
in regional employment growth in the United States which appear to be driven by demand. Employment has been growing in the oil states and in the
'sun belt', but declining in coal mining areas and the older industrial states
(the 'rust belt'). These employment changes have been matched by changes
in population, but in the United States there is much more migration than in
the United Kingdom. Blanchard and Katz (1992: 34) suggest that in the
United States as much as half of an employment shock is met by net out-
migration even in the first year, compared to one-sixth in Britain. The
remainder primarily takes the form of a change in unemployment, though
there are also small effects on participation. A given change in employment
would be fully offset within five to seven years by a change in population,
with no effect on wages or unemployment beyond this time.

The lower responsiveness of migration to unemployment in Britain than
in the United States may be ascribed to a number of factors. In the past, housing policies involving rent controls and rent subsidies have been associated
with severe shortages, with the result that tenants have wanted to stay put
rather than join the back of a queue for housing in another locality (Hughes
and McCormick (1981)). Though these particular rigidities have lessened, it
remains the case that housing supply is relatively inflexible in the United
Kingdom compared to in the United States, and it might be argued inevitably
so, given the greater need for land use planning on environmental grounds in
a densely populated country such as the United Kingdom. (The overall density of population is 239 people per 1,000 square kilometres in the United
Kingdom, as against only 28 in the United States.) Another important factor
is social security and unemployment benefits which provide a more effective
safety net for workers losing their jobs in the United Kingdom than in the
United States, and hence may weaken the incentive to migrate.[1]

It might be thought that housing reforms and the increased pressure on
unemployed people to find work in recent years might lead to a higher rate
of labour mobility. We therefore split the sample and looked at the relationship between unemployment and migration before and after 1986. Over
these time periods there appeared to be no change in the responsiveness of
labour mobility to unemployment. Thus, in the United States, there is great

---

[1] However, the bulk of migrants are employed rather than unemployed and the migration
rate of the unemployed has fallen relative to that of the employed people over the past twenty
years (see Green, Gregg and Wadsworth (1998: 76)).

flexibility of the labour supply and shocks to regional employment are met fully and quickly through the migration of workers from declining to growing regions. In Britain the same process can be observed but it works much more slowly and requires the emergence of large and persistent unemployment differentials across localities. Given the existence of such immobility, it might be asked whether other potential mechanisms of adjustment come into play in Britain, in particular wage adjustments.

The role of wage flexibility

There are two issues here, first whether or not wages in a region are in fact sensitive to that region's unemployment rate, and second, if they are, what effect the lower wages in a region of high unemployment have, either on the creation or retention of jobs or on migration. (In addressing the second question we also need to look at the effect on regional cost of living indices, because in depressed regions lower relative wages may buy more consumer goods.)

Figure 2.7 shows the relationship between unemployment and the rate of change of male wages over the last twenty-five years. Wages have been growing slowly in regions with high unemployment and most rapidly in regions where unemployment has been low. According to our calculations, the responsiveness of the rate of change of wages to the regional unemployment rate is about 0.3. That is, if a region's unemployment rate should increase by, say, 1 percentage point, then it will experience wages growing at 0.3 percentage points below the national average rate of wage inflation.

Figure 2.7 Unemployment rates and the change in male wages: 1974–97

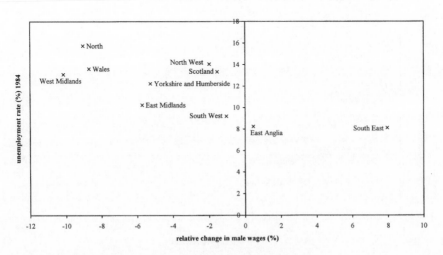

Source: Labour Market Trends, various issues, Office for National Statistics.

The relative inflexibility of regional wages to regional unemployment has often been ascribed to the influence of collective bargaining at the national level. It might then be thought that the decline in the power of the trade unions and the increase in plant level wage setting could be associated with a greater responsiveness of wages to labour market conditions at the local level. We find some support for this in the data, for example our estimates suggest that over the last ten years (post-1986) the impact of excess unemployment differentials on wages rises to 0.5. Our estimates suggest that cumulatively 6 percentage points of excess unemployment will reduce the regional wage by just under 2 percentage points. After 1986, the responsiveness of wages becomes more sensitive, falling by 3 percentage points for the same-size unemployment shock.

Wages and employment

These numbers look small, but the question is whether they have a significant impact on the number of jobs, and for this we also need to know the effect of relative wages on labour demand. Figures 2.8a and 2.8b examine the relationship between wages and jobs. The figures show the relationship between the region's wage and the difference between its employment growth and a baseline growth for employment in the region calculated on the assumption that each industry in that region grows at the national growth rate for that industry.

In this comparison the South East is clearly an outlier with much higher wages (and slower growth relative to its employment structure) than other

Figure 2.8a   Wages and employment growth: 1981–96

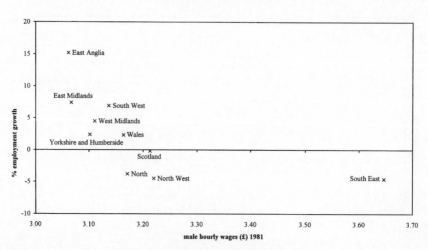

Source: Labour Market Trends, various issues, Office for National Statistics.

Figure 2.8b   Wages and employment growth: 1981–96, adjusted for industry mix

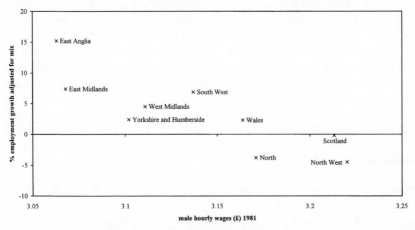

Source: Labour Market Trends, various issues, Office for National Statistics.

regions. But in Figure 2.8b, which makes the same comparison excluding the South East, an equally clear picture emerges of an inverse correlation between wages and employment growth adjusted for structure.

The magnitude of this effect appears to be of the order of 0.33: a reduction of wages of 1 per cent in a region will lead to employment growing at about one-third of 1 per cent more rapidly than otherwise. If we combine this with the estimated wage effect of unemployment (of 0.3), the total outcome is that a region with an unemployment rate 1 percentage point above the average will have wages falling by 0.3 per cent more than the average in the first year, this will cause employment to grow 0.1 per cent more rapidly than otherwise. When this figure is compared with the migration effect (of 0.15) it suggests that wage/employment growth effects are somewhat less important in the short run. However, the greater responsiveness of wages to unemployment in the latter part of the period suggests the wage/employment effects may now be at least as influential in the short run.

Conclusions

We began by asking whether Britain had solved its regional problem. The answer is that it has to some extent. There are two reasons for being reasonably optimistic in the UK context. First, the long historical experience of a declining manufacturing industry, which has been the main cause of regional imbalance, no longer dominates shifts in the employment structure to the same extent. This is, in part, simply because manufacturing now has a much smaller share of total employment, and in part because there seems less reason to expect the shocks to be as concentrated on this sector. It follows that future shocks will have a more balanced regional incidence than has been the case in the past. Second, the labour market is becoming more flexible. Our work suggests that the more important dimension of flexibility in the regional context is migration rather than wage flexibility, though the latter dimension appears to be the one within which most change has been observed. Even so, some of the factors discouraging migration in the past have been reduced or removed, so that on both dimensions the prospects are for a more rapid adjustment to internal regional imbalances.

References

Aldcroft, D. H. (1984), *Full Employment: the Elusive Goal*, Wheatsheaf Books, Brighton.

Blanchard, O. and Katz, L. (1992), 'Regional evolutions', *Brookings Papers on Economic Activity*, 1, 1–61.

Davis, S. and Haltiwanger, J. (1992), 'Gross job creation, gross job destruction and employment reallocation', *Quarterly Journal of Economics*, 107:3, 817–63.

Green, A., Gregg, P. and Wadsworth, J. (1998), 'Regional unemployment changes in Britain', in P. Lawless, R. Martin and S. Hardy (eds), *Unemployment and Social Exclusion*, Regional Studies Association, Jessica Kingsley Publishers, London.

Hughes, G. and McCormick, B. (1981), 'Do council housing policies reduce migration between regions?', *Economic Journal*, 91, 919–37.

Hughes, G. and McCormick, B. (1985), 'Migration intentions in the UK: which households want to migrate and which succeed?', *Economic Journal*, Conference Papers.

Jackman, R. and Savouri, S. (1992), 'Regional migration in Britain: an analysis of gross flows using NHS Central Register data', *Economic Journal*, 102:415, 1433–50.

Layard, R., Nickell, S. J. and Jackman, R. (1991), *Unemployment: Macroeconomic Performance and the Labour Market*, Oxford University Press, Oxford.

Nickell, S. J. and Bell, B. (1995), 'The collapse in the demand for unskilled labour and unemployment across the OECD', *Oxford Review of Economic Policy*, 11:1, 40–62.

Pissarides, C. and Wadsworth, J. (1989), 'Unemployment and the inter-regional mobility of labour', *Economic Journal*, 99, 739–55.

3 Paul Gregg and Jonathan Wadsworth

Economic inactivity

Keypoints

- There are now some 2.3 million men of working age (excluding students) who are economically inactive according to the Labour Force Survey (LFS). Twenty years ago there were around 400,000. The inactivity rate has risen for all men, but is highest amongst those aged 50 and over and amongst the least skilled.

- Inactivity is also concentrated in high unemployment regions, now typically urban areas.

- When the economy expands the incidence of economic inactivity usually falls. However, in the latest recovery this effect has been much more muted. Indeed male inactivity is higher than in 1993. Only in areas that have experienced large positive employment gains has male inactivity fallen. This failure of the inactive to reconnect with the labour market flatters the recent improvement in unemployment.

- Attachment to the labour market is actually more complicated than a simple dichotomy of unemployment and inactivity. Those that express a desire for work, but are not currently seeking work, have transition rates into employment of twice that of people who don't want work.

According to the LFS, around 23 per cent of the non-student working age population, some 7 million people, were out of work in 1975. In 1998, 25 per cent (8.2 million) were not in work (see Table 3.1). At first glance this seems to be a relatively modest change, not perhaps worthy of further investigation. Especially since the division of non-employment into its constituent components, unemployment and inactivity – those out of work but not actively seeking a job – has also remained broadly constant over the same period. Around one-fifth of the non-employed are unemployed and four-fifths inactive. So why the need for concern? The answer is that constant stocks of non-employment, unemployment and inactivity in the economy can obscure important changes in the composition of the individuals who form those stocks.

Table 3.1   Inactivity, unemployment and non-employment rates

	Non-employed	Inactive	Unemployed
All			
1975	23.4	18.8	4.6
	(7036)	(5644)	(1392)
1979	23.2	19.0	4.2
1983	29.5	20.8	8.7
1987	27.7	19.2	8.5
1990	23.4	17.5	5.9
1993	27.4	19.2	8.2
1998	24.6	19.7	4.9
	(8226)	(6595)	(1631)
Men			
1975	7.7	2.6	5.1
	(1208)	(402)	(805)
1979	9.1	4.7	4.4
1983	18.9	8.2	10.7
1987	19.6	9.6	10.0
1990	15.6	8.9	6.7
1993	22.3	11.3	10.7
1998	19.0	13.2	5.8
	(3345)	(2322)	(1023)
Women			
1975	40.6	36.5	4.1
	(587)	(5242)	(5829)
1979	38.5	34.6	3.9
1983	41.0	34.4	6.6
1987	36.6	29.8	6.8
1990	31.9	26.9	5.0
1993	35.4	27.9	5.5
1998	30.7	26.9	3.8
	(4881)	(4273)	(608)

Source: LFS, Spring quarter.
Note: Population numbers in thousands given in brackets for 1975 and 1998.

Rising male inactivity, falling female inactivity

The make-up of the inactive is radically different now because the composition has shifted dramatically toward men. Men have dropped out of the labour force in unprecedented numbers, while, as Chapter 10 explores, women have entered the labour force to such an extent that these two trends broadly offset each other (see Figure 3.1 and Table 3.1). In the mid-1970s, less than 8 per cent of men aged 16–64, some 1.2 million, were economically inactive and only around 400,000 of these were not in full-time education. In 1990 this figure had risen to some 1.5 million excluding students and now, in 1998, stands at around 2.3 million, more than 13 per cent of the potential

Figure 3.1   Non-employment, unemployment and inactivity by sex

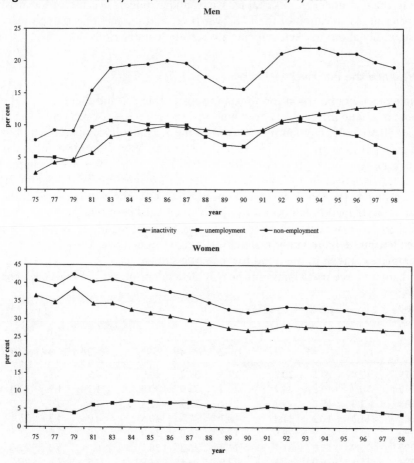

Source: Labour Force Survey.

workforce, an overall increase of nearly 2 million men since 1975. Since 1986, the inactivity rate, excluding students, has consistently exceeded the unemployment rate for men. An increase in economic inactivity, rather than an increase in employment, accounts for almost half the fall in male unemployment since 1993. The unemployment rate is no longer a good proxy for the extent of male labour market slack.

In contrast, the inactivity rate for women has fallen sharply from 37 per cent in 1975 to 27 per cent in 1998, an almost equal and opposite swing compared with men. There are now just 4.3 million inactive women of working age excluding students. Indeed most of the 900,000 net rise in female employment over this period has been met by increased economic activity from those previously outside the labour force. The proportion of the inactive that are male has risen five-fold since 1975, from 7 per cent to 35 per cent.

In the remainder of this chapter we exclude students because of inconsistencies in classification of the LFS over time, and the fact that though inactive in the labour market, students are actively gaining skills.

Who are the inactive?

Male inactivity has risen for all age groups (Table 3.2 and Figure 3.2). The most dramatic increase has been amongst the over-50s. 28 per cent of men over 50 are now economically inactive, some 1.3 million, compared with less than 7 per cent in 1975. However, this is not only a problem for older workers. Around 8 per cent of non-student men under 50, some 1 million, are now inactive. In 1975 less than 1 per cent of men under the age of 50 were outside the labour force and not in education. For women, most of the rise in participation has been amongst women aged between 25 and 49. For this group, inactivity fell from 3.2 to 2.5 million. Significantly there is a smaller, but definite fall in inactivity amongst women over the age of 49, in complete contrast to the trend for men of a similar age.

Labour force participation is heavily dependent on skill (Table 3.3). The

Table 3.2 Inactivity by sex and age

	All			Women			Men		
	16–24	25–49	50+	16–24	25–49	50+	16–24	25–49	50+
1975	12.0	20.0	20.7	23.3	39.2	40.0	0.9	0.9	6.6
1979	10.7	19.3	24.7	20.4	36.9	40.9	1.3	1.9	12.4
1983	12.3	19.8	29.7	21.2	35.9	42.3	3.6	3.4	21.0
1987	11.3	17.2	31.4	18.7	30.2	40.5	4.2	4.3	25.1
1990	10.9	14.9	29.9	18.3	26.0	38.2	3.9	3.8	24.1
1993	13.9	15.9	31.9	21.4	26.2	38.1	6.9	5.8	27.5
1998	15.1	16.0	31.5	22.9	24.6	36.2	7.8	7.6	28.2

Source: LFS, Spring quarter.

Figure 3.2 Male inactivity rates by age

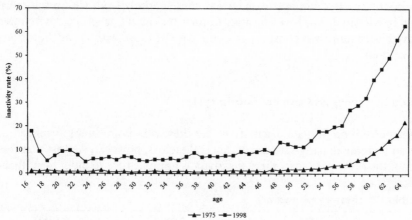

Source: Labour Force Survey.

lower the level of qualifications held, the more likely it is that an individual will be economically inactive. More than 30 per cent of men with no formal qualifications are now inactive. Less than 8 per cent of men with degrees are outside the labour force. For men, inactivity has risen amongst all education groups in roughly equal proportions, so that the share of different skill

Table 3.3 Inactivity by sex and qualification level

	Degree	'A' level and equivalent	'O' level and equivalent	CSE and equivalent	None
Men					
1979	0.8	1.6	1.5	1.6	4.9
1981	1.2	1.1	1.9	2.2	6.0
1984	3.8	3.8	5.8	5.1	14.5
1987	5.2	5.5	6.2	7.4	17.0
1990	4.7	6.0	6.0	7.6	17.3
1993	7.1	9.2	9.5	10.5	22.1
1998	7.4	9.4	10.7	13.2	30.4
Women					
1979	23.4	29.1	29.2	30.6	40.7
1981	23.2	26.6	28.4	28.9	41.2
1984	21.4	23.0	26.4	29.0	41.5
1987	17.8	20.9	23.4	27.6	40.8
1990	11.2	18.2	18.2	27.2	38.6
1993	14.3	20.6	24.1	29.5	42.5
1998	13.2	18.6	22.5	29.5	48.9

Source: LFS, Spring quarter.

groups in the inactive stock is little different than in 1979. In contrast the fall in inactivity rates amongst women has come entirely from within the more highly educated. For less educated women (below 'O' level) inactivity rates have either remained constant or in the case of those with no qualifications have risen.

Male inactivity and the economic cycle

One perception of male inactivity is that these trends are simply a reflection of an increase in early retirement. Several factors, however, suggest that this is not the principal cause. First, inactivity is not exclusive to older men. Inac-

Table 3.4 Reasons for inactivity

	Sickness	Home and family	Retired	Discouraged	Other
Men					
1993	59.6	6.1	16.7	4.7	12.9
1998	62.9	8.2	15.7	2.1	11.1
Age 16–24					
1993	43.5	2.6	0	11.2	42.7
1998	44.0	8.5	0	1.7	45.8
Age 25–49					
1993	68.6	13.4	0.2	3.4	14.4
1998	71.6	15.3	0.5	1.2	11.6
Age 50–64					
1993	71.4	4.6	11.5	4.6	7.8
1998	59.7	4.5	25.2	2.6	8.1
Women					
1993	19.3	66.0	3.2	1.4	10.0
1998	26.2	59.0	4.0	0.7	10.2
Age 16–24					
1993	8.9	78.8	0	0.8	11.5
1998	11.7	75.4	0	0.6	12.2
Age 25–49					
1993	14.8	75.8	0.2	1.1	8.1
1998	20.6	70.6	0.2	0.5	8.2
Age 50–59					
1993	33.6	39.0	11.3	2.2	13.9
1998	41.7	31.2	12.7	0.9	13.5

Source: LFS, Spring quarter.

tivity rises and falls for men under 50 in much the same way as the pattern of inactivity amongst older men. Second, inactivity is greatest amongst the least skilled. If inactivity were simply an early retirement effect we would expect to see inactivity concentrated amongst the wealthier groups of the workforce, the more highly skilled. This is not what we observe. Table 3.4 gives the self-reported reasons for inactivity in 1993 and 1998. It is clear that even amongst older inactive men retirement is rare. Less than 16 per cent of inactive men say that they have retired and only a quarter of men over 50. The dominant reason for inactivity is sickness. Some 63 per cent of men say they are out of the labour force because they are ill. True, the share in retirement has grown amongst older men since 1993, but it cannot account for most of the spells of inactivity amongst men. This raises the possibility that a growing number of sickness benefit claims may underlie much of the rise in inactivity. The move to sickness benefits may in turn reflect tougher access to other benefits or declining labour market opportunities.

That higher male inactivity is correlated with poor labour market performance and a lack of earning opportunities for men can be seen from Table 3.5 which outlines unemployment and inactivity rates for eighteen British regions. Areas with high male unemployment have higher male inactivity rates. The higher the unemployment rate, the higher the inactivity rate. This holds for all men as a group and less skilled men with no qualifications. The inactivity rate in 1998 for least skilled men in regions with an unemployment rate above 9 per cent is more than 40 per cent. Figure 3.1 indicates that when unemployment rises so does inactivity. So, can economic recovery help

Table 3.5 Unemployment and inactivity

Area male unemployment rate	Inactivity rate	Less skilled inactivity rate (men 25+)	5 year change in area male employment rate	5 year change in area inactivity rate	5 year change in less skilled inactivity rate
1998					
less than 5%	11.9	27.3	more than 5% rise	−0.6	+3.0
5–7%	13.9	32.6	3–5% rise	+0.3	+7.8
7–9%	15.1	33.6	1–3% rise	+2.1	+8.8
more than 9%	18.7	43.4	less than 1% rise	+3.0	+10.4
1990					
less than 5%	8.3	13.2	more than 6% rise	−1.2	+0.2
5–8%	11.1	18.3	4–6% rise	+0.6	+1.4
8–10%	12.9	23.1	2–4% rise	+0.8	+2.5
more than 10%	14.9	26.3	less than 2% rise	+1.0	+1.8

Source: LFS, Spring quarter.

reduce inactivity? The final two columns in Table 3.5 suggest that areas with the best employment performance during a recovery do have the best improvement in male inactivity rates. Even so, it requires the employment rate to rise by 5 percentage points or more to generate even a 1 percentage point fall in the inactivity rate. Few areas managed to improve employment by so much. Moreover the improvement during the current recovery has been smaller than in the 1980s. This suggests that many of the inactive are the last to benefit from an upturn. It may be then that for many, inactivity is akin to (very) long-term unemployment.

Flows into and out of unemployment and inactivity

The stocks of unemployment and inactivity are not static. Rather, workers move between the two states as well as in and out of employment over time. Table 3.6 maps the chances of leaving employment, unemployment or inactivity within a three-month period, beginning in 1992. The aggregate flows over the period map the process of labour market recovery. Outflows from employment fall and inflows into employment rise. The improvement in outflows from unemployment into work is larger for women. The flows also document the rise in male inactivity over the same period. Outflows from inactivity fall and inflow rates from unemployment rise. In 1998, some 15

Table 3.6   Labour market flows

				Percentage leaving each state within 3 months					
	E to U	E to N	Total E outflow	U to E	U to N	Total U outflow	N to E	N to U	Total N outflow
All									
1992	1.6	1.4	3.0	18.1	9.8	27.9	5.0	4.8	9.8
1994	1.3	1.3	2.6	20.8	11.1	31.9	5.0	4.8	9.8
1998	1.1	1.5	2.6	24.9	14.5	39.4	5.1	3.9	9.0
Men									
1992	2.0	0.9	2.9	17.3	6.4	23.7	4.9	7.0	11.9
1994	1.6	0.7	2.3	19.6	7.6	27.2	4.0	6.1	10.1
1998	1.2	1.0	2.2	23.1	10.6	33.7	4.6	4.2	8.8
Women									
1992	1.1	2.0	3.1	19.7	16.7	36.4	5.0	3.9	8.9
1994	1.0	2.0	3.0	22.9	17.7	40.6	5.4	4.2	9.6
1998	0.9	2.1	3.0	27.8	20.6	42.9	5.3	3.7	9.0

Source: LFS, Spring quarter.
Note: E = employed, U = unemployed, N = inactive.

per cent of the International Labour Organisation (ILO) unemployed[1] became inactive, around 37 per cent of the total leaving unemployment over the three months. At the same time, around 9 per cent of the inactive moved out, half into employment, the other half into unemployment. With an inactive stock of 7.4 million, this implies that around 700,000 move in and out of inactivity each quarter. This is the same size as the flows in and out of unemployment each quarter. Approximately 45 per cent of moves into work come from those inactive in the preceding quarter. 60 per cent of moves into unemployment are from inactivity. It seems that, for some, the distinction between unemployment and inactivity is somewhat blurred.

Who leaves inactivity?

To explore this issue we use LFS information on job search and availability for work, allowing us to identify four categories within the working age inactive. (1) Those who say they have searched for work but are not available to start within two weeks. (2) Those who say they want work but did not search because they believe no work was available, so-called 'discouraged workers'. (3) Those who want work, but are not searching for other reasons. (4) All other inactive workers. For comparison we split the unemployed into short-term (less than 6 months), medium term (6–12) and long term (12 months or more). Table 3.7, column 2 outlines the share of each group within the non-employed. Some 10 per cent of the non-employed are short-term unemployed, while discouraged workers and those searching but not available amount to less than 3 per cent of the non-employed.

Table 3.7 Unemployment, inactivity and the transition to work

	Share of those not in work	Status 3 months on		
		Employed	Unemployed	Inactive
Unemployed less than 6 months	9.6	35.1	46.2	18.7
Unemployed 6–12 months	4.3	23.6	58.2	18.2
Unemployed more than 12 months	10.2	11.0	70.4	18.5
Seeking work, not available to start	1.4	23.3	22.2	54.5
Discouraged workers	1.5	7.1	11.2	81.7
Others who want work	18.6	5.4	7.3	87.3
All those who do not want work	54.4	3.5	1.8	94.7
Total	100.0	8.9	17.0	74.2

Source: LFS, Spring quarter.
Note: All figures have been rounded up to the nearest decimal place.

[1] ILO standard definition of unemployment. For more detail see Chapter 1.

We then follow workers at three-month intervals and look to see whether their labour market status has changed. The results confirm that the chances of finding a job fall with the duration of unemployment. Some 35 per cent of the short-term unemployed have moved into work within one quarter, but only 11 per cent of the long-term unemployed. It is also clear that many of the inactive are in work within three months but that, similar to the unemployed, there is a hierarchy within the inactive stock. Those searching but not available to start are three times more likely to find work than discouraged workers who in turn are twice as likely to find work as those who say they do not want work. Those who are searching but not available have similar chances of moving into work as the medium-term unemployed. These results question the dividing line between inactivity and unemployment. Adding inactive searchers to the ILO unemployment count raises the jobless measure by around 100,000 (excluding students), or an additional 0.4 percentage points on to the unemployment rate.

Conclusions

While the numbers of economically inactive have not changed much in the last twenty years, the composition of inactivity has changed radically. There are now some 2.3 million men of working age, excluding students, who are economically inactive according to the LFS. Twenty years ago there were around 400,000. The inactivity rate has risen for all men, but is concentrated amongst those aged 50 and over and amongst the least skilled. Inactivity is also concentrated in high unemployment regions, typically urban areas. At the same time, inactivity rates for women have fallen. Most of this rising labour force participation is concentrated amongst more highly qualified women aged between 25 and 49. Female participation has risen least in households where men are not present or not in work. When the economy expands the incidence of economic inactivity normally falls. However, in the latest recovery this effect has been much more muted and confined to women. Indeed male inactivity is now higher than in 1993. Only in areas that experienced employment growth in excess of 5 percentage points over five years did male inactivity fall. This failure of the inactive to reconnect with the labour market flatters the improvement in the unemployment count as employment increases.

We have also shown that entry rates into employment for the section of the inactive who are searching but not available to start work in the next two weeks are broadly the same as those in medium-term unemployment. These results question the accuracy of the current measure of unemployment. Adding inactive searchers to the ILO unemployment count raises the current jobless measure by around 100,000, or an additional 0.4 percentage points on to the unemployment rate. Those that want work, especially those described as discouraged workers, are more likely to gain employment or start searching in the near future. Britain's inactive are a serious and growing problem. Reconnecting these people with the labour market or preventing disconnection needs to be a serious target for government policy in order to reduce poverty and social exclusion.

4 Richard Disney

Why have older men stopped working?

Keypoints

- The proportion of men over 50 in employment has dropped precipitously over the last twenty years.

- It is often held that this trend merely reflects a desire for voluntary early retirement arising from increased access to private pension schemes. This is far from reality. Rising pension access actually has two opposite effects on the retirement decision. The higher prospective income makes people want to retire earlier but, with final salary schemes linked to years of accrual, an extra year of work earns not just a wage but a rise in the future pension incomes from extra accrual.

- A major cause of the increase in early retirement is the behaviour of firms, which often use the pension scheme as the means of shedding unwanted labour. There is clear evidence of a demand shift against older workers.

- Apart from early retirement, the inactive over-50s end up on sickness or disability benefits. This is most often the destination of those who were unemployed or do not have occupational pension rights. It is clear that this, in part, reflects patterns of joblessness and restricted employment opportunities.

- Reform of the benefit system, changes to occupational pension schemes, tougher legislation against age discrimination, and training of older workers, are policies which may reverse the trend to earlier retirement amongst men.

The evidence

Older people in Britain, especially men, now stop working at an increasingly early age. As Figure 4.1 illustrates, the labour force participation rate of

Figure 4.1 Labour force participation

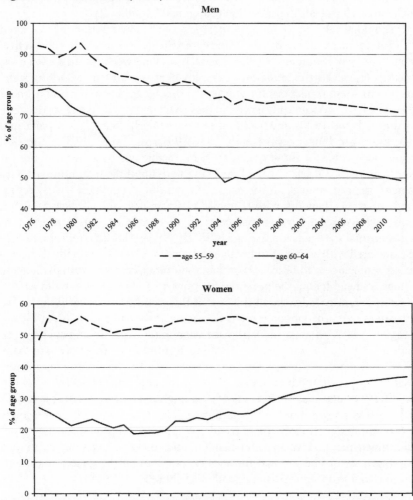

men aged 60–64 has fallen from around 80 per cent to under 50 per cent during the last two decades, while for men aged 55–59, the rate has fallen from over 90 per cent to 75 per cent. Projections do not suggest any secular upturn in participation in the future, although the precipitate decline is expected to end. For women, there is no evidence of a trend in Figure 4.1, but such data conceal age and cohort effects and, in fact, there are systematic forces operating in the female labour market as well which are discussed later in Chapter 10 (see also Disney, 1996: Figures 7.1 and 7.2).

It should also be borne in mind that 'economic activity' cannot be equated with employment: many people who report themselves 'economically active' in later life may be unemployed and actively seeking work (in their own eyes, at least). However, the cessation of employment is often an 'absorbing state' (i.e. a permanent transition) for workers in this age group, and many of those who appear as 'economically active' in these data may in fact never work again.

Although the 1970s and 1980s saw a particularly sharp fall in participation, there are longer-term trends at work across most OECD countries. Employment rates of those over state pensionable age have been falling for over forty years (OECD, 1992), largely as the result of the maturation of public pension programmes. However, private pension programmes, early retirement, disability benefits within public programmes and implicit taxes on continued work are strong disincentives to continued employment even below normal state pensionable age (OECD, 1996). Although retirement may be associated with strong disincentives to continued work, individuals nevertheless often appear to retire earlier than they anticipated and with inadequate savings, so heightening the potential for poverty and insecurity in old age.

An apparent paradox in all this is that this trend towards earlier effective retirement from the labour force is occurring at the same time as people are living longer. With most industrialised economies experiencing ageing populations due to a combination of falling fertility after the post-war 'baby boom' and increased longevity, an increased number of older economically inactive people should be a matter of social and economic concern. Notwithstanding over-alarmist predictions of a demographic 'ageing crisis', it is clear that pension programmes and health care delivery systems will increasingly be brought under strain by these trends. What may be optimal for the individual, given prospective pension benefits and effective taxes on continued working, may not be optimal for society, especially if the generational burden of social programmes is unequally distributed.

The case for a policy focus on the inactivity of older people

In recent years, OECD governments have intervened with active labour market programmes mainly aimed at the young unemployed. It is often implicitly assumed that older inactive people have chosen to retire voluntarily and that there is less need for intervention at this later stage of the life-cycle. However, as we will demonstrate, the transition to inactivity amongst older workers is not always voluntary. Older people often respond to survey questions in a manner indicating that they feel that they have retired too early or have been subject to 'age discrimination' in employment. While I return to the problematic concept of 'age discrimination' below, it is apparent that there is a widespread perception amongst older inactive people that they have been marginalised, and therefore not all economic inactivity amongst this age group can be considered as 'voluntary'. In any event, with some 2.5 million inactive people in Britain aged between 50 and the state pensionable age (currently 60 for women and 65 for men), the size of the population eligible for active policy dwarfs other target groups.

A second concern is that, once older workers cease employment, even those that continue to search for employment face a much lower re-employment probability than young people. This may arise because older people search for jobs at similar wage levels to those in jobs held previously and re-entry jobs are only available at considerably lower levels of pay. On the other hand, there is also evidence from the United States that only a limited range of industries and occupations hire older workers, compared with hires of young workers which are much more representative across industries as a whole (Hutchens, 1988). A particular concern for retirement incomes is that households typically save for retirement in the second half of their working life, starting in their mid-40s. If individuals lose their job at, say, 50 and are unable ever to find an adequate career job thereafter, their prospect of a low retirement income is high. However, as we shall see in the next section, this link between early retirement and low incomes later in life is hard to decipher in the data, because people retire early at both ends of the income distribution: there are both positive and negative shocks to income over the working life.

Finally, it is important to examine the way in which demand shocks impact on the labour market. Suppose that the average individual age–productivity profile is as exhibited by the line $f'(l)$ in Figure 4.2 (which is the marginal productivity schedule). This implies that an individual's productivity is quadratic, rising steeply in the early part of the working life and levelling out and ultimately declining later in life as skills depreciate. In some jobs, the age–wage relationship may exactly match the age–productivity profile but this need not be the case. In Figure 4.2, a linear age–remuneration profile is drawn in which the wage plus pension accrual ($w + \Delta ssw$ 'change in social security wealth') rises with age. Clearly, the employer benefits in the early years by paying a wage below the marginal product of labour, which may cover the cost of training, with the faster growth of wages over the lifetime acting as an incentive for the employee to remain with the firm. Beyond the age where $f'(l) = w + \Delta ssw$, the firm has an incentive to terminate the employment contract. Thus a demand shock, reducing the marginal product of labour from 1 to 2 in the figure, will induce the firm to get rid of older workers.[1]

---

[1] This issue becomes even clearer where the age–remuneration profile actually increases faster towards the end of the working life. This may, for example, be a product of final salary private pension schemes, where accruals are non-linear with age (see Disney and Whitehouse, 1996 for illustrations for the UK). It is then straightforward to demonstrate that employment contracts will, on average, be terminated at an earlier age, but that the volatility of employment to demand shocks is lower.

Figure 4.2   A downward shock to labour demand

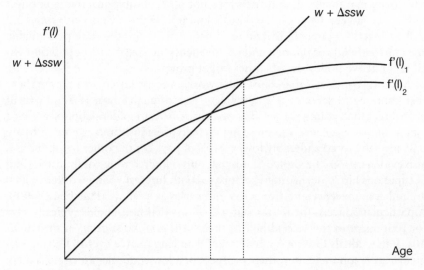

Source: Author's own figure.

The case for public intervention in favour of older workers when there are demand shocks is heightened if there is evidence that these demand shocks exhibit *skill bias* in favour of skilled workers. Typically, skill acquisition is cohort-specific and each new generation enters the labour market with new skills. Skill-biased change in the demand for labour hurts older workers in three ways. First, earlier cohorts have greater proportions of unskilled workers, because they have lower average levels of educational attainment. Second, technological innovation in the form of skill bias hits older unskilled workers because they are competitors for young unskilled workers, and hits older skilled workers because they are *not* competitors for young skilled workers.[2] Third, given the ageing 'baby-boom' generation, there are at present simply more older workers than there are young workers. Thus older workers are in greater supply at a point at which there is a demand shock in favour of younger, skilled workers.

Why are there high rates of economic inactivity amongst older people?

What explains the rate of exit from the labour force, and the declining rates of cohort participation by men? As suggested in the previous section, a

---

[2] Disney (1996: Chapter 6) summarises the many interesting studies in the US on substitutability between age and education groups within the labour force.

common explanation is that it is an outcome of choice by older workers faced with various disincentives to continued work and, in particular, with the growth in coverage of successive cohorts by private pension schemes. This last facet is well documented. For example, the average real pension income per person amongst male pensioners born between 1925 and 1929 is nearly double that of the cohort born between 1905 and 1909 (Dilnot *et al.*, 1994: Figure 2.11).[3] It should be noted that coverage in the workforce has now levelled out, although later cohorts will continue to retire with higher *average* pensions by virtue of having been in schemes for longer durations.

The impact of occupational pensions on early retirement is often regarded as merely increasing the amount of 'unearned income', thus inducing a reduction in hours. This is misleading and simplistic. Accrual of pension benefits in a typical 'final salary' scheme is highly non-linear, with each extra year's work adding disproportionately to the value of the final pension (Disney and Whitehouse, 1996). Thus, in principle, the calculations involved in deciding on an extra year's work should include evaluating the marginal disutility of one year's extra work against the marginal utility of the extra income which arises both from the extra year's work and from the increment of pension rights over the rest of the lifetime. In these circumstances, generous pension schemes are just as likely to induce the individual to stay on at work as to retire early. Ultimately, of course, the prospect of imminent mortality induces the individual to retire, but the relationship between scheme generosity and retirement date is a complex one.

In any event, it is not clear that individuals understand these calculations well enough to evaluate the optimal point at which to retire. For example, there is plenty of evidence that the annuitisation process is not well understood and that in particular people are unable to distinguish clearly between indexed and unindexed annuities. However, it is possible that firms do understand the incentives involved. If the pay and pension profile is similar to that in Figure 4.2, firms might impose mandatory retirement ages as a way of limiting pension obligations. Alternatively, if there are downward shocks to real productivity, as arguably occurred in the 1970s, or a rise in the effective real wage, as occurred in the UK in the early 1980s with the rise in the value of sterling, there is a strong incentive for employers to offer early-retirement 'windows' as a means of downsizing the workforce before 'normal' retirement age (Lumsdaine *et al.*, 1990).

The consequences of these various points are three-fold. First, any corre-

---

[3] This type of comparison must be treated with caution. If those with the most generous pensions retire earlier, the rise in 'implicit' pension wealth is overstated by observations only on pensioners. On the other hand, there is differential mortality by level of income and wealth, so that, for older cohorts, the probability of being observed at all due to continued life is positively related to having occupational pension wealth. This biases the pension wealth of older cohorts upwards. These biases work in opposite directions in these kinds of calculations, but it cannot be assumed that they entirely cancel out *a priori*.

lation over time between the growth of occupational pension rights by cohort and earlier retirement has to be treated cautiously, as the effect of rights accrual need not, theoretically, lead to early retirement. Secondly, insofar as the growth of rights has, behaviourally, induced individuals to retire earlier, it may be that individuals do not fully understand the accrual and annuitisation procedures (which could be why they are subsequently disappointed by their pensions). And third, the driving force behind early retirement through occupational pension schemes in the 1970s and 1980s has almost certainly been firms, which have utilised the schemes to shed expensive and unwanted labour. In these circumstances, earlier retirement through occupational pension schemes does not inevitably generate high levels of income in retirement.[4]

There is a second 'economic' incentive behind earlier retirement, which arises from public provision of social security. In many countries in Europe, there are comprehensive schemes of earnings replacement by social security, and provisions for early retirement through the state scheme (Gruber and Wise, 1997). Whether these are sustainable in the long run as populations age is extremely doubtful. However, in the UK, as is well known, the generosity of real social security benefits has been falling for more than a decade, and there is also no explicit opportunity for 'early retirement' within the UK system of state pension benefits. The route to early inactivity which appears to have been exploited over time in the UK is via long-term disability benefits such as Invalidity Benefit (IVB), now Incapacity Benefit.

During the twenty-five years from the mid-1960s to the late 1980s, recipients of IVB trebled in number. In the early 1990s, the rate of increase in claimant numbers slowed down, but there are still well over a million claimants. Furthermore, although there was a rise in the inflow probability in the early 1980s, the main reason for the increase in the stock figure has been a fall in the outflow probability. This arises, in part, because the age composition of IVB recipients has gradually increased, so that by 1994 about a quarter of men aged 60–64 and nearly 20 per cent of those aged 55–59 were in receipt of IVB. There is strong evidence that the probability of a person receiving IVB is related to local unemployment rates, although there are locational-specific variations in receipt which are hard to explain (Disney and Webb, 1991). Furthermore, there is no one-to-one relationship between measures of individual disability and receipt of IVB.

There is, therefore, evidence that IVB receipt has been used as an early-retirement vehicle, at least until benefit reforms in the early 1990s which

---

[4] A further consequence of the structure of occupational pension schemes is that the *distribution* of post-retirement benefits is highly unequal as a result of a combination of 'backloading' and penalties to early leavers. Thus *average* occupational pension entitlements conceal a wide variance (see Disney and Whitehouse, 1996).

tightened up eligibility and also made IVB liable to tax.[5] There is also some casual evidence that measures designed to limit long-term unemployment, such as the Restart Programme, encouraged individuals to flow out of unemployment-related benefits and into IVB.

Taking occupational pensions and invalidity benefits together, a common picture emerges. Both have been used as early-retirement vehicles by firms anxious to unload 'surplus' labour, and as a response to depressed labour markets. Transitions into inactivity in response to such incentives represent a 'rational' short-term response to depressed job opportunities and to financial inducements that might not be available in the long run. In the case of IVB, the generosity of benefits has been reduced in the last few years. Considering the ageing workforce and increased opting-out of company pension plans in favour of Personal Pensions, especially amongst young men, it is hard to believe that in the case of occupational pensions such generous early-retirement benefits will be available in the future. Hence, there are two conclusions: first, the relative importance of the above-mentioned 'routes' into economic inactivity is likely to decline in the future and, secondly, retirement by these 'routes' in the past has not guaranteed adequate incomes in retirement.

What do we know about retirement other than through these 'routes'?

Figure 4.3 illustrates how different the exit hazards from employment are for men and women who are covered, or not covered by, occupational pension schemes. Typically, such pension schemes disproportionately cover white-collar men and public-sector workers. Employment rates remain high by age until early-retirement benefits come into operation, usually at discrete ages such as 55 and 60, or at a given number of years' service. After that point, employment rates fall sharply. Conversely, for people who do not belong to occupational pension schemes, exit rates exhibit no such 'kink' (i.e. the hazard rate is flat), so that, as can be seen in Figure 4.3, these workers exhibit a faster exit rate before 55 and a slower rate than occupational pension members thereafter. Indeed for the 'No occupational pension' group, the rate of attrition after age 40 is quite startling. In Figure 4.3, by age 55 around one-half of men have left employment and by age 60 (still five years before state pensionable age), only one-third of men are left in regular employment.[6] This acceleration of the exit rate amongst pension scheme members at later ages is one reason why clear differences between manual/non-manual and skilled/unskilled workers do not show up in age-cohort activity rates.

[5] Until that time, IVB was tax-free and could also be received instead of the basic state pension for five years after state pensionable age. Clearly, if entitlement had been granted prior to pensionable age, it was attractive to remain on IVB for the full five years after that age.

[6] These charts are derived from Retirement Survey data. For further discussion and interpretation, see Meghir and Whitehouse, 1997.

Figure 4.3 Survival probabilities by whether entitled to occupational pension

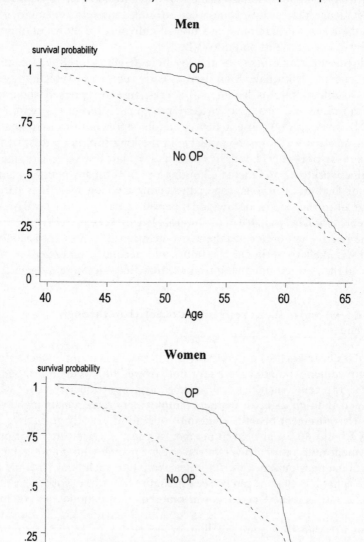

Source: Retirement Survey data, figure from R. Blundell and P. Johnson, 'Pensions and Labour Market Participation in the UK', *American Economic Review Papers and Proceedings*, 1998, No. 88, P168–72, Figures 1 and 2.
Note: OP = occupational pension.

This discussion confirms that employment exit rates are not the same as transitions from 'activity' into 'inactivity', as mentioned in the introductory section. Individuals who move onto IVB, or who receive an occupational pension, often leave the labour market permanently and report that they have done so. Individuals who leave their last job without an occupational pension, or without moving onto IVB, may continue to report that they are 'economically active' even though they subsequently never work again, or to report destinations other than 'retirement' for their subsequent behaviour.

This is illustrated in Table 4.1, taken from Tanner (1998), for men in the Retirement Survey who were observed in both the first (1988–89) and second (1994) waves. It shows different exit patterns between those who were eligible for an occupational pension and those who were not. In particular, the transition destinations of those who initially report themselves as 'working' and 'unemployed' are of interest. A lower proportion of those eligible for an occupational pension report themselves 'retired' or unemployed in 1988, with a correspondingly higher proportion still in work (confirming the difference in survival probabilities in Figure 4.3). Conversely, amongst those without an occupational pension a far greater proportion of transitions out of unemployment and 'working' are into the 'other' category. Around three-quarters of these people are moving into disability and disability-related benefits, thus around a half of these unemployed men and 15 per cent of working men ultimately retire by this route rather than by a directly self-reported transition into 'retirement'. Even amongst those with occupational pension entitlements, of whom 50 per cent remained at work five years on, only three-fifths directly moved into self-reported 'retirement' – the remainder

Table 4.1 Transition states: men aged 55–59 in 1988–89

Status in wave 1 (1988–89)	% of sample	Status in wave 2 (1994) (%)			
		Working	Unemployed	Retired	Other
With occupational pension					
Working	76.4	50.2	6.9	30.0	12.9
Unemployed	6.0	13.9	15.4	39.8	30.9
Retired	6.3	0.0	0.0	82.0	18.1
Other	11.4	0.0	4.8	29.3	65.8
No occupational pension					
Working	68.8	60.5	1.1	17.7	20.7
Unemployed	20.1	9.4	8.9	24.7	57.0
Retired	0.8	0.0	0.0	100.0	0.0
Other	10.3	7.0	0.0	17.2	75.9

Source: Tanner (1998), Table 6. The Retirement Survey.

moved via spells of unemployment, ill health or other forms of inactivity not considered by the respondent to be 'retirement'.

This complexity of the 'retirement' transition is reinforced elsewhere. Tanner also examines data on men from the second wave of the survey, who were asked about their main reason for retiring from the labour force, leaving the respondent to provide their own assessed date and interpretation of 'retirement'. Answers were provided for the 70 per cent of those in the second wave of the Survey who had left employment before age 65, the age at which the state pension could first be received. In addition, individuals are asked to say whether there was a 'fixed retirement age' at the firm they worked for and whether they retired at this age.[7] The main reasons given are summarised in Table 4.2. Not surprisingly, given Table 4.1, those with occupational pensions are less likely than those without to cite ill health and involuntary redundancy, and more likely to cite voluntary redundancy. These differences imply a greater degree of voluntarism in the retirement decisions of those who have an occupational pension, but in fact the differences are not statistically significant and even so a third of occupational pensioners cite ill health or involuntary redundancy as the reason for retiring before 65.

Overall, the message of this section is that it is highly misleading to think of the retirement decision amongst men as one in which individuals move

Table 4.2   Reasons for retirement

	With occupational pension (%)	Without occupational pension (%)
Own ill health	22.5	32.2
Ill health of others	2.7	8.3
Involuntary redundancy	12.3	21.0
Voluntary redundancy – reasonable financial terms	26.4	6.3
Spend more time with family	2.5	2.1
Enjoy life while young and fit	6.0	3.3
Fed up with work/wanted change	4.0	4.6
Other	7.8	8.0
Fixed retirement age	11.2	4.3
Missing	4.6	9.9

Source: Tanner (1998), Table 7. The Retirement Survey.
Note: For a comparison with self-reported reasons for women, see Disney, Grundy and Johnson (1997), Table 2.19.

[7] In cases where individuals give no other reason for retiring, and the firm-level retirement age was less than 65 and where individuals actually retired at the specified age, 'fixed retirement age' is assigned as the reason for retirement. It is not always clear what individuals mean when they refer to 'fixed retirement ages', not least because of the degree of divergence between 'fixed retirement ages' and individuals' actual retirement ages. Tanner (1998) discusses alternative interpretations.

seamlessly from work into 'retirement' with a decent income. Even amongst those with occupational pensions, a significant fraction move to retirement via unemployment and ill health, and often at the behest of employers rather than as the outcome of an individual decision-making process governed by the 'option value' of continued work. Even so, many older men with occupational pensions probably have a reasonable standard of living. In contrast, for men who are not covered by occupational pensions, attrition from employment starts at an earlier age, often taking the route of unemployment and/or ill health. This last route was particularly favoured in the 1980s when IVB was paid more generously than the state pension.

Over time we are observing a retrenchment in social security programmes and probably also in occupational pension schemes, as the traditional 'final salary' defined benefit scheme is replaced by alternative arrangements. The 'carrot' aspect of such retirement 'routes' will thereby be eroded, but while this may serve to decelerate the fall in labour force participation of older workers (as projected in Figure 4.1), it would be foolish to assume that retirement ages will rise as a result without additional policies. This is because, as this section has demonstrated, much of the recent trend in earlier retirement has not been associated simply with the attractions of early retirement, but rather arises involuntarily as a result of changes in the demand for skills, loss of jobs, lack of re-employability and employer behaviour in the face of adverse macroeconomic shocks. Policies to combat this trend will have to be assessed in this light.

Policies to keep older men working: what are the options?

Here we consider a range of four policy options required to keep older men in work. They include altering the benefit system, changing occupational pension incentives, anti-age discrimination legislation and training or retraining.

The benefit system

A range of policies can be suggested here, all sharing the common aim of persuading individuals to work for a longer period, whether part-time or full-time, than they had otherwise intended. Some of these, such as replacing IVB with the less generous Incapacity Benefit, and abolishing the 'earnings rule' for the Basic State Retirement Pension, have already been enacted. But the pitfalls that arise from a partial analysis of the retirement decision can be illustrated by a consideration of the latter policy.

Until October 1989, men aged 65–69 and women aged 60–64 who earned more than £75 per week would have their state retirement pension withdrawn, initially at 50 pence per pound and, above £79, at a pound for a pound under the pensions 'earnings rule'. Not unnaturally, the government felt that this was a major discouragement to continued work in the five years after reaching state pensionable age. They therefore abandoned the rule, expecting to see an increase in participation amongst this group from the simple operation of the substitution effect in a labour supply model.

This increase did not materialise for a very simple reason. Retirement pensioners had another option, which was to defer receipt of their pension for up to five years, thereby receiving an extra 7.5 per cent addition to their ultimate pension for each year of deferral. Since over 200,000 people deferred their pension whereas only 2,500 were affected by the 'earnings rule' (Whitehouse, 1990), the disproportionately large number of beneficiaries from its abolition would be deferrers. But once the 'earnings rule' no longer operated, then, so long as deferral was actuarially unfair (which, at 7.5 per cent it is, for men although approximately neutral for women), the effect of the abolition of the 'earnings rule' would be to make *immediate* reductions in hours more attractive due to a pure income effect! This is another example of a misleading inference drawn from a partial analysis of retirement as a static labour supply decision.[8]

Nevertheless, this episode does raise another policy option, which is to make later retirement more attractive by increasing the deferral rate for pension accrual. Indeed this policy has been adopted recently, by raising the deferral rate from 7.5 per cent to 10 per cent. Given life expectancy for men and women, this makes deferral reasonably attractive. But, as we have seen, attrition from the labour force occurs long before state pensionable age is reached and has a strong involuntary component. Those who are likely to take advantage of the more attractive deferral rate are those with a strong preference for continued work who already have a well-paid job. As a means of reincorporating those who are already inactive, favourable deferral rates are an irrelevance.

There is a second route, however. Many older people engage in low-paid or even unpaid work, such as working for charities and voluntary organisations. Although any earnings are not now subject to the 'earnings rule' they are still liable to income tax (although not, unlike some countries, liable to social security contributions). Given starting tax rates, this should not be a major deterrent. But it may be that, for low-paid jobs, the deduction of taxes at the margin is an irritation to people for whom continued work is at best a marginal decision. Increasing the age allowance or perhaps simply exempting such earnings from tax might be a possible policy option. But the net effects on participation are likely to be small.

Unlike other countries, the UK does not offer an explicit early-retirement option through the state pension programme. In other countries, notably the United States, it is possible to retire earlier with an actuarially reduced pen-

---

[8] It should not be inferred from this discussion that abolition of the 'earnings rule' was a bad policy; merely that the incentive effects of the policy were not analysed properly.

sion. It has sometimes been argued that this option is overly attractive given the insufficient actuarial deduction, making early retirement the norm. But, given the UK system, in which Income Support (plus housing and council tax benefits) may actually be more generous than the basic state pension, early retirement with a reduced pension would simply be 'topped up' by income-tested benefits, where the individual had no other resources. Again, therefore, ideas of a 'decade of retirement' and of actuarial incentives within the state pension programme to vary retirement behaviour, are likely to have very little impact.

Incentives in occupational pension schemes

The discussion in the previous section suggested that early-retirement 'windows', or use of occupational pension schemes to cushion involuntary separations, were a significant cause of reduced labour force participation amongst older men in particular (given the lower coverage of women by schemes). At the same time, it was argued that individuals were often confused about entitlements from pension schemes; for example, as to the consequences of indexation, or its absence. A logical response to the problem of inaccurate information would seem to be greater transparency in occupational pension schemes so that accrual structures are better understood. Although this seems an uncontroversial recommendation, there are several problematic issues here.

Most occupational pension schemes are of the 'defined benefit' (DB) form, in which the scheme commits to a target benefit outcome, conditional on a number of unknowns, such as years of service, age–earnings profiles, and so on. *Accrued* rights, particularly in the early years of pension scheme tenure, rise very slowly as a result of the phenomenon of 'backloading' described earlier. Schemes much prefer to detail *projected* rights, based on, say, an uninterrupted career history through to retirement. As we have seen, actual *ex post* pension payments are often much lower than these projected rights due to career breaks, job mobility, and so on. Thus, there is an intrinsic difficulty in persuading DB schemes to provide useful information on the 'option value' of continued work. In contrast, 'defined contribution' (DC) schemes are intrinsically more transparent, since the pension depends only on contributions and projected returns. Although DC funds are typically somewhat opaque about effective transaction costs, the potential volatility of investment and annuity *rates*, the 'option value' of continued work is usually easier to calculate for the individual.

To pursue this line of argument therefore, if there is a DC basis to pension calculations rather than a DB basis, individuals may be able to make a more informed choice and therefore, by extension, not retire from active work 'prematurely' (relative to realised pension benefits). Firms are increasingly moving toward offering new employees DC rather than DB plans (including

Personal Pensions amongst DC plans), which might by this argument facilitate rational retirement planning.

Unfortunately, there are three difficulties with this chain of reasoning. First, it is obvious that much of the problem of inactivity amongst older workers arises amongst those with no occupational pensions (although in the long run, a shift to DC plans may broaden coverage). Second, occupational pensions, of whatever form, are often used to cushion involuntary retirement, and the 'transparency' of the benefit is a second-order problem. And thirdly, many firms that *have* switched from DB to DC plans have done so to reduce pension entitlements (most clearly when DB plans are wound up and individuals are invited to purchase a Personal Pension without a matching contribution from the employer).

In the light of these points, the major policy issue would seem to be whether it is feasible to deter firms from using existing occupational pension plans as a cheap means of retiring workers prematurely. Restrictions on the form in which pension benefits can be offered seem largely unenforceable, but the question of tax relief could be looked at again. At present, pension contributions up to a ceiling are tax-relieved, but there is little else in the way of special treatment of pension funds since the abolition of dividend tax credit in 1997. On the other hand, part of an employee's benefits can be taken in the form of tax-free cash lump sum up to a ceiling multiple of their final salary. This, and other lump sum *ex gratia* or redundancy payments, are probably a major incentive to individuals to take early retirement and restrictions of tax reliefs here might be a feasible direction for policy, especially if the tax reliefs were retained for 'normal' retirement. However, it is hard to obtain any empirical 'feel' of how large an impact such a policy would have, and it is again a policy primarily targeted at voluntary retirements rather than the involuntary inactivity that causes much of the concern here.

Age discrimination legislation?

It was suggested above that many older 'retired' individuals feel that they have become marginalised in the labour market through no fault of their own. Although explicit age ceilings on job advertisements are illegal (as a form of indirect discrimination on grounds of gender), many employers, it is argued, implicitly operate such age ceilings in their hiring policy. Would tougher legal measures to combat 'age discrimination' therefore be the answer? There are several reasons for being sceptical about an extension of such legislation in the case of older people.

To the economist, discrimination arises when an employer selects between two workers, identical in terms of productive characteristics, on grounds that are irrelevant to their productivity, such as their gender or the colour of their skin. The difficulty in applying such a concept in the case of older workers is that they typically *are* different in terms of productive characteristics from younger workers. This is not to suggest that older workers are less productive than young workers, merely that they have different skills, perhaps less dexterity but greater experience, for example. The argument that there is age discrimination is therefore harder to pin down, and must arise because it is believed that employers undervalue skills more common to older workers and overvalue the skills of young workers.

Why should employers undervalue the skills of older workers, particularly when hiring? There are three possible reasons. First, given the pace of technological change, the skills of older workers are regarded by employers as obsolete and it is too costly, in present value terms, to retrain them. Second, older workers simply demand wages that are too high relative to young workers. Third, past unemployment and redundancy amongst older workers are taken as an adverse signal of worker quality by prospective employers. Little evidence on these points is available for Britain, although, as mentioned previously, there is evidence from the United States that older workers are typically *hired* into a smaller set of industries and occupations either than those hiring young workers or those in which older workers are *employed*. Fixed costs such as initial training costs, as well as the industrial and occupational incidence of private pension and health benefits (Scott *et al.*, 1995), may be causes of these unequal opportunities for displaced older workers.

In the light of these points, it seems likely that the main beneficiaries from new legislation on 'age discrimination' will be lawyers, since it appears hard to prove a *priori* that there is discrimination on grounds solely of age. It is true that the penalties to unfair dismissal could be toughened up, and that, for workers who can show that they have been made redundant prematurely, continued employment rather than lump sum compensation could be the more frequent sanction than it is at present. But neither legal policy is likely to have a large impact on the activity rates of the elderly.

Training and retraining

The case for greater public involvement in training or retraining older workers is implicit in the discussion earlier in this chapter of skill-biased shifts in labour demand. The private returns to training workers late in life are low, unless prospective wages (to the trainee) are high, but high prospective wages discourage firms from undertaking the training themselves or from hiring retrained workers. Thus, by undertaking to subsidise employer training of older workers, the government reduces the marginal cost of training to the firm. Also the trainee does not then require such high wages to recoup any training costs incurred themselves. Although basic training in new technologies (such as computers or automated systems) is desirable not least because innovations of this type often prove to be a mental stumbling block to older workers, it is likely that the training would have to differ for older workers, including training based on 'life-long learning' and strategies with a strong educative function for employers. Of particular interest is that, just as the workforce is ageing, so are consumers, with predictable effects on expenditure patterns. For example, consumers are likely to shift toward expenditure on services, some of which may provide outlets for older workers. There is scope for further analysis of these likely changes and of the costs and benefits of training strategies. But of the options considered here, this seems the most fruitful approach to what may be the most pressing labour market problem facing Britain today.

References

Dilnot, A., Disney, R., Johnson, P. and Whitehouse, E. (1994), 'Pension Policy in the UK: an Economic Analysis', Institute for Fiscal Studies, London.

Disney, R. (1996), 'Can We Afford to Grow Older?: A Perspective on the Economics of Aging', MIT Press, Cambridge Massachusetts.

Disney, R., Grundy, E. and Johnson, P. (eds) (1997), 'The Dynamics of Retirement: Analyses of the Retirement Surveys', Department of Social Security Research Report No. 72, HMSO, London.

Disney, R. and Webb, S. (1991), 'Why are there so many long term sick in Britain?', Economic Journal, 101:405, 252–62.

Disney, R. and Whitehouse, E. (1996), ' What are occupational pension plan entitlements worth in Britain?', Economica, 63:250, 213–38.

Gruber, J. and Wise, D. (1997), 'Social Security Programs and Retirement Around the World' , Working Paper No. 6134, National Bureau of Economic Research, Cambridge, Massachusetts.

Hutchens, R. (1988), 'Do job opportunities decline with age?', Industrial and Labor Relations Review, 42:1, 89–99.

Lumsdaine, R., Stock, J. and Wise, D. (1990), 'Efficient windows and labor force reduction', Journal of Public Economics, 43:2, 131–59.

Meghir, C. and Whitehouse, E. (1997), 'Labour market transitions and retirement of men in the UK', Journal of Econometrics, 79:2, 327–54.

Organisation for Economic Co-operation and Development (OECD) (1992), 'Employment Outlook', Paris.

OECD (1996), 'Employment Outlook', Paris.

Scott, F. A., Berger, M. C. and Garen, J. E. (1995), 'Do health insurance and pension costs reduce the job opportunities of older workers?', Industrial and Labor Relations Review, 48, 775–91.

Tanner, S. (1998), 'The dynamics of male retirement behavior', Fiscal Studies, 19:2, 175–96.

Whitehouse, E. (1990), ' The abolition of the pensions "earnings rule"', Fiscal Studies, 11:3, 55–70.

5 Paul Gregg, Kirstine Hansen and Jonathan Wadsworth

The rise of the workless household

Keypoints

- Employment is as plentiful now as it was thirty years ago, but despite this both the number of adults living in workless households and the number of workless households have roughly quadrupled.

- Workless households are now much more common across all family types than they were in the 1970s. Work has polarised across households. There has been a simultaneous rise in households that are fully employed and in those with no access to earned income.

- 50 per cent of the poor live in workless households and 70 per cent of workless households are poor.

- The presence of children increases a workless household's chance of living in poverty to 90 per cent. In Britain one in five children are growing up in workless households, a higher percentage than in any other Organisation for Economic Co-operation and Development (OECD) nation.

- Adults in workless households are spending increasingly long periods out of work. 60 per cent have not worked in at least three years.

- The workless household rate falls as the size of the household increases; thus single parents and single adults have the highest workless household rates.

- Only about one-third of the rise in the number of workless households observed over the last thirty years can be explained by changes in family structure and the economic cycle. Most of the change is caused by differential access to work by household status.

We know that male and female employment rates have converged (Chapters 3 and 10). Male employment has fallen mostly amongst the over-50s, and female employment has risen most for women aged between 25 and 40. These increases for women have been almost entirely amongst those with a working partner. Employment amongst lone mothers and those with unemployed partners has changed little. This chapter examines the consequences of these changes for the distribution of work across households. In doing so we encounter what is, we believe, one of the most profound developments in the labour market over the past thirty years – the rise of the workless household.

The bold facts

Given the demographic make up of these trends in male and female employment it is no surprise that we do not see the rise in female employment occurring in the same households where male activity rates have fallen. These trends, together with a move to smaller household size, lie behind one of the major shifts in the distribution of work over the last thirty years. Figure 5.1 shows how the proportion of households containing no adult in work has risen from 4 per cent in 1968 to 17 per cent in 1996, according to the Family Expenditure Survey (FES).

The definition of a workless household used here excludes students and households where the head is over retirement age. It also excludes those where the household head is absent or no data are available. The more up-to-date Labour Force Survey (LFS) shows a very similar pattern over time, but at a slightly higher rate. Even at the end of the 1990s recovery, 18 per

Figure 5.1   The rise of the workless household

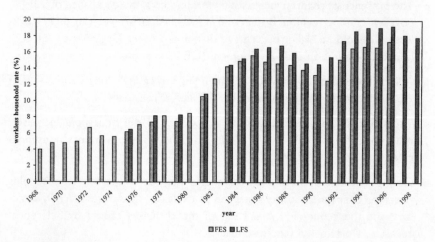

Sources: FES and LFS.

Table 5.1 Workless households

	Workless households (000s)	%	Households where all adults work (000s)	%	Working age adults in workless households (000s)	%	Children in workless households (000s)	%	All individuals in workless households (000s)	%	Employment rate
FES											
1968	540	4.0	7146	52.8	800	2.6	520	4.0	1320	3.0	76.3
1975	870	6.2	7802	55.5	1330	4.4	990	7.2	2320	5.3	77.7
1981	1530	10.6	7996	55.4	2540	8.1	1730	13.2	4280	9.6	73.1
1985	2370	15.7	8025	53.6	3730	11.6	2090	16.9	5830	13.1	70.8
1990	2180	13.3	10340	63.1	3200	9.6	1890	15.6	5090	11.2	76.7
1995	2870	16.7	10473	61.2	4110	12.6	2400	18.3	6520	14.2	75.1
1996	2990	17.4	10567	61.5	4330	13.2	2560	19.6	6890	15.0	75.7
LFS											
1975	900	6.5	7770	56.1	1240	4.4	–	–	–	–	76.6
1981	1570	10.9	7460	51.8	2360	7.8	–	–	–	–	72.9
1985	2530	16.5	7940	51.8	3820	12.1	–	–	–	–	71.6
1990	2360	14.6	9620	59.5	3300	10.2	–	–	–	–	76.9
1995	3290	19.1	10370	60.2	4480	14.1	2880	20.4	7360	16.0	73.9
1998	3150	17.9	11120	63.2	4270	13.2	2700	19.0	6980	15.1	75.8

Sources: LFS 1975–98, Spring quarter. FES 1968–96.
Note: – = data not available.

cent of working age households have no one in work. The chart also highlights that while the proportion of households with no work rose rapidly in
all three recessions over the last thirty years, the share of workless households
did not fall back by a corresponding amount during recovery. The effect is to
ratchet up the workless household rate. So, as noted in Table 5.1, while overall employment has moved with the economic cycle, returning with each
recovery to around the same rate (about 77 per cent), the workless household
rate has not. At the end of the 1990s' boom, workless households are four
times as common as in the late 1960s.

Table 5.1 shows something more. At the same time as the workless household share has risen, so has the share of households where every adult occu-
pant is in work. Households have polarised into the work-rich and the
work-poor. Households containing a mixture of adults in and out of work
are diminishing rapidly – down from 37 per cent of households in 1975 to
20 per cent in 1998. Women have typically gone out to work where their
partner is already in work, not from households where women are alone or
have a partner out of work. The 3.1 million workless households in 1998
contained nearly 7 million people, including 2.7 million children (one in five
British children). OECD (1996) international comparisons show that Britain,
despite its high employment rate, has the fourth highest workless household
rate (see Figure 5.2).

In comparison with other OECD countries, Britain has by far the greatest
proportion of children growing up in workless households (Figure 5.3). In
other countries, workless households tend to contain adults just short of
retirement age rather than those with dependent children. In Britain, over 30
per cent of our workless households contain children (half of whom are in
lone parent families), whereas in France this figure is just 14 per cent, 11 per
cent in Germany and 18 per cent in Spain.

Figure 5.2 Workless household rate by country in 1996

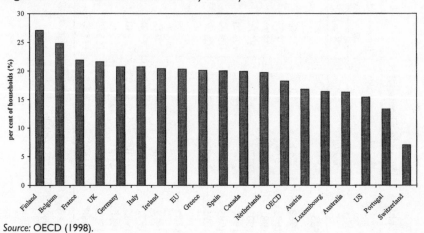

Source: OECD (1998).

Figure 5.3 Workless household rate by country for households with children in 1996

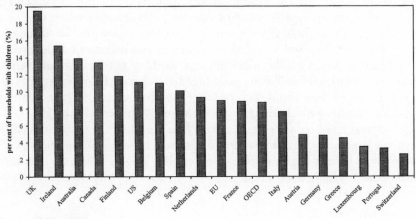

Source: OECD (1998).

Resulting poverty

It is no surprise that lone parent households have the highest propensity to be workless at any point in time. The more adults there are in a household, the more chance there is that one is in work; therefore, it follows that work-

Table 5.2 Workless households by family type

	Total	By family type			
	%	Single adult	Single parent	Couple, no children	Couple with children
FES					
1968	4.0	11.3	23.4	2.7	1.6
1975	6.2	13.2	36.5	3.4	3.0
1981	10.6	17.5	40.7	5.8	7.3
1985	15.7	22.1	30.2	11.0	10.5
1990	13.3	19.2	48.8	7.9	6.1
1995	16.7	26.5	50.4	9.3	7.3
1996	17.4	26.2	51.4	10.4	7.5
LFS					
1992	17.5	35.2	60.8	7.2	8.9
1994	19.1	34.3	60.0	8.1	9.4
1996	19.3	34.8	56.7	7.8	8.3
1998	17.9	31.8	54.1	7.8	6.8

Sources: LFS 1992–98, Spring quarter. FES 1968–96.

less household rates are higher for households with only one adult. It is less obvious, however, why worklessness has risen over time for all household types and especially rapidly amongst couples, with or without children.

Table 5.2 shows how the incidence of worklessness varies across family type. While poverty and benefit dependence do not necessarily follow from worklessness, poverty is the norm amongst workless families. Around three-quarters of workless families are poor (defined as having below half the average equivalised household income after housing costs), 90 per cent of workless families with children are poor and just 40 per cent of workless couples without children are poor. For this latter group, many will have early retirement incomes, perhaps on top of sickness benefits. Around half of all the poor in Britain live in workless households, a figure which rose sharply during the 1970s, but remained broadly constant over the 1980s and 1990s (see Table 5.3).

Table 5.3 Poverty rates in workless households

| | Workless household poverty rate | By family type | | | | Proportion of the poor living in workless households |
		Single adult	Single parent	Couple, no children	Couple with children	
1968	70.8	59.3	81.9	61.0	75.0	29.3
1975	62.2	46.9	82.3	41.5	60.4	37.8
1981	62.5	47.4	66.9	40.7	71.2	46.8
1985	69.0	56.4	73.7	47.3	85.1	58.0
1990	77.4	68.2	89.7	49.5	84.3	43.2
1995	76.2	61.3	90.2	40.9	90.3	51.7
1996	74.9	60.6	89.1	40.1	89.2	51.2

Source: FES 1968–96.

Unemployment and workless households

As the share of households which are workless has risen, so those out of work have become increasingly concentrated in workless households. The proportion of the unemployed in workless households has risen from 40 per cent in the 1970s to 60 per cent in the 1990s. This trend is even more dramatic amongst those not looking for work – the inactive (see Figure 5.4).

In two-thirds of workless households in Britain no one is looking for work. This concentration is more marked than in most other countries (except Finland – see Figure 5.5). This again shows how high Britain's workless household rate is, given its strong employment position.

Adults in British workless households have usually not worked for more than three years (see Table 5.4), a figure which, again, is increasing, as is the length of separation from work. In 1992, some 45 per cent of adults had not worked in three years. This pattern of long periods of worklessness holds for all households with children, and older or younger households.

Figure 5.4   Percentage of inactive and unemployed living in workless households

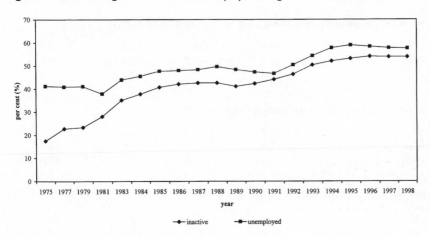

Source: LFS.

Figure 5.5   Likelihood of living in a workless household for the unemployed and inactive in 1996

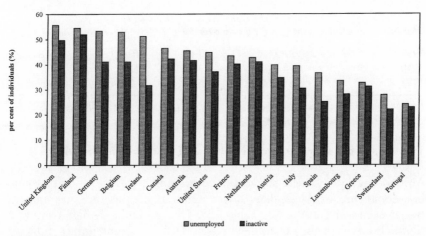

Source: OECD (1998).

Table 5.4 Minimum time since any adult in a workless household was in work

	Less than 1 year	1–2 years	2–3 years	More than 3 years
All workless households				
1992	32.0	13.2	9.6	45.3
1995	20.5	14.1	11.7	53.7
1998	18.9	12.6	9.0	59.5
Workless households containing at least 1 unemployed person				
1992	52.8	16.4	8.3	22.5
1995	35.2	17.9	13.3	33.7
1998	39.7	16.1	7.2	36.9
Workless households containing a single parent				
1992	18.2	10.8	11.3	59.7
1995	12.8	11.4	10.4	65.4
1998	13.0	12.6	9.5	65.0
Workless households with children				
1992	32.3	13.4	9.5	44.8
1995	19.6	12.4	10.5	57.5
1998	18.6	12.2	8.4	60.7
Workless households containing at least one person over 50				
1992	24.2	11.1	9.1	55.7
1995	16.2	14.2	11.1	58.2
1998	13.0	10.6	9.3	67.1
Workless households containing no one over 50				
1992	37.5	14.7	10.0	37.8
1995	23.2	14.0	12.1	50.7
1998	23.0	14.0	8.7	54.3

Source: LFS 1992–98, Spring quarter.

Where are the workless households, and who lives in them?

Around one in two local authority and housing association non-pensioner households are workless. This is four times as high as the rates amongst owner-occupied housing (see Table 5.5). This astoundingly high concentration helps explain the government's New Deal for Communities initiative. For if this is the average, there will be some estates in the more depressed

Table 5.5 Workless households by housing tenure

	Owner	Council	Private
1979	4.7	14.2	9.7
1987	8.2	38.5	20.0
1995	9.2	48.8	27.9
1998	9.2	47.5	28.2

Source: LFS 1979–98, Spring quarter.
Note: table shows per cent of each housing type.

Table 5.6 Regional variation in workless households

Region	Workless household rate				Employment rate			
	1979	1990	1998	79–98 change	1979	1990	1998	79–98 change
Tyne & Wear	10.9	25.9	26.2	+15.3	73.5	66.9	68.2	−5.3
Rest of Northern Region	12.2	17.7	21.4	+9.2	72.8	71.8	71.4	−1.4
South Yorkshire	7.5	21.2	23.6	+16.1	76.5	70.5	68.4	−8.1
West Yorkshire	7.9	16.1	18.8	+9.9	79.4	77.1	75.9	−4.5
Rest of Yorkshire & Humberside	10.3	14.0	16.6	+6.3	73.4	76.1	76.9	+3.5
East Midlands	7.5	12.4	15.6	+8.1	77.4	78.0	78.2	+1.2
East Anglia	6.3	9.6	12.8	+6.5	77.5	82.1	79.4	+1.9
London (inner & outer)	7.9	14.3	20.8	+12.9	79.2	77.7	73.2	−6.0
South East (except London and East Anglia)	6.2	8.2	12.2	+6.0	79.3	82.2	81.2	+1.9
South West	9.1	11.0	13.9	+4.8	76.7	80.4	79.9	+3.2
West Midlands (metropolitan)	8.3	15.8	19.7	+11.4	78.3	74.2	73.8	−4.5
Rest of West Midlands	6.6	9.9	13.9	+7.3	77.7	80.2	79.1	+1.4
Greater Manchester	10.0	18.8	21.5	+11.5	77.2	73.9	72.8	−4.4
Merseyside	12.9	22.9	28.2	+15.3	72.9	68.9	65.6	−7.3
Rest of North West	6.9	14.1	19.3	+13.6	78.1	77.1	74.8	−3.3
Wales	10.7	16.7	22.7	+12.0	72.1	71.9	70.8	−1.3
Strathclyde & Central Clydeside	11.5	24.8	26.8	+15.3	73.1	66.6	69.0	−4.1
Rest of Scotland	8.0	14.5	15.8	+7.8	77.4	76.3	77.2	−0.2
Northern Ireland	12.0	22.2	20.8	+8.8	68.7	67.9	70.6	+1.9
United Kingdom	8.3	14.6	17.9	+9.6	77.0	76.9	75.8	−1.2

Source: LFS, Spring quarters.

cities with a far higher incidence than this. Yet this rising trend is common to all housing types.

Regional variation in the incidence of workless households is quite large (Table 5.6). Merseyside has the highest incidence at 28 per cent, Tyneside and Strathclyde also have over 25 per cent of households workless. The South East (excluding London and East Anglia) has the lowest rate at about 12 per cent. These variations and those across time reflect employment patterns. On average, a one percentage point fall in the employment rate leads to a one point rise in the workless household rate. Yet all regions show a rise in workless households over time.

Table 5.7 shows that the proportion of workless households where no adult has any qualifications has risen from 9 per cent to 29 per cent, far faster than for any other education group. Yet as a share of workless households the proportion with no qualifications has fallen from three in every four to well under half. This apparent contradiction can be explained by the rapid rise in educational attainment in Britain in the last twenty years (see Chapter 11). Splitting the population according to educational attainment shows that, for that half of the population with the lowest qualifications in each year, the workless household rate rose from 9 per cent in 1979 to 24 per cent in 1998. For the most highly educated quarter the rate rose from just under 5 per cent to 12 per cent. The divergence has been especially marked since 1990: amongst the most educated households the workless household rate has risen by a quarter since 1990, for the least educated half it has increased by nearly 40 per cent. So education does matter.

Table 5.7 Workless household rate by highest qualification within the household

Qualification	1979		1990		1998		79–98 change	
	Rate	Share	Rate	Share	Rate	Share	Rate	Share
Degree / higher voc.	4.3	4.3	7.4	5.3	8.9	7.8	+4.6	+3.5
'A' level / advanced voc.	5.6	2.7	9.2	4.1	13.3	5.3	+7.7	+2.6
'O' level / intermediate voc.	4.6	10.5	10.1	19.4	14.3	25.7	+9.7	+15.2
CSE / lower voc.	5.6	6.2	12.4	12.2	16.6	17.8	+11.0	+11.6
None	8.5	76.3	19.0	59.0	29.3	43.4	+20.8	−32.9

Source: LFS 1979–98, Spring quarter.

What explains rising workless households?

What is driving the rise in the workless household and why is the trend so strong in Britain? It is reasonable to consider whether the causes are related to changes in the availability of jobs and patterns of household formation.

Chapter 3 shows that there has been little change in the aggregate employment rate. So the overall availability of jobs is unlikely to be a major factor. The breakdown of the nuclear family, rising divorce rates and later marriages have all encouraged a trend towards households made up of fewer adults than in the past. Both the LFS and FES show a decline in the average number of adults in each household in the last thirty years. This will obviously reduce the likelihood that a person out of work will be supported by someone else in work.

However, changes in family composition alone cannot explain the rise in workless household rates. Table 5.2 has already shown that there have been increases in workless households in all family types. One way of assessing how important these forces are is to think about how the world would look if work were distributed randomly. Thus, if a quarter of the population of working age were workless then a quarter of single adult households would not work. For couples it would be one in sixteen, as each person has a one in four chance of being out of work and so on. Over time an increase in single adult households would generate a higher workless household rate, fewer jobs would also have the same effect. Hence we can predict a workless household rate and see how it differs from what we observe in reality. If married women have a low propensity to work, then the random allocation will over-predict the number of workless households. However, if the tendency is for couples to both work, or both not to work, the opposite will be true – so this will be a useful indicator of trends in polarisation.

Figure 5.6 illustrates the gap between the random and actual workless household rates since 1968 using the FES and from 1975 using the LFS. Both data sets tell the same story. In the 1970s there were fewer actual workless households than there would have been by chance. Those in large households had a lower likelihood of being in work than single adult households, this was no doubt driven by the lower incidence of women with children who worked. In the 1990s there are many more workless households than there would be by chance. The rise has been continuous although it may have slowed down somewhat since the mid-1980s. The implied trend in each year produces a rise in the workless household rate of 0.3 percentage points above what would have been predicted by changing employment patterns or household formation. Thus polarisation of work across households accounts for

Figure 5.6   Difference between random and actual workless household rates

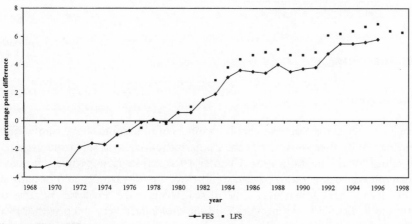

Source: LFS and FES.

about two-thirds of the 13-percentage-point rise in workless households since 1968. Of the remaining 5 percentage points, the bulk has been driven by changing household composition.

When the gap between predicted and actual workless household rates is compared across the OECD countries (Figure 5.7) it becomes clear that in some countries, such as Ireland and the United States, the rate is consistent with a random distribution. Other countries, such as Spain and Luxembourg, have far fewer workless households than they would if every adult had equal access to work. Spain keeps its workless household rate down despite very low employment rates. This may in part be explained by the fact that unemployment in Spain is concentrated on youths who tend to live with their working parents. Britain has by far the largest gap between actual and predicted workless household rates, given our employment and household formation record. It is therefore important to try and establish what forces cause this situation.

Figure 5.7   Difference between random and actual workless household rates in 1996 across countries

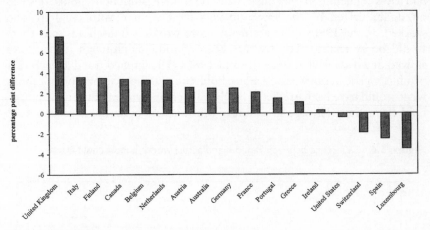

Source: OECD (1998).

Polarisation

The evidence above suggests that if members of households have similar ages and educational characteristics then polarisation could result from regional or educational concentrations. Chapter 14 describes how people who have been out of work get jobs paying well below typical earnings and how these entry wages have fallen over time in real terms and even faster relative to other jobs. People living in workless households face very steep withdrawal rates in Income Support, Family Credit and Housing-related benefits when moving into low-paid work. In contrast, those with working partners, or younger workers living with their parents, face no such work disincentives. Table 5.8 highlights results taken from Gregg, Johnson and Reed (1998), and gives the average gains to taking a job at typical entry wages across different family circumstances, derived from the Institute of Fiscal Studies Tax and Benefit Model (TAXBEN). It shows that men with working partners are around £115 a week better off on entry into full-time work, whereas those with a non-working partner are just £52 a week better off. For women, those with working partners gain about £80 a week. This is lower than for men because more women move into part-time jobs, thus lowering the average entry wage. The gains for those with non-working partners are just £27 and £43 for lone parents. None of these calculations consider the child-care and travel to work costs that would also have to be met if in work. Taking all these factors into account, low-paid work may, in many cases, simply not be financially worthwhile.

One way of exploring how important these factors are is to look at who moves back into work and to what extent these moves can be explained by region, education and financial incentives. Table 5.9a gives the probability of moving back into work within the next three months conditional on household status, in 1997. Around 9 per cent of jobless men, on average, move back into work in three months. However, for men with working partners the entry rate is almost twice as high as for those living alone or with non-working partners. These entry rates, conditional on partner's status, are similar for women. Table 5.9b introduces controls for the key forces considered to be driving these differences. The observed gaps decline as control factors

Table 5.8 Weekly incomes and expected gains from work under initial tax-benefit regime (£)

	Average income out of work	Average expected gain to work
Men		
All single men	86.6	82.9
Single, living with parents	39.8	82.7
Couple, partner working	227.9	115.0
Couple, partner not working	178.2	51.7
Women		
All single women	126.1	44.0
Lone parent	147.1	43.0
Single, living with parents	44.1	75.2
Couple, partner working	337.6	78.4
Couple, partner not working	185.3	27.7

Source: Family Resources Survey. 1993–94 data, indexed to 1997 prices.

Table 5.9a Quarterly entry rates

	All	Single adult households	Multi-adult households	
			Workless	Non-workless
Men	9.2	5.7	7.9	13.0
Women	7.1	5.6	3.4	9.2
– with children		5.2	3.6	8.9
– without children		6.2	3.5	9.7

Source: LFS 1997.

Table 5.9b Difference in entry rates

	Difference between entry rates for:	
	single adult and non-workless households	workless and non-workless households
Men	–0.064	–0.042
With controls for:		
recent displacement	–0.059	–0.037
age	–0.045	–0.032
qualifications	–0.042	–0.026
region	–0.042	–0.025
Women	–0.031	–0.052
With controls for:		
children	–0.031	–0.052
recent displacement	–0.029	–0.048
age	–0.027	–0.045
qualifications	–0.021	–0.036
region	–0.020	–0.035

Source: LFS 1997.

are added, but the key forces, age and region, do little to explain the differences across household types. The combined effect of all the controls is to reduce the gaps by about a third. In addition to these factors Gregg, Johnson and Reed (1998) estimate that about a quarter of these gaps can be explained by financial incentives.

Conclusion

Both the number of adults living in workless households and the number of workless households have quadrupled in the last thirty years, despite the fact that employment is as plentiful now as it was then. Households have polarised into the work-rich and the work-poor. Women have gone out to work from households where other occupants are already in work and not from households where women are alone or where other occupants are out of work. The workless household rate falls as the size of the household increases. Thus, single parents and single adults have the highest workless household rate. However, workless households are now more common amongst all family types. 50 per cent of the poor live in workless households and 70 per cent of workless households are poor. The presence of children raises a workless household's likelihood of living in poverty to 90 per cent. One in five children are growing up in workless households: this rate is higher than in any other OECD nation. Adults in workless households are enduring increasingly long spells without work: 60 per cent have not worked in at least three years.

Changes in family structure and the availability of work explain about one-third of the rise in the number of workless households observed over the last thirty years. Most of what we observe, however, is caused by differential access to work by household status – the polarisation of work. These events can only be partially explained by the characteristics of household members (age, education and region). For many benefit-dependent households, the interaction of low-paid jobs with the tax and benefit system ensures that many low-paid jobs do not pay. Low-paid jobs can be more easily taken with the support of another income.

Despite improving employment rates, the number of workless households will continue to remain high until efforts are made to help ensure that work is more evenly distributed. This danger has, in part, motivated the government's attempts to re-evaluate the tax and benefit system that currently discourages participation in the labour market if no one else in the household is in work.

References

Gregg, P., Johnson, P. and Reed, H. (1998), 'Entering Work and the British Tax and Benefit System', mimeo, Institute of Fiscal Studies, London.
Organisation for Economic Co-operation and Development (OECD) (1998), *Employment Outlook*, Paris.

Further reading

Gregg, P. and Machin, S. (1998), 'Poor Kids: The Trends in Child Poverty in Britain 1968–96', Working Paper No. 1005, Centre for Economic Performance, LSE, London.
Gregg, P. and Wadsworth, J. (1996), 'More work in fewer households?', in J. Hills (ed.), *New Inequalities*, Cambridge, Cambridge University Press.

Working 9 to 5?

Keypoints

- The average number of hours worked each week has increased over the last decade, with more men and women working over fifty hours a week.

- The working week has become longer because the number of hours of paid and unpaid overtime worked has increased. In 1998 the average full-time male worked seven hours overtime a week, three more than in 1988, while for women, the average number of hours overtime worked increased from three to six hours a week.

- Ten years ago women worked little overtime compared to men, but by 1998, while they were as likely as men to be working overtime, it was much more likely to be unpaid.

- One in six employees work during the evening, and one in sixteen work at night. However, there is little evidence of an increase in the numbers working during these hours.

- Only a small proportion of evening and night workers are employed in the sales sector. Personal service workers and machinery and plant operatives make up the biggest shares of evening and night workers.

- Within occupations, the biggest change in proportions working evenings and nights has been in sales and professional occupations. From 1992 to 1998 the proportions working evenings increased from 15 per cent to 20 per cent of professionals and from 14 per cent to 17 per cent of sales staff.

- Evening and night workers are paid less than those who work during the day, although there is an important gender difference. Full-time male night workers are no more likely to be low paid than other men, while full-time women are twice as likely to be low paid if they work nights (with one in five full-time women who regularly work nights paid less than the proposed minimum wage compared to one in sixteen full-time men).

- Women in couples are 50 per cent more likely to work evenings if they have children.

- In a quarter of two-parent households at least one parent regularly works during the evening.

The '24-hour economy' is a subject which has recently attracted a great deal of media interest. We can now bank or shop at any time of the day or night, and this has important implications for the times people work in these services. Changes in the occupational structure of the economy, increases in part-time employment and higher rates of female labour market participation, alongside increased job insecurity and greater labour market 'flexibility', mean that far fewer people now work 9 a.m. to 5 p.m., Monday to Friday. In 1998, only 51 per cent of employed men, and 38 per cent of employed women, worked full-time for five days a week, with no regular weekend, evening or night work. This chapter describes some of the recent changes in patterns of working, looking at changes in the length of the working week (and in particular at the increasing importance of overtime), times of the day worked, and the influence of family structure on working hours.

Why do we care about working times?

Working times are interesting for two main reasons. First, the times when people work affect economic well-being, and are therefore an important aspect of non-wage labour market inequalities. For example, cleaners who work through the night are badly off not only in terms of pay but also in terms of working conditions. Measures of wage inequality could therefore understate the true degree of labour market inequality. Second, the decline of the traditional working week has important implications for the organisation of society and in particular for family life. The length of parents' working weeks and the times at which parents work are important to our understanding of how families balance work and family responsibilities.

Work in the United States by Bell and Freeman (1994), and in Britain by Gregg (1994), shows that the number of hours people work are becoming increasingly dispersed, with both those at the bottom and those at the top of the wage distribution working longer hours than before. The authors suggest that these changes have been a response to rising wage inequality, with those at the top of the wage distribution working longer hours because the rewards for doing so are so high or to secure future promotion, while those at the bottom work longer hours to make ends meet or to protect employment.

Research on days of the week and times of the day worked by Hamermesh (1995, 1996) shows that in the United States the trends in times of work have reinforced trends in wage inequality. Those at the bottom of the wage distribution are not only getting paid less than before but are also more likely to work at less desirable times of the day (evenings, nights and weekends). Hamermesh also looks at the variations in working time across households with and without children, and finds that women are much more likely to work evenings and nights if they have young children in the household.

Throughout, the chapter uses data drawn from the Labour Force Survey (LFS) on all employees of working age. Hours of work are defined for the main job only. Where times of the day and days of the week worked are discussed, figures are reported only for those who say they are usually working at these times only. Definitions of full-time and part-time work are self reported.

Differences in the length of the working week

Tables 6.1a and 6.1b look at changes in weekly working hours since 1988, reporting figures for 1988 and 1998 (similar points in the economic cycle) for male and female employees. 'Normal hours' are defined as the number of hours usually worked per week, excluding all overtime. For men working full-time, normal hours fell by almost one hour, from 40.2 hours to 39.3 hours, between 1988 and 1998. We observe a clear compression in normal hours, with the proportions working 30 hours to 39 hours a week rising from 54 per cent to 59 per cent over the decade. There are marked declines in the proportions working fewer than thirty hours and over fifty hours.

The most striking changes in hours, however, have been in the amount of overtime worked. Over the decade the proportion of full-time men usually working any paid overtime increased by 12 percentage points, to 55 per cent of all employees, while the proportion working unpaid overtime grew even faster, by 16 percentage points, to 41 per cent. As a result, the average number of paid overtime hours worked rose from 3.3 hours to 4.5 hours a week, while average hours unpaid overtime increased from 1.8 hours to 3.2 hours amongst men working full-time. The fall in the number of normal hours worked per week was therefore more than offset by the rise in overtime hours. In 1998 the average full-time male worked a total of forty-seven hours a week, two hours more than a decade earlier. Men working part-time also saw an increase in overtime work. The distribution of hours worked by men including overtime has lengthened over the decade, with only 16 per cent of male employees usually working fewer than forty hours a week and 30 per cent working more than fifty hours (comparative figures in 1988 were 27 per cent and 24 per cent).

For full-time women there has been a small fall in normal weekly hours

Table 6.1a Hours of work

Hours	Men						Women					
	Hours not including overtime		Hours including paid overtime		Hours including paid and unpaid overtime		Hours not including overtime		Hours including paid overtime		Hours including paid and unpaid overtime	
	1988	1998	1988	1998	1988	1998	1988	1998	1988	1998	1988	1998
<20	1.1	1.0	1.1	0.6	1.0	0.5	21.9	14.7	20.6	11.3	20.1	9.8
20–29	2.2	1.7	2.0	1.5	1.7	1.1	16.9	17.5	17.0	17.6	16.2	16.2
30–39	53.8	58.8	33.1	32.5	24.1	14.8	48.4	55.5	42.1	45.8	36.6	28.7
40–49	35.8	34.7	46.0	46.8	49.4	54.0	11.6	11.7	17.9	22.1	23.1	35.2
50+	7.2	3.8	17.8	18.6	23.8	29.6	1.2	0.7	2.4	3.2	4.0	10.1
Total	100.0	100.0	100.0	100.0	100.0	100.0	100.0	100.0	100.0	100.0	100.0	100.0
Average hours worked												
Full-time	40.2	39.3	3.3	4.5	1.8	3.2	37.4	36.8	1.2	2.2	1.4	4.0
Part-time	19.8	19.7	0.7	3.5	0.6	1.3	17.5	19.3	0.8	2.3	0.3	1.1

Source: LFS, Spring quarters.
Note: Figures are a percentage of the working age population.

Table 6.1b Overtime hours

	Men				Women			
	Full-time		Part-time		Full-time		Part-time	
	1988	1998	1988	1998	1988	1998	1988	1998
% working paid overtime	43.0	55.2	12.1	53.5	24.3	38.5	19.8	50.1
% working unpaid overtime	25.2	40.6	10.4	28.5	27.0	57.8	11.0	34.0

Source: LFS, Spring quarters.

(from 37.4 hours to 36.8 hours a week). As with men, however, overtime has become increasingly important. In 1988 around one-quarter of full-time women worked paid and unpaid overtime, but by 1998 these proportions had increased to 39 per cent and 58 per cent respectively. Average hours of paid overtime rose from 1.2 hours to 1.4 hours a week, while unpaid overtime increased sharply from 2.2 hours to 4 hours. Including overtime hours raises average hours of work for full-time female employees from 40 hours to 43 hours over the decade. A striking change, therefore, is that full-time female employees are now much more likely to work overtime than before, and are much less likely than men to get paid for it.

Amongst part-time working women, hours too have lengthened over the decade and overtime has become more common. Just over one-half of part-time women worked paid overtime in 1998 (compared with fewer than one in five a decade earlier). The greater prevalence of paid overtime amongst female part-timers than full-timers may reflect occupational differences between these workers.

For the full hours distribution across women, there is again compression in normal working hours over the decade. The proportion working between 30 hours and 39 hours a week increases from 48 per cent to 56 per cent. The proportions working over forty hours fell marginally (although only around 12 per cent of women have a standard working week longer than thirty-nine hours), while the proportion working fewer than thirty hours a week dropped from 41 per cent to 33 per cent. Adding in overtime hours, however, as with men, increases the working week over the period, with the numbers working under thirty hours a week including all overtime falling from 36 per cent to 26 per cent. In 1998, 45 per cent of female employees worked more than forty hours a week and 10 per cent over fifty hours, compared with 27 per cent and 4 per cent respectively a decade earlier.

The evidence therefore shows that, for both men and women, there has been a compression in the standard working week when we exclude over-time. Overtime work has, however, become much more important, with hours of unpaid overtime increasing particularly fast. When we include over-time hours we observe a clear lengthening of the working week. The increasing importance of overtime hours is likely to reflect both increased labour market 'flexibility', which may have led to greater demand from employers for paid overtime, and greater job insecurity, which may have affected the number of hours of unpaid overtime individuals work.

Hours and occupations

If we believe that hours of work have changed most for those at the top and bottom of the wage distribution, as Bell and Freeman (1994) and Gregg (1994) suggest, then we would expect to see significant differences in the number of hours of paid and unpaid overtime worked across occupations. Amongst men, regular working hours are fairly homogeneous across occupations, but there are notable differences in the patterns of overtime worked. Those in professional and managerial occupations rarely get paid for working overtime, while unpaid overtime is relatively rare in other occupations. Moreover, the last decade has seen a rapid growth in unpaid overtime amongst professionals and managers, and in paid overtime amongst those in other occupations (in particular amongst those working in personal services and as machinery operatives). One interpretation of this could be that unpaid overtime has grown because these workers see this as increasingly important to their career prospects in the face of increasing labour market competition, while paid overtime has become more common as those in lower paid occupations increasingly need to work extra hours in order to make ends meet.

Amongst women, the distribution of hours across occupations varies considerably, with those in sales and personal service occupations much more likely to work short hours. However, those in managerial occupations, machine operatives and clerical workers are predominantly full-time. Professional women are predominantly full-time, although more were working shorter hours in 1998 than 1988. The number of hours of unpaid overtime worked by professional women has grown considerably, from an average of 4 hours to 10 hours a week. Comparable figures for men were 5 hours and 7 hours respectively. Hours of paid overtime have also increased in other occupations.

Holidays

Another important aspect affecting the amount of leisure time people have is holiday entitlement. Table 6.2 reports the number of days' holiday for full-time and part-time permanent and temporary employees. 4 per cent of full-timers have no annual holiday entitlement, and 16 per cent are entitled to fewer than two weeks' holiday a year. 40 per cent of temporary full-time employees have no holiday entitlement. Part-timers fare even worse, with one-third having no holiday entitlement. Even amongst permanent part-time employees as many as 28 per cent are not entitled to any annual leave. This lack of holiday entitlement reinforces inequalities in the labour market, and it is notable that part-timers (who have low average wages) are particularly likely to have no paid holiday.

Table 6.2 Holiday entitlement by employment status

	Full-time			Part-time		
	Permanent	Temporary	All	Permanent	Temporary	All
% in each status	94.8	5.2	100.0	86.4	13.6	100.0
No holiday entitlement	2.3	41.3	4.3	27.5	73.6	33.8
I week or less	2.7	42.8	4.8	31.6	75.9	37.7
I–2 weeks	4.9	45.8	7.0	41.6	80.1	46.8
2–3 weeks	12.0	50.8	14.0	55.6	83.8	59.5
3–4 weeks	34.8	64.3	36.3	72.7	89.1	74.9
4–5 weeks	73.4	84.9	74.0	89.4	93.3	90.0
5–6 weeks	91.2	93.9	91.3	94.9	94.7	94.9
6–7 weeks	94.5	95.1	94.5	95.7	95.0	95.6
7–8 weeks	95.3	95.9	95.3	96.2	95.2	96.1
8–9 weeks	95.8	96.3	95.9	96.5	95.7	96.3
9–10 weeks	96.3	96.7	96.3	96.7	96.3	96.7
Average days' holiday	24.1	14.1	23.6	14.4	6.3	13.3

Source: LFS 1997, Spring quarter.

So when are people working?

Times of work: evening, night and weekend work

The evidence so far has shown that the working week has lengthened over the last decade. Given this change, it is interesting to ask whether the rising number of people working long hours has been accompanied by a rise in the numbers working weekends and evening/nights. Alternatively, it may be that it is part-time workers who are particularly likely to work at these times. This section looks at day, evening, night and weekend work by full-time/part-time employment status, gender and occupation and at earnings by times of day worked. Day, evening, night and weekend work is defined for those who usually work these hours. Including those who report sometimes working at these times leads to a large increase in these numbers (for example, while 16 per cent of employees report usually working evenings in 1998, this number rises to over 50 per cent if we include those who sometimes work these hours. The numbers working nights would also show a comparable rise, from 6 per cent of employees to over 20 per cent.) Shift work accounts for a significant proportion of those working evenings and nights. In 1998, 40 per cent of those regularly working nights and 34 per cent working evenings worked time-varying shifts.

Over the period 1992–8, the proportion of employees working nights remained virtually unchanged, at around 6 per cent, while the numbers working evenings increased only from 14 per cent to 16 per cent of employees. The proportions working Saturdays also remained almost constant, with just under one in four workers regularly employed on a Saturday. Sunday work showed a small increase from 10 per cent to 12 per cent of employees.

Of course, times of work may vary greatly for different groups of workers. In Table 6.3 we therefore report the proportion of employees

Table 6.3 Timing of work by sex and employment status

	All		Men				Women			
			Full-time		Part-time		Full-time		Part-time	
	1992	1998	1992	1998	1992	1998	1992	1998	1992	1998
Day only	91.5	91.6	92.1	91.7	80.2	79.6	96.0	95.7	84.1	86.7
Evening	14.1	16.3	14.7	16.7	23.1	25.3	11.6	13.5	17.3	17.9
Night	6.0	6.4	7.1	7.9	8.0	7.5	4.3	4.3	6.2	5.4
Saturday	21.4	21.9	23.4	24.2	29.4	28.1	19.1	18.4	20.5	19.7
Sunday	10.2	11.7	10.8	12.1	12.5	14.8	9.6	11.0	10.6	11.4
Share of group as a proportion of all employees	100.0	100.0	50.6	51.4	1.4	2.5	28.6	27.6	19.4	18.6

Source: LFS, Spring quarters.

working during the day, evening and night, and at weekends, by full- and part-time employment status and gender in 1992 and 1998. In each of these groups, there was some increase in evening and Sunday work, but little change in night or Saturday work between 1992 and 1998. Comparing working times across these groups we can see that full-time women work the 'best' hours – they are the most likely to work during the day and less likely to work evenings, nights or weekends than any other group of workers. Women who work part-time are more likely to work evenings than full-time men and women (18 per cent compared to 17 per cent and 13 per cent respectively in 1998). Men, however, whether full-time or part-time, are twice as likely as women to work nights, with almost one in twelve regularly working at this time. It is part-time men who fare worst of all in terms of working times – they are less likely to work during the day and much more likely to work evenings (one in four are employed during the evening) and weekends than other workers. Note, however, that part-time men make up only 2.5 per cent of all employees.

Times of work and occupations

The fact that there is no large change in working time in aggregate does not mean that there have been no important changes in working times for different groups of workers. Increases in demand for 24-hour services (from shopping to telebanking) are thought to have been important factors contributing toward the erosion of the traditional working week for workers in this sector. It is perhaps less well recognised that these workers, in highly visible service sectors, account for only a small proportion of those working during the evening and night. Far more night workers are employed in manufacturing occupations, and the declining importance of this sector may have tempered the perceived shift toward the 24-hour economy.

Table 6.4 shows little change in the occupational structure of evening, night and weekend work. In 1998, amongst evening workers, one-fifth were employed in personal services (which include occupations such as cleaners and security guards), with managerial, professional, associated professional, and plant and machinery operatives making up the other largest occupational shares. Together these occupations account for 70 per cent of evening workers. Sales occupations account for only 7 per cent of those working during the evening. The occupational composition of night workers is even more concentrated, with personal service occupations and plant and machinery operatives together accounting for almost one-half of all night workers. 'Associated professionals' (which includes occupations such as nursing) account for a further 13 per cent of those working nights. Sales workers make up just 3 per cent of all night-time employees. Weekend work is dominated by managers and administrators, personal services and sales workers. It is notable that the only significant change in occupational structure between

Table 6.4   Occupational composition of employees by times of work (percentages)

	Day		Evening		Night		Saturday		Sunday	
	1992	1998	1992	1998	1992	1998	1992	1998	1992	1998
Managers	14.9	16.5	12.2	12.3	7.6	6.3	15.7	14.5	11.4	11.5
Professionals	11.0	11.5	10.6	12.9	5.1	5.1	4.7	5.6	8.2	10.2
Associated professionals	9.0	9.9	10.7	10.4	12.7	13.0	7.7	7.8	12.6	11.1
Clerical	18.4	17.6	7.1	7.4	5.2	6.0	7.6	8.0	5.3	5.9
Craft	12.7	11.0	7.0	6.7	8.9	8.9	11.1	11.2	8.0	6.6
Personal services	8.9	10.0	20.8	20.6	27.3	25.5	17.6	17.6	26.3	26.5
Sales	7.6	7.2	7.5	7.2	3.9	3.3	13.8	13.8	5.1	7.0
Machinery operatives	9.4	9.3	13.1	13.7	19.7	23.1	10.2	10.2	11.2	10.7
Other occupations	8.0	7.0	11.0	8.7	9.5	8.8	11.5	11.5	12.0	10.5

Source: LFS, Spring quarter.

Figure 6.1   Times of work by occupation

Evenings

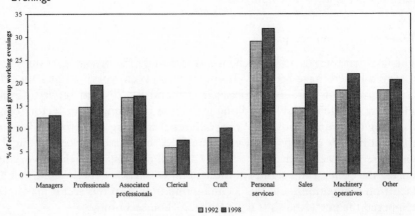

Nights

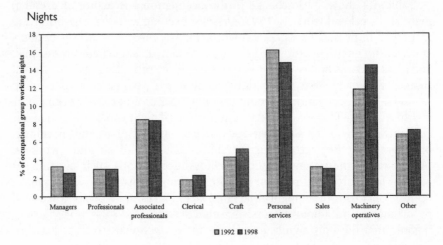

1992 and 1998 was in Sunday working, with sales increasing their share of Sunday workers (from 5 per cent to 7 per cent). This is likely to have been a result of relaxations in Sunday trading legislation in 1994.

The fact that we have not observed a change in the occupational composition of workers by times of the day worked does not mean that the probability of working evenings or nights has not changed within occupations. Figure 6.1 plots the proportions working during the evening, night, Saturday and Sunday by occupation in 1992 and 1998. The first panel shows the proportions working evenings, and there is clearly considerable variation by occupation. Personal services workers are the most likely to work evenings, with 30 per cent of this occupational group working at this time in 1998. Around one-fifth of professionals, sales staff and plant and machinery operatives were also regularly at work during the evening, but those in clerical or

Saturdays

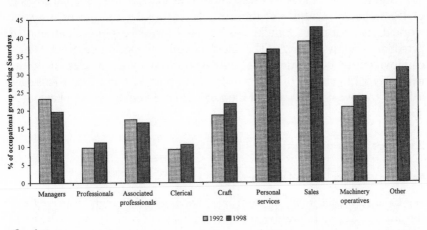

Sundays

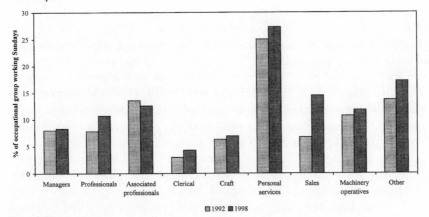

Source: LFS.

craft occupations were much less likely to work at this time. The most notable changes in evening work were amongst professionals and sales staff, who both saw an increase in the proportions at work during the evening, from 15 per cent to 20 per cent of professionals and 14 per cent to 17 per cent of sales staff. All other occupations also saw small increases in evening work. While not shown in the figure, it is notable that professional full-time women are much more likely to report that they regularly work during the evening than professional men (23 per cent compared to 17 per cent).

Amongst night workers it is clear that occupation is even more important. Night work is common amongst personal services workers and plant and machinery operatives (with around 15 per cent in both occupations working nights), and amongst 'associated professional' occupations where around 10 per cent work nights. In all other occupational groups (with the exception of 'other' occupations) fewer than 5 per cent of workers regularly worked nights. Weekend working is prevalent across all occupational groupings, although it is most likely amongst employees in sales and personal services. In 1998 almost two-fifths of those employed in sales and personal services worked on a Saturday. Sunday work is also particularly prevalent amongst personal services workers. The most notable change in rates of Sunday employment by occupation was amongst those working in sales, up from 7 per cent to 12 per cent of sales workers between 1992 and 1998. This again is likely to have been a result of the relaxation of Sunday trading laws.

Earnings and working time

Number of hours worked and earnings

We have seen that hours of work have become increasingly dispersed over the last decade. An interesting and related question concerns what the correlation between hours of work and earnings looks like. Unfortunately, LFS wage data only go back to 1992, so we have chosen to look at evidence from 1998 only. Figure 6.2 plots the estimated relationship between hours of work and hourly earnings for men and women. The top two graphs show the relationship between the number of hours of paid work and average hourly pay. For both men and women, earnings rise steadily with hours up to around thirty-five hours a week, when earnings start to fall. This indicates that those who are best remunerated are most likely to work a standard full-time working week. Those working longer or shorter hours than this are significantly less well paid. This fits well with earlier work of Harkness (1996) which has shown a growing gap between the earnings of full-time and part-time employees. It should, however, be noted that the chart does not control for any differences in the characteristics of workers and therefore does not tell us anything about any causal relation between hours of work and earnings.

Figure 6.2 Wages by hours of work

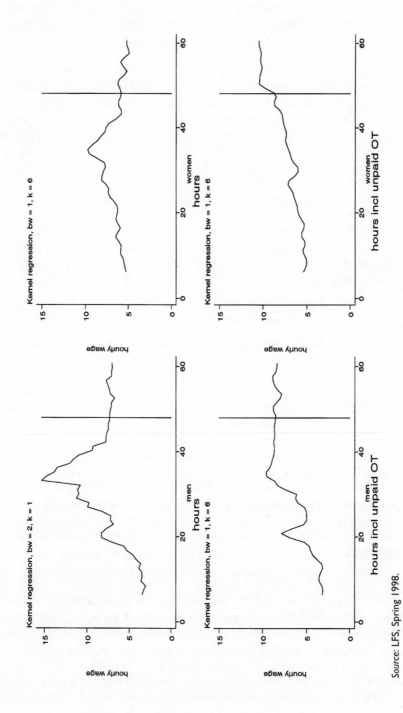

Source: LFS, Spring 1998.

We saw earlier that unpaid overtime is particularly important amongst the higher paying professional and managerial occupations. The observed relationship between paid hours of work and average hourly pay may therefore be substantially tempered if we add unpaid overtime to hours of work in calculating hourly wages rates. The bottom two graphs in Figure 6.2 chart this relationship. They show that at the upper end of the wage distribution earnings no longer fall with hours of work. Instead hourly earnings rise and then flatten out at around thirty-five hours a week for men, but grow consistently with the number of hours worked each week for women over the plotted 0–60 range. Of course, if we think that unpaid overtime is at least in part 'voluntary', we need to treat any interpretation of the hours/earnings relationship observed here with caution.

This relationship between hours and earnings holds even after account is taken for occupational differences. The only exception is amongst professionals, whose earnings are inversely related to hours of work. These professionals, who work relatively short paid hours, may include those who hold more than one job or who are paid high consultancy rates for a relatively short number of working hours.

Earnings and times of day worked

Is there a link between times of work and wage inequality? How well or how badly paid are those who work antisocial hours? Table 6.5 reports average earnings, the proportions of men and women in the top and bottom fifth of the hourly earnings distribution, and the proportions paid below the proposed minimum wage (of £3.60 an hour) in 1998. With the exception of full-time women, workers who are regularly employed during the evening have lower average earnings than other workers while those who work nights earn even less. Amongst full-time males, average earnings are £9.18 for those who regularly work during the day, £9.08 for those who regularly work evenings, and just £7.88 for those who work nights. Comparable figures for full-time women are £7.51, £7.89 and £6.60. Amongst full-timers, therefore, average earnings are substantially lower for those regularly working nights. Part-timers on the other hand tend to be badly paid regardless of the time at which they work.

The second and third panels of Table 6.5 report the proportions in the top and bottom fifth of the hourly wage distribution, while the bottom panel shows the proportions paid below the proposed minimum wage of £3.60 an hour. It is notable that part-time men, whatever time of day they work, are likely to be low paid. It should be remembered, however, that these workers constitute only a small proportion of employees. Looking at full-time men, those working evenings and nights are no more likely than other workers to be low paid, but those who work nights are much less likely to be high paid.

The position amongst women, whether full-time or part-time, is strikingly

Table 6.5 Earnings distribution and average wages

	Men		Women	
	Full-time	*Part-time*	*Full-time*	*Part-time*
Average hourly wage (£)				
Day	9.2	8.0	7.5	5.9
Evening	9.1	5.4	7.9	5.4
Night	7.9	5.5	6.6	5.8
All	9.2	7.3	7.4	5.9
Proportion in bottom quintile (%)				
Day	11.0	44.0	17.8	40.3
Evening	11.7	51.6	21.2	45.5
Night	11.0	41.4	26.8	37.5
All	11.0	46.7	18.2	41.2
Proportion in top quintile (%)				
Day	27.4	13.9	18.1	8.3
Evening	24.9	8.9	23.8	5.7
Night	14.0	0.0	10.8	6.0
All	26.8	11.8	17.4	8.0
Proportion earning below minimum wage (%)				
Day	6.4	30.0	9.7	23.9
Evening	7.0	29.6	14.2	28.4
Night	5.9	23.7	19.0	26.5
All	6.4	31.0	10.1	25.1

Source: LFS, Spring quarters.

different. Amongst full-time women, those working evenings are disproportionately likely to be high paid (reflecting the fact that a disproportionate number of professional women work evenings). Looking at the proportions paid
below the proposed minimum wage we find that 10 per cent of full-time
women working during the day had hourly earnings below £3.60 an hour, but
this increased to 15 per cent of evenings workers and 19 per cent of night
workers. Note too that women are much more likely to be low paid than full-
time men whatever time of the day they work. Part-time women are even more
likely to have earnings below the level of the proposed minimum wage, with
the probability of being low paid being higher if evenings or nights are worked.

Full-time female night workers, in contrast to men, are twice as likely to
be low paid as those who work days. It may be that men who work nights are

likely to be employed in traditional male occupations, which pay significant wage premiums for night work, while women working nights are employed in occupations which rarely pay a wage premium. When we look at differences in the proportions paid under the proposed minimum wage by occupation, those in associated professional occupations (a predominantly female occupational group) who work nights are eight times more likely to be low paid than those working during the day. Amongst those employed in sales, 25 per cent of evening and night workers are paid less than £3.60 an hour, compared with just 12 per cent of those who work during the day. In the predominantly male occupational group of plant and machinery operatives, low pay is much less prevalent amongst those employed during evenings or nights (5 per cent of night workers earn under £3.60 an hour compared with 27 per cent of day workers). On the other hand, those in personal services occupations are the most likely to be low paid (one in four workers earning under £3.60 an hour), with the prevalence of low pay being little affected by the time of day worked.

Times of work and the family

There has been a great deal of concern about the impact of changes in working times on the quality of family life. This section looks at how working times vary across different family types. Table 6.6 shows that, in 1998, fathers worked an average of forty-seven hours a week (including all overtime), which is almost two hours longer than a decade previously. One-third of men with children in the household were employed for over fifty hours a week, a 6-percentage-point increase over a decade. Fathers were also more likely than men without children to work over fifty hours. Amongst women, average working hours increased over the decade, from 27 hours to 33 hours a week for mothers, and from 35 hours to 39 hours for women without children. Mothers are of course much more likely to work part-time than those without children (57 per cent compared to 27 per cent in 1998), and their distribution of working hours is wider. There was, however, a notable increase in the numbers working long hours, with the proportion working more than fifty hours rising from 3 per cent to 7 per cent. The proportion of mothers working more than forty hours also increased dramatically, from 19 per cent to 33 per cent.

Table 6.7 looks at the times of day worked by family type. Men who are married with children are most likely to work evenings and nights. Amongst women, hours of work are strongly influenced by household type, with those who are married with children or single and childless most likely to work evenings and nights. 18 per cent of married female employees with children regularly worked evenings, and 6 per cent regularly worked nights in 1998. Comparable figures for married or cohabiting childless women were much

Table 6.6 Hours worked by parental status

	Men				Women			
	with children		without children		with children		without children	
	1988	1998	1988	1998	1988	1998	1988	1998
% working less than 20 hours	0.7	0.3	1.2	0.7	32.2	16.5	11.4	5.2
% working 20–29 hours	1.2	0.9	2.0	1.3	21.5	24.7	12.3	10.3
% working 30–39 hours	21.5	13.0	26.1	16.0	27.5	26.2	43.2	30.4
% working 40–49 hours	49.0	52.9	49.7	54.9	15.9	25.3	28.4	42.1
% working more than 50 hours	27.6	33.0	20.9	27.1	2.9	7.3	4.8	12.0
Average hours excluding overtime	40.1	39.1	39.3	38.9	25.2	27.7	32.6	33.8
Average paid overtime hours	3.5	4.7	3.1	5.3	1.0	2.2	1.1	2.7
Average unpaid overtime hours	2.1	3.5	1.5	3.8	0.8	2.7	1.1	3.3
Average total hours	45.7	47.3	43.9	47.8	27.0	32.6	34.8	39.3
% working paid overtime	43.1	53.9	41.5	56.8	21.0	44.1	23.5	40.9
% working unpaid overtime	27.5	42.8	22.7	38.7	17.9	47.0	22.6	52.6
% working part-time	1.7	3.6	3.3	3.5	58.0	57.4	26.6	26.6

Source: LFS, 1998, Spring quarter.

Table 6.7 Times of work by family type, 1998

	Men			Women			
	Married/cohabiting		Single	Married/cohabiting		Single	
	Children	No children	No children	Children	No children	Children	No children
Day	90.7	91.8	91.4	88.8	95.0	89.3	94.2
Evening	18.5	16.1	16.6	17.8	12.3	17.8	14.1
Night	8.6	7.8	7.0	5.7	3.6	5.5	4.5
Saturday	24.0	23.9	24.3	17.6	16.4	22.3	21.4
Sunday	13.0	11.9	11.2	11.7	8.9	14.0	11.4
Total	34.7	26.2	30.5	32.1	27.5	13.1	27.4

Source: LFS 1998, Spring quarter.

lower, at 12 per cent and 4 per cent respectively. Thus, amongst couples, the chances of working evenings or nights are 50 per cent higher if there are children in the household.

Of course amongst couples working time is likely to be strongly influenced by the hours the partner works. Table 6.8 therefore looks at the joint labour supply of couples. The first two panels show the joint employment decisions of all couples with and without children, by the time they work. Two things stand out. First, in households with children men and women are much more

Table 6.8 Joint labour supply of couples

	Neither work*	Man works*	Woman works*	Both work*
All couples without children (%)				
Day	22.8	20.1	11.9	54.2
Evening	82.2	9.9	5.8	2.1
Night	93.2	4.7	1.8	0.4
All couples with children in household (%)				
Day	13.5	27.2	9.1	50.2
Evening	74.8	13.5	8.9	2.9
Night	90.0	6.3	3.2	0.4
All employed couples, both working full-time, with children in household (%)				
Day	2.6	23.9	10.0	63.6
Evening	73.7	14.1	8.0	4.2
Night	89.4	6.8	3.2	0.6
All employed couples, woman working part-time, with children in household (%)				
Day	2.8	25.0	8.7	63.5
Evening	69.2	14.9	12.5	3.3
Night	87.9	7.1	4.6	0.4

Source: LFS 1998, Spring quarter.
Note: Neither work* refers to neither member of the couple working the time specified in the left column. Man works* refers to only the man working the time specified in the left column etc.

likely to regularly work during the evening or night. Second, in one in four households with children at least one parent regularly works during the evening. The third and fourth panels show employment patterns in families with children where both parents work full-time, and where the man works full-time and the woman part-time. It is clear that the probability of working during the evening is much higher for women who work part-time, with 12 per cent of part-time women working evenings compared to 8 per cent of those working full-time. Night work is also more prevalent among women who work part-time. The results here are similar to those of Hamermesh for the United States. He suggests that the availability of affordable alternative child-care may be an important factor in shaping (particularly women's) decisions about the times of day worked. Our results suggest that for women in Britain this is also likely to be the case.

Conclusions

One of the most striking findings to emerge from this analysis was the dramatic increase in both paid and unpaid overtime hours. Thus, while we observed a compression in the working week when overtime was excluded, when overtime was included the working week clearly lengthened. In 1998 only 16 per cent of men worked fewer than forty hours a week, while 30 per cent worked more than fifty hours (this compares with 27 per cent and 24 per cent respectively a decade earlier). Amongst women, too, the working week is longer. In 1998, 45 per cent of women worked over forty hours a week, and 10 per cent worked over fifty hours (compared to 27 per cent and 4 per cent respectively in 1988). There is also an important gender difference in patterns of overtime work. Ten years ago women worked little overtime compared to men, but by 1998 while women were as likely as men to be working overtime it was much more likely to be unpaid.

In 1998 one in six employees regularly worked evenings and one in sixteen nights. There was, however, only a small change in the proportions working at these times between 1992 and 1998. This is because, while there has been a rapid increase in the number of retail outlets 'open all hours', the impact on employment has been limited because sales employees make up only a small share of those who work during the evenings and nights. In 1998 only 7 per cent of those employed in the evening and 3 per cent of those employed at night worked in sales. The majority of those working at these times were employed in personal services occupations and as plant and machinery operatives. Within these occupations the '24-hour' working culture is nothing new. It is notable, however, that within occupations the biggest changes in proportions working evenings and nights have been in sales and professional occupations. Between 1992 and 1998 the proportions working evenings increased for professionals and sales staff. It is likely that increased evening work amongst professionals, alongside increased female employment, is likely to have contributed toward the growing demand for 24-hour services. There is also an important gender difference in rates of pay by times of work. While full-time men who work nights have lower average earnings than other men, they are no more likely to be low paid. Amongst full-time women the story is quite different. Those who work nights are twice as likely to be low paid as those working days. This suggests that men who work nights are much more likely to be employed in occupations which pay a premium for working antisocial hours.

Women with children are much more likely to work evenings and nights than those without. Mothers who work part-time are particularly likely to work evenings (and many of the jobs they work in are low paid). Availability of quality, affordable child-care has an important impact on the times at which parents, and particularly mothers, work. In one in four families with children at least one parent regularly works during the evening and this has potentially important implications for the quality of family life.

References

Bell, L. and Freeman, R. (1994), 'Why Do Americans and Germans Work Different Hours', Working Paper No. 4808, National Bureau of Economic Research, Cambridge, Mass.

Gregg, P. (1994), 'Share and Share Alike', *New Economy*, Spring 1994, 1:1.

Hamermesh, D. S. (1995), 'Who Works When? Evidence from the US and Germany', Working Paper No. 2508, National Bureau of Economic Research, Cambridge, Mass.

Hamermesh, D. S. (1996), 'The Timing of Work Time over Time', Working Paper No. 5855, National Bureau of Economic Research, Cambridge, Mass.

Harkness, S. E. (1996), 'The Gender Earnings Gap: Evidence from the UK', *Fiscal Studies*, 17:2, 1–36.

7 Paul Gregg and Jonathan Wadsworth

Job tenure, 1975–98

Keypoints

- The typical new job lasts just fifteen months. However, the average length of a job in progress is around five and a half years. This is because most workers eventually find a long-term job match. Only one-fifth of new jobs last five years, whereas only a third of the jobs that have lasted five years will break up within the next five years.

- Despite public perception to the contrary, average job tenure has remained relatively stable since 1975. However, stability at national level disguises sharp contrasts across gender: job tenure has risen amongst women with children, but fallen for men and women without dependent children.

- Job stability for many women with dependent children seems to have been bolstered by the increased provision and use of maternity leave.

- For young workers, below the age of 25, median tenure fell by 30 per cent between 1975 and 1985, and by a further 7 percentage points in the years to 1995. This is due, in part, to this age group having the largest increases in the share of short-term jobs (from 36 per cent to 50 per cent for young men and from 34 per cent to 49 per cent for young women).

- The largest fall in tenure has been amongst men aged 50 and over, down from 15 years and 3 months to 13 years and 8 months between 1975 and 1995. This appears to be driven primarily by a fall in the share of long-term jobs. This trend is not related to levels of educational attainment.

Recent media attention – with some dissenting voices – has focused on the idea that the job for life is in decline. Aside from obvious concerns over the possible unemployment consequences, the issue of job stability also concerns policy makers in the debates over job insecurity, pension entitlements and the provision of insurance to cover earnings interruptions. Job stability is often measured in one of two principal ways – the average tenure of all jobs in existence and the probability of continued job survival. The average length of time a worker has held a job in Britain is currently just over five years. However, the typical new job lasts just fifteen months. This is because most workers move on from new jobs and find good, long-term job matches.

However, the debate over job stability is not quite so straightforward. Falling job stability could simply mean that workers are able to change jobs more frequently. If this were a means to ensure better wages and working conditions then declining stability may not always be a bad thing. What matters more from the worker's perspective is whether stability has declined for involuntary reasons. Job security and job stability are related, but they are not the same thing. The OECD (1997) felt moved to investigate the issue of insecurity across its member countries, concluding that average job tenure or the likelihood of staying in a job had changed little, despite the widespread perception of job insecurity.

Perhaps more important, for policy makers and the public alike, is whether measures of job tenure have changed over time. Is there any evidence from this aspect of the labour market to support popular notions that job stability has decreased?[1] If so, which groups have been affected most and what factors are responsible? Has average tenure changed because of a change in the share of long-term jobs or because of a change in the share of short-term jobs? The distinction matters because the implications for policy are different. There may be concerns over falling stability caused by a decline in the share of long-term jobs. Long-term jobs typically pay higher wages and are less likely to break up. New jobs may be used as a springboard to better things, but equally they may be of poorer quality than in the past (see Chapter 14).

Gregg and Wadsworth (1996), using data from the British Labour Force Survey (LFS), have suggested that job tenure has fallen in the 1990s. In contrast, using data drawn from a different source, the General Household Survey (GHS), for the period 1975–92, Burgess and Rees (1997) conclude that average job tenure has not fallen much in Britain. In what follows we update and bring together these two separate data sets to try to settle the issue. We show that small changes in national job tenure statistics disguise larger changes across age and gender that offset each other when aggregated. Women with dependent children are increasingly much more likely to be in

[1] See OECD *Employment Outlook* (1997).

longer-term jobs, whilst job tenure is falling amongst men and amongst women without dependent children. This appears to be more than just cyclical variation.

How long do new jobs last?

We begin by analysing the process of job separation conditional on tenure, using information in the LFS from 1992 onward. Table 7.1 and Figure 7.1 outline how new jobs break up.

Table 7.1 How long do new jobs survive?

Year/quarter	% of new jobs surviving	% of 5-year-old jobs surviving	% of 10-year-old jobs surviving
1992 Spring	100.0	100.0	100.0
Summer	83.1	94.1	89.0
Autumn	68.4	88.6	83.0
Winter	62.1	84.5	80.5
1993 Spring	57.9	84.4	83.8
1994 Spring	33.8	74.8	75.8
1995 Spring	29.3	67.7	67.1
1996 Spring	25.3	67.1	64.9
1997 Spring	22.3	68.0	64.3

Source: LFS.

Around 870,000 workers were in new jobs in the spring of 1992. Seventeen per cent of these jobs ended within three months and around 42 per cent within twelve months. The typical (median) survival time of these new jobs is around fifteen months.[2] Half of all jobs still in existence at this point will break up within the following four years. Only one-fifth of new jobs last five years. The third column of Table 7.1 undertakes a similar exercise but follows those beginning a new job in the spring of 1987, picking them up in the spring of 1992. By 1992 the survivors have amassed five years' tenure. The decay is much less steep than that observed for the first five years. Only a third of jobs that have lasted five years will break up within the next five years. Column 4 shows that the pattern of separations is similar for jobs that were ten years old by the spring of 1992.

Table 7.2 outlines the chances of separating from a job over the next three months at different levels of job tenure in the years 1992 and 1997. On average around 5 per cent of workers separate from their jobs every

[2] These numbers are consistent with the findings of Booth, Francesconi and Garcia-Serrano (1997) who use the British Household Panel Survey (BHPS) work history data to analyse job separations.

Figure 7.1 Decay functions
Jobs created between December 1991 and February 1992

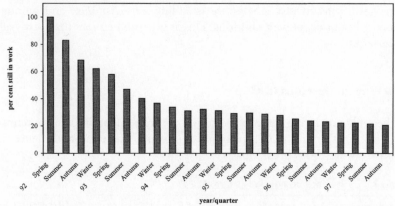

Jobs created in 1981

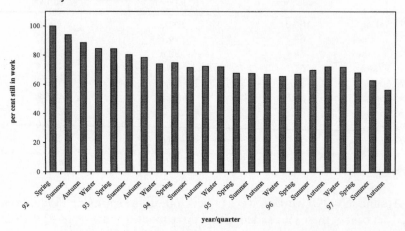

Jobs created in 1986

Jobs created in 1981

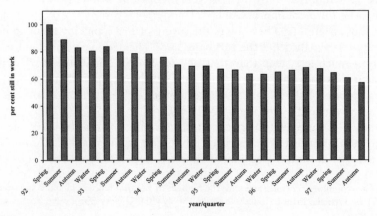

Source: LFS.

Table 7.2 Percentage of workforce separating from jobs by length of job tenure

Length of current job	All		Male		Female	
	1992	1997	1992	1997	1992	1997
Months						
1 month	20.5	24.9	20.4	23.8	20.6	26.4
2 months	22.2	21.8	23.9	21.3	20.7	22.4
3 months	16.9	18.8	16.7	18.8	17.2	18.8
4 months	15.8	15.3	15.1	17.7	16.5	12.8
5 months	16.5	15.2	18.2	15.4	15.0	15.0
6 months	14.6	14.8	13.8	13.7	15.2	15.9
Years						
<1 year	14.1	15.1	14.5	15.1	13.7	15.0
1–2 years	7.8	8.0	6.9	7.7	8.5	8.2
2–3 years	5.8	5.9	5.9	5.6	5.7	6.2
3–4 years	4.4	4.6	4.7	4.5	4.2	4.6
4–5 years	3.5	4.0	3.2	3.5	3.9	4.5
9–10 years	1.9	2.6	1.4	1.8	2.7	3.5
14–15 years	1.8	0.7	2.0	0.8	1.5	0.6
20 years +	2.4	1.8	2.9	1.3	1.4	2.9
Total	5.5	5.9	4.9	5.6	6.1	6.3

Source: LFS.

three months. However, this masks large variations in the separation rate according to length of tenure. The probability of separation falls four-fold from around 20 per cent during the first two months to around 3.5 per cent after the first five years, it then falls by half as much again for jobs of between five and ten years' tenure and levels off at around 2 per cent thereafter. Table 7.3 shows that separations decline with age. The chances of leaving new jobs are around 50 per cent higher for the youngest age group, those under 25, but do not vary much across the older age cohorts at any level of tenure. Job tenure is a better predictor of separation than age after the age of 25.

Table 7.4 outlines the pattern of job separations caused by dismissal or redundancy, the end of a temporary contract, resignations and quits for any other reason. Both quits and lay-offs fall with time spent in a job. Workers with less seniority are more likely to lose their jobs, but are also more likely to quit. 55 per cent of all lay-offs and 45 per cent of all quits are from jobs that have lasted less than one year.[3] There are more quits than lay-offs at all

[3] If we restrict the definition of lay-offs only to those made redundant or dismissed then 38 per cent of these lay-offs occur amongst those with tenure less than one year.

Table 7.3 How do separation rates vary by job tenure and age?

Length of job	Age			
	16–24	25–34	35–49	50–59
<1 year	18.5	13.4	12.8	14.2
1–2 years	11.0	7.8	6.1	5.9
2–3 years	8.6	5.6	5.0	4.6
3–4 years	8.0	4.2	3.9	3.3
4–5 years	8.5	3.4	2.8	4.9
9–10 years		2.8	2.4	3.0
14–15 years			0.7	0.5
20 years +			1.2	3.0

Source: LFS, 1997.

Table 7.4 Separation rates by reason

Length of job	Lay-off	Temporary contract	Resign	Other
Less than 1 year	1.6	2.9	3.4	4.9
1–2 years	1.0	0.5	2.0	2.6
2–3 years	0.8	0.5	1.5	2.2
3–4 years	0.6	0.2	1.2	1.5
4–5 years	0.5	0.2	1.1	1.4
5 years or more	0.5	0.1	0.4	1.0

Source: LFS, 1997.

tenures. The aggregate quarterly quit rate, at 3.2 per cent, is around twice that of the aggregate quarterly lay-off rate.

Changes in job stability, 1975–98

Our main aim is, however, to establish whether job stability has changed over recent years, in addition to the changes associated with the economic cycle. Since this could arise from either a change in the extent of job creation or a change in the pattern of job separation, which can occur anywhere in the tenure distribution, we look at both changes in average (median) job tenure and changes in the share of new and long-term jobs. We take the proportion of workers with tenure less than one year as a measure of the share of new jobs, the sum of hires made as a result of firm relocation and worker replacements, as well as the creation of genuine new vacancies. The five- and ten-year thresholds are used to identify the changing share of long-term jobs in the economy. Cumulative evidence from Hall (1982) through to this chapter suggests that job survival rates begin to stabilise somewhere between these points. The estimates are restricted to the population of working age (men aged 16–64 and women aged 16–59).

Tables 7.5a and 7.5b, and Figure 7.2 highlight changes in job tenure over the past twenty years. The estimates vary with the state of the economic cycle. Since quits dominate lay-offs and there are more quits in good times

Table 7.5a Distribution of job tenure by sex

	Average	Per cent of working population with tenure:		
		less than 1 year	more than 5 years	more than 10 years
All				
1975	4 yrs 9 months	18.7	47.8	–
1985	5 yrs 6 months	18.5	52.2	31.1
1990	4 yrs 4 months	19.8	45.8	30.0
1995 – GHS	5 yrs 7 months	18.5	52.5	30.1
1995 – LFS	5 yrs 6 months	17.4	53.1	29.2
1998 – LFS	4 yrs 10 months	20.3	48.8	28.6
% change 1985–95	1.5	0	0.6	–3.2
% change 1975–95	17.5	–1.1	9.8	–
Men				
1975	6 yrs 6 months	15.7	56.1	–
1985	7 yrs 2 months	14.9	59.0	38.4
1990	6 yrs	16.5	53.2	37.0
1995 – GHS	6 yrs 10 months	16.8	57.5	36.8
1995 – LFS	6 yrs 6 months	15.7	58.0	35.6
1998 – LFS	5 yrs 9 months	18.9	52.2	33.3
% change 1985–95	–4.7	12.8	–2.5	–4.2
% change 1975–95	5.1	7.0	2.5	–
Women				
1975	3 yrs 7 months	23.3	34.7	–
1985	3 yrs 10 months	22.9	43.8	20.9
1990	3 yrs 9 months	23.9	36.5	21.2
1995 – GHS	4 yrs 6 months	20.1	47.6	23.2
1995 – LFS	4 yrs 5 months	19.4	47.3	21.6
1998 – LFS	4 yrs 4 months	22.0	44.8	23.0
% change 1985–95	17.4	–12.2	8.7	11.0
% change 1975–95	25.6	–13.7	37.2	–

Sources: GHS, 1975–95, LFS, 1995–98.

Table 7.5b Distribution of women's job tenure by presence of dependent children

	Average	Per cent of working population with tenure:		
		less than 1 year	more than 5 years	more than 10 years
Women with no children				
1975	4 yrs 10 months	16.3	48.8	–
1985	5 yrs 8 months	17.1	53.3	29.9
1990	4 yrs 6 months	19.9	46.2	29.6
1995 – GHS	5 yrs 8 months	17.1	53.2	28.9
1995 – LFS	5 yrs 5 months	17.7	52.6	27.2
1998 – LFS	4 yrs 11 months	19.7	49.7	28.2
% change 1985–95	0	0	–0.2	–3.3
% change 1975–95	17.2	4.9	9.0	–
Women with children				
1975	1 yr 8 months	16.3	48.8	
1985	3 yrs 1 month	22.9	43.8	22.0
1990	3 yrs	28.0	27.6	13.1
1995 – GHS	3 yrs 11 months	24.1	41.1	15.9
1995 – LFS	3 yrs 8 months	22.7	40.8	14.7
1998 – LFS	3 yrs 10 months	24.7	39.1	17.1
% change 1985–95	17.4	5.2	–6.2	–2.8
% change 1975–95	25.6	47.9	15.8	–

Sources: GHS, 1975–95, LFS, 1995–98.

when there are more jobs around, the stock of those in new jobs rises in buoyant labour markets and so average tenure falls. Has there been any decline in average tenure over and above that associated with the economic cycle? According to the GHS, job stability measured by average tenure has increased at the aggregate level, subject to the cycle, with nearly all of the increase occurring before 1985. Average job tenure rose by 17 per cent between 1975 and 1985, from around 4 years and 9 months to 5 years and 6 months, and by just 1 per cent from 1985 to 1995, to 5 years and 7 months. This aggregate pattern, however, disguises a large difference across gender. For men, job tenure rose by 10 per cent up to 1985 and fell by 5 per cent thereafter. The average job length for men is now 6 years and 10 months. In contrast, average tenure for women grew by 8 per cent during the first half of the sample period and continued to grow thereafter by 17 per cent, reaching 4 years and 6 months by 1995.

According to Table 7.5a, the share of new jobs in Britain is around 19 per cent and the share of long-term jobs around 30 per cent. Again there is little

Figure 7.2 Median job tenure

All

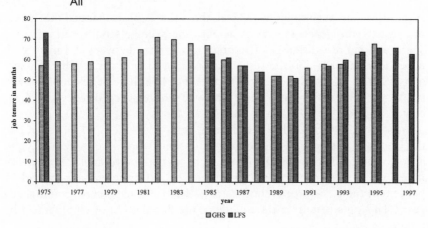

Male

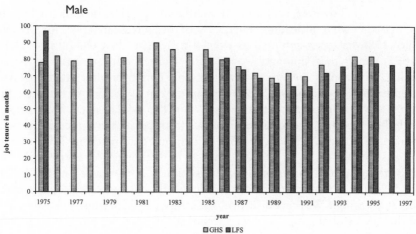

Female

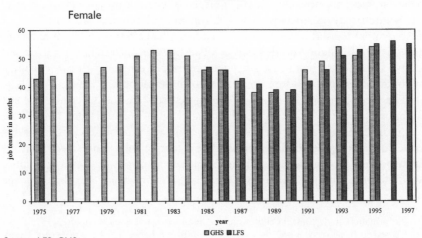

Sources: LFS, GHS.

suggestion that, at the aggregate level, these shares have changed much over the past twenty years. However, as with the average tenure estimates, the aggregate figures disguise offsetting movements between women with dependent children and the rest of the employed workforce. The LFS suggests that this has continued beyond 1995. The LFS share of new jobs in 1998 is 20.3 per cent, whilst the share of jobs with tenure over ten years is 28.6 per cent.

According to OECD (1997) estimates, countries with rapid turnover, like the United States have over one-quarter of their workforce in new jobs and average tenure of around four years. Countries with more stable jobs, or with more employment protection legislation, such as Germany, have around 15 per cent of the workforce in short-term jobs and average tenure around seven years. This puts Britain in the middle of the distribution of employment by tenure.

There are, however, reasons to think that these aggregate data for Britain may be somewhat misleading. First, most of the increase in tenure for women since 1985 has been confined to women with dependent children.[4] McRae (1997) shows that, amongst women who worked full-time prior to pregnancy, the proportion returning to the same employer after childbirth has risen from 18 per cent in 1979 to 69 per cent in 1996. For part-timers the increase was from 37 per cent to 64 per cent. The evidence here is consistent with these findings. Using survey evidence from Japan, the United States and Britain, Waldfogel, Higuchi and Abe (1998) find that maternity leave coverage has a strong effect on women's chances of retaining a job after childbirth. In Britain, national maternity leave legislation was first passed in 1978, but less than half of working women were eligible for cover. In 1993, in line with the EC Pregnant Workers directive, maternity leave coverage was extended in the UK as qualifying rules were relaxed. All working women with two years' service[5] are now eligible for fourteen weeks' statutory maternity leave. So women may be increasingly utilising one of the few major pieces of employment legislation remaining – maternity leave rights – to maintain continuous employment, and this may be offsetting any decline in overall job stability. This seems most likely since job tenure patterns over time for women without dependent children are similar to those of men.

The second reason to question the aggregate statistics is because the age composition of the workforce is changing. Tables 7.6a and 7.6b, and Figure 7.3 indicate that tenure patterns differ across age groups. Younger workers have lower average tenure, because they change jobs more frequently. A higher share of younger workers in employment means that average tenure will fall, other things being equal. So failure to control for the changing age

---

[4] Information on dependent children and qualifications is not available in 1975.

[5] Working 16 hours or more: those working less than 8 hours must have five years' service to qualify.

Table 7.6a Job tenure by age

	Age 16–24			Age 25–34				Age 35–49				Age 50–64			
	less than 1 yr (%)	more than 5 yrs (%)	Average tenure (yrs, mths)	less than 1 yr (%)	more than 5 yrs (%)	more than 10 yrs (%)	Average tenure (yrs, mths)	less than 1 yr (%)	more than 5 yrs (%)	more than 10 yrs (%)	Average tenure (yrs, mths)	less than 1 yr (%)	more than 5 yrs (%)	more than 10 yrs (%)	Average tenure (yrs, mths)
All															
1975 – GHS	40.1	12.1	1, 10	22.3	36.7	–	3, 9	12.9	56.4	–	6, 4	6.7	73.1	–	11, 7
1985 – GHS	41.7	13.9	1, 5	19.7	45.6	17.3	4, 5	11.9	63.4	41.5	8, 1	5.9	77.8	59.8	12, 11
1995 – GHS	45.7	11.0	1, 3	20.6	44.6	15.5	4, 4	12.1	62.8	38.5	7, 8	9.3	71.7	53.5	11, 1
1995 – LFS	–	–	1, 5	–	–	–	4, 3	–	–	–	6, 0	–	–	–	10, 11
1998 – LFS	–	–	1, 0	–	–	–	3, 6	–	–	–	7, 0	–	–	–	10, 9
Men															
1975 – GHS	38.6	12.8	1, 11	18.8	44.7	–	4, 5	10.0	67.8	–	9, 7	5.2	79.8	–	15, 3
1985 – GHS	39.3	15.2	1, 7	14.8	53.2	21.8	5, 6	8.6	72.4	52.9	10, 9	5.3	79.7	65.2	15, 3
1995 – GHS	45.2	11.0	1, 3	18.8	50.0	17.8	5, 0	10.2	69.9	49.0	9, 9	8.5	73.6	60.0	13, 8
1995 – LFS	–	–	1, 4	–	–	–	4, 11	–	–	–	9, 2	–	–	–	12, 10
1998 – LFS	–	–	1, 2	–	–	–	4, 0	–	–	–	8, 5	–	–	–	11, 8

Sources: GHS, 1975–95; LFS, 1995–8.
Note: Average tenure figure is in years, months.

Table 7.6b Job tenure by age for women with and without children

	Age 16–24			Age 25–34				Age 35–49				Age 50–59			
	less than 1 yr (%)	more than 5 yrs (%)	Average tenure (yrs, mths)	less than 1 yr (%)	more than 5 yrs (%)	more than 10 yrs (%)	Average tenure (yrs, mths)	less than 1 yr (%)	more than 5 yrs (%)	more than 10 yrs (%)	Average tenure (yrs, mths)	less than 1 yr (%)	more than 5 yrs (%)	more than 10 yrs (%)	Average tenure (yrs, mths)
Women with no children															
1975 – GHS	49.9	15.5	2, 2	16.1	39.8	–	4, 1	11.0	58.5	–	6, 11	8.9	63.7	–	8, 6
1985 – GHS	37.7	16.2	1, 8	15.8	46.9	14.7	4, 7	11.8	65.2	39.8	7, 9	6.0	77.4	53.6	10, 7
1995 – GHS	40.3	14.0	1, 5	18.1	40.9	11.0	4, 0	12.4	62.7	36.3	7, 2	10.9	68.9	45.0	8, 11
1995 – LFS	–	–	1, 7	–	–	–	4, 2	–	–	–	7, 6	–	–	–	9, 3
1998 – LFS	–	–	1, 1	–	–	–	3, 6	–	–	–	7, 2	–	–	–	9, 5
Women with children															
1975 – GHS	36.6	4.6	1, 0	35.2	13.6	–	2, 2	20.2	30.6	18.3	3, 5	–	–	–	–
1985 – GHS	56.1	5.6	0, 10	36.9	24.5	7.0	1, 11	19.0	43.1	18.3	3, 9	–	–	–	–
1995 – GHS	55.5	6.4	1, 1	26.7	36.8	15.0	3, 4	15.6	48.6	19.1	4, 8	–	–	–	–
1995 – LFS	–	–	1, 0	–	–	–	3, 1	–	–	–	4, 7	–	–	–	7, 1
1998 – LFS	–	–	0, 10	–	–	–	3, 0	–	–	–	4, 10	–	–	–	7, 4

Sources: GHS, 1975–95; LFS, 1995–98.
Note: Average tenure figure is in years, months.

composition of the workforce may lead to incorrect inference about aggregate tenure patterns. The average age of the employed workforce fell by around two years between 1975 and 1984, caused by the arrival of the 'baby-boom' generation in the labour market.[6] As this generation aged and the number of people staying in education after the age of 16 increased (see Chapter 9), the average age of the workforce grew by a similar amount over the next ten years. So aggregate tenure estimates will rise because there are now more older workers, who on average are in longer-term job matches and so have longer job tenure. This shifting age pattern produces unwarranted

Figure 7.3   Average tenure by age and gender
Age 16–24

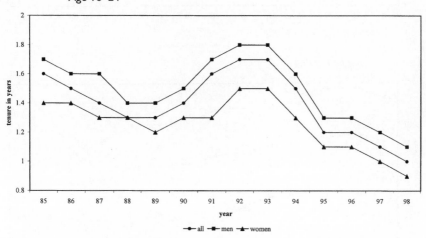

Age 25–34

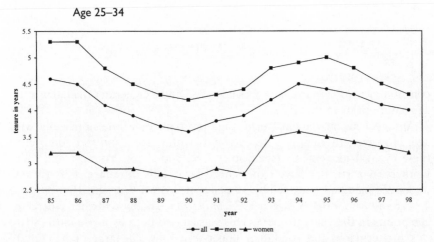

[6] Median age of the employed workforce was 39 years and 1 month in 1975, 37 years and 3 months in 1985 and 38 years and 9 months in 1995.

Figure 7.3 (continued)
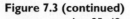

Age 35–49

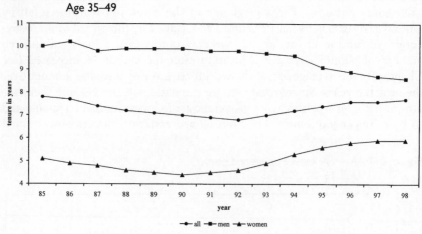

Age 49–59/64

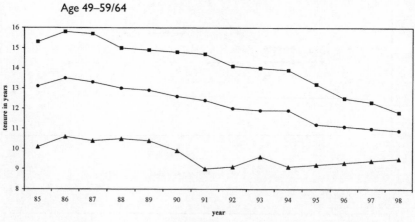

Source: LFS.

consistency in job tenure patterns since 1985 and exaggerates the fall in average tenure prior to that date.

Any cyclical movements in average job tenure decline noticeably with
age. However, there appear to be trends within age groups in addition to
these cyclical movements (see Tables 7.6a and 7.6b). Younger and older
workers in particular have experienced large falls in tenure. For workers
under 25, median tenure fell by 30 per cent, from 1 year and 10 months to
1 year and 5 months, between 1975 and 1985, and by a further 7 percentage points in the years to 1995. This was caused both by a rise in the share
of short-term jobs and by a fall in longer-term jobs. The largest fall in tenure
has been amongst men over the age of 50. Average tenure for these workers
has fallen by 14 per cent since 1985, to around eleven years. The share of

Table 7.7 Change in the share of short-term jobs

	Total		Qualification level				Age group	
		Degree	Higher intermediate	Lower intermediate	None	16–24	25–49	50–64
All								
1985 share	17.5	16.5	15.4	25.2	14.5	38.5	14.9	5.8
1989	21.0	18.0	18.6	25.6	20.0	42.4	18.5	8.0
1992	15.5	15.3	14.4	18.4	13.8	33.1	14.1	7.1
1995	17.4	16.3	15.8	20.2	15.9	40.7	15.7	8.7
1998	20.3	19.6	19.1	23.2	19.1	51.7	17.5	9.8
Men								
1985 share	14.2	12.2	12.8	22.9	11.6	36.5	11.1	5.0
1989	17.3	14.3	15.9	21.8	16.6	39.2	14.5	7.0
1992	13.0	12.4	12.0	15.5	12.6	31.1	11.3	6.5
1995	15.7	14.4	14.3	19.2	14.8	40.3	13.5	9.1
1998	18.9	16.7	17.5	22.7	18.5	49.8	15.8	9.9
Women without children								
1985 share	16.7	23.0	18.7	20.6	10.9	33.8	12.8	6.7
1989	20.8	24.4	22.5	23.5	15.6	40.6	17.0	9.1
1992	15.6	21.2	16.7	16.4	11.3	31.3	13.5	7.5
1995	16.7	23.6	17.0	17.5	10.6	38.2	14.7	7.7
1998	19.7	27.4	21.0	18.2	13.4	49.0	17.4	8.8
Women with dependent children								
1985 share	27.3	24.9	23.5	32.6	25.8	50.2	23.8	7.9
1989	30.0	22.9	24.8	33.1	31.5	51.5	27.0	11.8
1992	22.5	19.1	21.2	25.0	21.0	45.1	20.1	9.0
1995	22.7	14.0	20.1	25.1	26.1	50.2	20.7	8.9
1998	24.7	16.9	21.6	28.0	28.3	57.1	20.0	11.5

Source: LFS, 1985–98, Spring quarter.
Note: Short term is defined as tenure less than one year.

jobs with a tenure of more than ten years fell by 6 percentage points in the years 1985–95.[7] Job tenure for workers in the middle of the age distribution has risen. The largest rise in tenure is amongst women aged 25–34 with children. Again the LFS indicates that these trends have continued through to 1998.

[7] The LFS suggests a larger fall of 7.5 points over the same period. There was a further 3-point fall between 1995 and 1998.

Table 7.8 Change in the share of long-term jobs

	Total	Qualification level				Age	
		Degree	Higher intermediate	Lower intermediate	None	25–49	50–64
All							
1985 share	37.5	34.3	38.6	31.2	40.5	30.0	58.8
1989	36.7	33.2	39.0	32.2	39.2	30.0	58.4
1992	34.3	30.8	37.8	29.6	35.7	28.4	53.7
1995	33.1	30.0	36.3	28.5	37.7	27.5	51.7
1998	32.9	28.3	35.0	30.3	38.7	27.1	49.8
Men							
1985 share	45.3	39.8	43.1	43.2	50.8	38.0	63.9
1989	44.2	38.9	43.5	43.3	48.5	37.8	62.5
1992	42.0	37.3	43.2	39.2	45.4	36.3	58.6
1995	40.2	36.1	42.1	35.4	48.4	34.6	56.3
1998	38.1	32.8	39.2	36.0	47.3	32.3	53.1
Women without children							
1985 share	37.1	20.2	35.2	35.2	41.9	28.1	51.5
1989	38.2	21.4	37.3	35.8	43.5	29.8	53.6
1992	32.9	20.3	34.0	33.2	36.0	25.5	47.6
1995	32.5	20.0	33.0	32.2	39.4	25.6	46.0
1998	33.1	21.9	32.7	34.9	39.3	24.7	47.1
Women with dependent children							
1985 share	14.5	17.0	17.7	11.9	14.4	13.0	36.5
1989	13.2	15.6	17.9	10.6	11.9	12.4	29.2
1992	13.8	15.4	17.8	11.0	11.7	13.4	25.2
1995	15.5	18.4	18.4	14.2	11.8	14.6	32.9
1998	19.3	20.7	22.9	16.8	17.4	18.7	29.3

Source: LFS, 1985–98, Spring. Age 25 and over.
Note: Long term is defined as tenure greater than ten years.

If job turnover and instability have grown, then the fraction of the work-force with tenure less than one year should have risen and the fraction with tenure more than ten years should have fallen. We use LFS data for more information on turnover at the top and bottom ends of the tenure distribution up to the latest available point, Spring 1998 (Tables 7.7 and 7.8). The share of long-term jobs is now estimated on the employed population aged 25 and over. The numbers confirm that the share of short-term jobs rises in good times, but that the overall share is no different in 1998 than it was in

1985.[8] The aggregate share of new jobs is no higher than at the height of the previous economic boom in 1989. There are more new jobs for men and women without children, but fewer new jobs amongst women with children. The results for the share of jobs with tenure above ten years do suggest that, between 1985 and 1998, there has been a decline in the proportion of long-term jobs. A rising share of long-term jobs, of around 4 points amongst women with children, is now insufficient to offset a 7-point fall for men and a 4-point fall for women without dependent children.[9]

In order to see whether these changes are concentrated on certain sections of the workforce within these gender groups, Table 7.7 and Table 7.8 also track the share of short-term and long-term jobs within three 'age' and four 'education' categories. For men, and women without dependent children, the rise in the share of short-term jobs does not appear to be concentrated in any education category. Whilst all ages in these groups have experienced a rise in the share of short-term jobs, the largest increases have been amongst those under the age of 25 (from 36.5 per cent to 49.8 per cent for young men and from 33.8 per cent to 49 per cent for young women). The fall in the share of short-term jobs for women with children does, however, appear to be largest amongst women with degrees. Furthermore, the decline is concentrated in the 25–49 age group. For younger and older women with children the trends in the share of short-term jobs mirror those of men and women without children. This again suggests that maternity leave explains much of what we observe.

According to Table 7.8 there is little evidence that the falling share of long-term jobs amongst men and women without children or the rise amongst women with children is influenced by the level of education. Nor is the decline in long-term jobs confined to those over the age of 49. This would indicate that early retirement is not the sole cause of these trends.

Conclusions

There may be some reason to think that job stability is falling for nearly three-quarters of the workforce; men, and women without dependent children. This declining stability is due to there being fewer long-term jobs and more short-term jobs around than before. At the aggregate level these changes have been largely offset by rising job stability amongst women with dependent children. It seems that one of the remaining aspects of job regulation, provision of maternity leave, may well be responsible for rising tenure amongst women with dependent children.

[8] Estimation of the short-term job share over the period 1985–98 suggests that the share of new jobs continued to rise up to 1998, reaching the same level as in 1989. At the aggregate level, there is no suggestion that this is anything other than a cyclical movement.

[9] GHS estimates for 1985–95 also confirm the steady fall in the share of long-term jobs.

For most groups, changes in tenure are not large, in the order of 2 per cent to 5 per cent since 1975. However, the fall in long-term job stability does appear to be worthy of concern, particularly for older men, where the chances of being in a job for more than ten years have fallen by around 9 percentage points since 1985. This does not seem to be related to levels of educational attainment. Whilst higher turnover need not necessarily be a concern, it may be if we think that a long-term job match is a good thing. If so, then many older workers are losing out more than ever before.

References

Burgess, S. and Rees, H. (1997), 'Job tenure in Britain, 1975–92', *Economic Journal*, March, 334–44.
Gregg, P. and Wadsworth, J. (1996), 'A short history of labour turnover, job tenure and job security, 1975–93', *Oxford Review of Economic Policy*, 11:1, 73–90.
Hall, R. (1982), 'The importance of lifetime jobs in the U.S. economy', *American Economic Review*, 72:4, 716–24.
McRae, S. (1997), 'Maternity Rights in Britain', Policy Studies Institute, London.
OECD (1997), 'Is Job Insecurity on the Increase in OECD Countries?', *Employment Outlook*, Paris.
Waldfogel, J., Higuchi, Y. and Abe, M. (1998), 'Maternity Leave Policies and Women's Employment after Childbirth: Evidence from the United States, Britain, and Japan', CASE Paper No. 3, ESRC Research Centre for Analysis of Social Exclusion, LSE, London.

Further reading

Diebold, F., Neumark, D. and Polsky, D. (1997), 'Job stability in the United States', *Journal of Labor Economics*, 15:2, 206–54.
Farber, H. (1998), 'Job Creation in the United States: Good Jobs or Bad?', Working Paper No. 341, Industrial Relations, Princeton University.

8 Francis Green

Training the workers

Keypoints

- On average, employees in Britain spend around one hour in training each week, of which roughly two-thirds is spent in off-the-job training.

- Training in Britain is very unequally distributed, with most of it going to those who are already highly educated, in higher-status occupational groups, unionised and not working in small firms.

- Despite all the policy changes and the hype, training volume for all employees is probably no higher than it was a decade ago.

- Nevertheless, the amount of *continuing* training – after the apprenticeship or initial stage – is relatively high in Britain compared with much of the rest of Europe.

- Training has many objectives, comprising both technical skills and knowledge, and social skills, including values and behaviour patterns. The vast majority of training produces transferable skills.

- Most, but by no means all, training is employer-sponsored.

- On average, employees benefit from training by gaining higher wages.

- The deficiencies of the British economy in relation to other advanced nations are primarily in terms of educational qualifications and outputs, and in apprenticeships. These deficiencies are only likely to be remedied in the long term if the education system is successfully upgraded to address poor results amongst lower achievers.

There is a certain evangelistic tone to be found in many discussions about the role of training in Britain. The prosperity of employees and the 'competitiveness' of individual companies and of the British economy as a whole are said to depend on firms adequately training their workforces. Many words and much public money have been spent trying to persuade private businesses that they ought, in everybody's interests as well as their own, to devote more resources to training.

Hyperbole about training can be traced to several sources. Politicians who say they want to stimulate a more highly skilled workforce may be reluctant to enact levies or taxes with which to finance training subsidies, and may prefer to refrain from intervening in private decisions. Their only recourse is to try to persuade the private sector to pay by marketing the learning process. As with any marketing strategy, whose tools are frequently those of image and insecurity rather than scientific evidence, it is understandable if those charged with the promotion of training assert its ubiquitous benefits, including the risks of remaining unskilled, without any real evidence that the training will always deliver enough to justify its costs. In addition to politicians, private or quasi-autonomous public organisations which supply training and education services often have a stake in talking up their product. Meanwhile, training and education is widely touted as *the* solution to long-running British economic problems, indeed the only solution within an increasingly global economy. Unfortunately, proponents regularly fail to note that enabling a substantive upskilling of the workforce requires as much attention to the demand for skills by British-based employers, as to skills supply (Keep and Mayhew, 1996).

Despite the exaggerations, there is plenty of sense in the proposition that good-quality work-related training is a necessary ingredient for companies aiming to compete in higher value-added product markets. Knowledge acquired in early life needs to be regularly updated as technology advances. Much of the required knowledge is hard or impossible to codify and could not therefore be constituted and tested as a qualification, and taught in a classroom or lecture hall. As well as technical skills, social skills (including attitudes and norms of behaviour) are acquired, often exclusively, at work. And even those technical skills that could be imparted through public training centres usually make heavy calls on the public purse if equipment is to be kept at the forefront of technology. It follows that no government can bypass employers in the attempt to raise work skills. Individuals can choose to invest more in gaining qualifications at colleges, and the government can support them, but any such gains are, on their own, not enough.

This chapter focuses therefore on the training and education received by people who are at work in Britain. More than a decade ago the government surveyed employers, individuals and various agencies in order to arrive at an understanding of the role of training in Britain (Deloitte Haskins and Sells, 1989). Despite showing that there was indeed already a larger-than-expected volume of training going on in British companies, the decade since has seen many policy developments partly or wholly aimed at employee training – Career Development Loans, Modern Apprenticeships, Investors in People, the National Vocational Qualifications (NVQ) system and, not least, the creation of the Training and Enterprise Councils (TECs) in England and Wales and the similar Local Enterprise Councils (LECs) in Scotland. The new Labour Government, with education and training at the centre of its strategy, has embarked on a 'renaissance' in lifelong learning, with Individual Learning Accounts (ILAs) and a University for Industry (UfI) as the main innovations. The scope of the renaissance is said to extend to the whole range of learning activities through life, including learning at work.

The aims of this chapter are: first, to look at how the quantity and quality of training in Britain have been changing and hence to gauge what effect, if any, the policy changes have had on employees' training; secondly, to chart the provision and distribution of training, including an assessment of how Britain compares internationally; thirdly, to review the impact of this training provision on firms, workers and society generally; and finally, to consider the importance or otherwise of training for the future of the British economy.

How much training in Britain?

The trends

For a long time, commentators and some policy makers used to be worried about the decline of training in Britain. The principal focus of concern was on the decreasing numbers of apprenticeships for young workers, both within the manufacturing industry and overall, as de-industrialisation took place. Apprentice numbers steadily declined in the late 1960s and early 1970s, and then dropped sharply in the 1980s in the course of a major economic recession. By the second half of the decade apprenticeship and young trainee numbers had dwindled to below 100,000, no more than a fifth of their numbers at their peak in the 1960s. Where, then, were those deep craft-based skills going to come from as older skilled workers retired?

Against this decline, however, is set the apparently comforting notion that continuing training for all workers has been taking the place of apprenticeships. In this notion, even if a deep training in intermediate skills is being provided to smaller proportions of young people, compensation is afforded to the British economy by the fact that participation in at least some training is offered to a broader range of young people and to more adult workers later in their working lives. No reasonably reliable figures are available before 1985, but since that date the Labour Force Survey (LFS) has registered an increase in the proportions of employees who report receiving work-related training or education over a four-week period (see Figure 8.1a).

Figure 8.1a Rate of participation in any training over a 4-week period

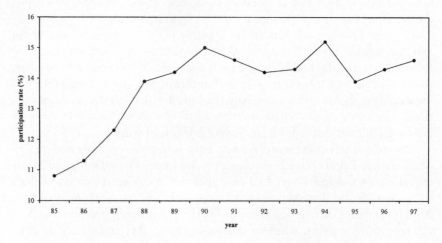

Figure 8.1b Off-the-job training volume, minutes per employee per week

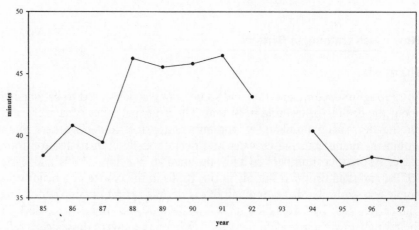

Source: LFS.
Note: Figure 8.1b, 1993 data unavailable.

The rise in participation was most marked in the late 1980s. From 1990 to 1992 there was a small setback coinciding with economic recession. Since 1992, if one allows for a small discontinuity in the series between 1994 and 1995, which shifted the rate downwards by about 1.5 percentage points, the series shows a slow but steady increase in training participation. These trends in the four-week training participation rate are widely used to support the view that, at least as far as quantity is concerned, training in Britain is improving.

The decline in training duration

Unfortunately, this conclusion is wrong. The conclusion rests on the presumption that there has been no decline in the length of training people actually receive during the said four-week period. We do not have any direct measure of this volume of training. We do, however, have from the same LFS a measure of participation in off-the-job training courses over a one-week period, and a measure of the time trainees have been spending in those off-the-job training courses. We can use these measures to compute the average time spent in off-the-job training per employee every week. This series, which is the best available covering a reasonably long period, registers no net change between 1985 and 1997 (Figure 8.1b). In both these years average off-the-job training time was thirty-eight minutes, while in between 1988 and 1991 the volume hovered around forty-six minutes.

Remarkably, what was apparently the most important structural policy change designed in part to stimulate private sector training – namely, the founding of the TECs and LECs – occurred when training volume was at its peak. The subsequent decline till 1995 in off-the-job training hardly speaks for a successful outcome, at least in volume terms, of this major policy initiative.

One weakness of the volume series shown in Figure 8.1b is that it only covers off-the-job training. Could it be that higher training participation over a four-week period derives from there being more on-the-job training? The answer is no: in 1985 some 31 per cent of training episodes took place exclusively on-the-job; by 1997 this proportion was 29 per cent. The real reason why the volume of training has stagnated, even though the four-week participation rate is higher than in the mid-1980s, is that training courses have become shorter. To illustrate: in 1985, some 26 per cent of training courses were less than a week long, but by 1994 the proportion of courses less than a week long was 45 per cent.[1]

The LFS also permits a brief time series for participation in all training (whether on- or off-the-job) over a one-week period: it shows a small rise from 7.4 per cent in 1992 to 7.7 per cent in 1997 which, taking into account the small discontinuity over 1994–5, means the one-week total training participation rate increased slightly over that period as the economy went through a prolonged expansion. The best estimate of total training volume in 1997 shows employees getting an average of one hour's training each week.

Uncertainty over the extent of training

Before proceeding it is necessary to record two caveats to these conclusions. First, the definition and meaning of 'training' are often interpreted differently by different respondents. Typically, one can increase the positive responses to LFS-type survey questions on training by a couple of percentage points

[1] A more detailed explanation is given in Felstead et al. (1997).

simply by suggesting concrete examples of varying types of training. Many workers engage in informal self-taught learning or professional development. Second, more than four out of ten LFS respondents have their details gleaned from a proxy; usually another member of their household. Proxy respondents may not get to hear about some of their household member's work-related training, and accordingly the proxy respondents are a lot less likely to respond positively to training questions than those who are questioned directly. Thus, for female employees, proxy respondents reported a four-week participation rate some 2 percentage points less than direct respondents; while for males the difference was as much as 5 percentage points.

Together, these two caveats render an unfortunate degree of uncertainty in our knowledge of the training market in Britain. This uncertainty has not been adequately resolved by successive government-sponsored surveys of establishments since 1991 (entitled 'Skill Needs In Britain'). The trend revealed in these surveys is for little change in the average number of days spent on off-the-job training annually in the years 1991 to 1994, then an upward jump in 1995 which coincided with the use of a new survey company which renders year-by-year changes somewhat less reliable. The survey covers only employer-sponsored training, and does not pick up what happens in smaller establishments employing less than twenty-five staff which cover more than a third of the labour force.

International comparisons

Even though the volume of work-related training in Britain in 1997 was no higher than in the mid-1980s, recently published findings suggest that the amount of continuing training may compare favourably with that received elsewhere in the European Union (European Commission, 1996). The survey, based on a sample of 50,000 enterprises with ten or more employees across member states, recorded instances and duration of continuing vocational training in 1993 that were wholly or partly funded by the enterprises. The survey excluded initial training and apprenticeships but encompassed formal vocational training courses, informal planned learning at work and other specified forms of self-directed continuous training. Figure 8.2 shows that the United Kingdom had an above-average volume of training. Other high trainers in this league table are Greece (where, though participation is low, the length of time per participant is high), France (which has a compulsory minimum spend on training) and the Netherlands.

One interpretation of these comparative figures would see high training levels in Britain as indicative that British companies are aiming at higher skill levels than their overseas counterparts. However, there is no other evidence to support this interpretation. A plausible alternative explanation is that, for any given skill requirement, continuing company-based training can act as a partial

Figure 8.2   Continuing vocational training in Europe, 1993

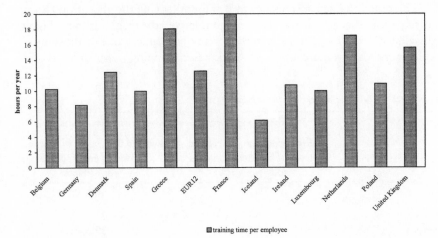

☐ training time per employee

Source: European Commission, 1996.

substitute for prior education or apprenticeship. Senior managers of multi-national companies have opined that more in-plant training is required in order to bring UK-educated recruits up to required skill levels, compared to workers in France, Germany, Singapore and the United States (DfEE and Cabinet Office, 1996). If this subjective response is accepted, we could have one reason why there is a relatively high amount of continuing training in British companies: it is there to make up for past shortcomings in education and initial training.

Who gets training?

Training in Britain is mainly left to market forces, with relatively little intervention from government. Since training will normally only take place if either the firm or the employee can see a return for their investment, it is not surprising that there are considerable inequalities in access. There are large numbers of jobs which do not require high levels of technical skill. Firms that have no intention of upgrading the markets they are operating in, and individuals who see no prospect of advancement to higher grade jobs, may correctly perceive that there is little advantage from training. Although their decisions are rational from their own angle, the amount of training may not be optimal from society's angle. Owing to the possibilities of 'poaching' skilled labour in imperfect labour markets, or to complementarities between innovation and upskilling of the workforce, it is likely that firms will under-invest in training, though by how much is hard to estimate. The remedy lies in some form of social intervention in the market for training.

Educational attainment

The chief identifiable consequence in Britain of leaving the allocation almost entirely to market forces is a chain of cumulative advantage for more highly educated workers, with the converse for the less educated. For those more skilled jobs that require a lot of work-based training, companies recruit

Table 8.1   The distribution of training, Spring 1997

	Training incidence	Training volume
	Proportions in job-related training or education over four weeks (%)	Average time spent in off-the-job training per employee per week (minutes)
All	14.6	38
males	13.5	37
females	15.8	39
full-time workers	15.4	38
part-time workers	11.9	37
Type of contract		
permanent	14.5	37
fixed	21.6	59
casual/seasonal	12.8	49
Size of establishment (no. of workers)		
1 to 24	12.1	31
25 to 49	15.3	37
50 or more	16.2	43
Highest qualification		
degree or equivalent	23.3	63
'A' level or equivalent	19.9	59
GCSE grades A–C or equivalent	13.1	32
NVQ1 or equivalent	9.7	23
no qualification	4.0	6
Occupation		
professional	23.1	67
intermediate	20.2	49
skilled non-manual	14.6	35
skilled manual	9.8	30
partly skilled	8.5	24
unskilled	4.2	13

Source: LFS, Spring 1997.
Note: The base is all employees in Great Britain excluding full-time students; percentages unweighted.

workers with more general education because they are likely to be more efficient at work-based learning. Amongst cross-sections of employees it is almost always the better educated ones who receive more training. The differences in access to training in Britain are startling (see Table 8.1): on average those with 'A' level qualifications or above spend roughly ten times as much time on off-the-job training courses as those with no qualifications. The inequality is reflected again in the occupational classifications: professional grade workers (including managers) receive about five times as much off-the-job training time as unskilled workers (sixty-seven minutes compared with thirteen minutes), and participate about six times as frequently in all job-related training (23 per cent compared with 4 per cent).[2]

Small firms

The other striking difference that generates justified concern is the relatively low amounts of training afforded to workers in small businesses. The comparisons in Table 8.1 show that employees in large establishments (fifty or more workers) receive about a third more training than those in smaller ones (less than twenty-five workers). However, many small establishments are part of larger firms, and the differences by establishment size are only a pale reflection of the problem that worries policy makers. In 1993, while around half the employees in large firms (with more than 500 workers) received employer-sponsored continuing training, for those in firms with between ten and forty-nine workers only one in five received such training (Government Statistical Service, 1977). This pattern is replicated in all other countries. It has been argued that, despite low formal training in small businesses, a great deal of informal training makes for a complex heterogeneous picture that defies any summary statement of the problem. The evidence just cited, however, encompasses various kinds of informal training in a fairly broad definition, for example to include planned learning through job rotation or quality circles. We know very little about the quality of training that occurs in small firms, but there remains little doubt that low levels of training are presently a fact of life in small businesses (Westhead and Storey, 1997). There may, however, be plenty of learning taking place through informal, often unplanned, processes that cannot in any way be described as training.

The fact that smaller firms seem less committed to training reflects, on the one hand, their higher training costs: a frequent reason advanced by small businesses for not training is the difficulty of sparing employees from the production line. Larger firms can reap scale economies both with lower

[2] Despite these imbalances, training could still be a substitute for education. In order to reach any given skill level, training could to some extent make up for lack of prior education. But across a cross-section of individuals, the higher educated get more training because they are generally involved in more highly skilled jobs.

opportunity costs and with cheaper training delivery. Low training also reflects problems of high labour turnover: if trained workers leave for higher paid jobs in larger firms, the small firm loses its investment. Small firms are especially disadvantaged in this respect by their low levels of union recognition. Unions, it has been shown, have a substantial positive impact on the quantity of training (Green *et al.*, 1999). For example, across a representative sample of establishments in 1991, union recognition was associated with about one full day's extra employer-sponsored training per year, that is, about half the average that manual workers receive and more than a third that non-manual workers receive. Although union leaderships have taken a very positive stance towards encouraging training, they have not yet succeeded in making access to training a regular item on the bargaining agenda. Unions' positive effect on training probably derives from their providing a voice for their members, their downward impact on labour turnover and their consequent positive impact on the returns to worker training.

Gender

Apart from differences according to education level, occupation, union recognition and size of business, there has been progress in Britain in widening access to training across a broader spectrum of the population. Most strikingly, training is now no longer a male-dominated affair – which it certainly was in the days when apprenticeship was the main form of training taking place, and still even in the mid-1980s when younger women appeared to face discriminatory barriers to work-based training. By 1997 women's participation in training marginally exceeded men's (15.8 per cent compared with 13.5 per cent), although the average training volumes barely differed between men and women. There is now little evidence of sex discrimination over the quantity of training received, though there remains the issue of occupational segregation which is often reinforced rather than challenged by the distribution of training places.

Part-time and temporary jobs

Table 8.1 also shows that part-time workers and those on non-permanent employment contracts are not badly off for access to training: indeed, fixed-term employees receive a good deal more training on average than permanent employees. Much of this difference is due to the fact that many non-permanent workers are receiving induction training in the early stages of their jobs. Another factor is that non-permanent and part-time workers may be more likely to be following training courses outside their present jobs but nevertheless related to potential future work.

The distribution of training shown in Table 8.1 is just a snapshot at one time, with consequent limitations. It might be less of a problem that certain groups received low training if, over the course of time, everyone at least had their turn, albeit with those stuck in lower occupational groups being obliged to take less frequent turns at training. The fact that only about one in three employees receives any training in the course of a year would be of little concern if the remaining two-thirds had their share of training in subsequent years. Unfortunately, training sharing is not the reality. For example, amongst a cohort who were 23 years of age in 1981, more than one in two males received no training courses of three or more days in the course of a whole decade (Arulampalam *et al.*, 1995). Tables 8.2 and 8.3 indicate a similarly poor situation in the 1990s. Utilising the British Household Panel Study, which has annually tracked more than 12,000 individuals from 1991 onward, Table 8.2 shows that training, far from being shared, is concentrated more or less in the same group of recipients year in, year out. One half of all those people who might at some point have received job-related training in fact received no training during five years. Meanwhile, about one in six had work-related training in at least three out of the five years. Table 8.3 shows that long-term deprivation of training is far higher for those in lower status jobs, and especially for those with low prior levels of education. Seven out of ten employees with no qualifications in 1992 did not receive any training at all in the subsequent five years. Three out of five employees in the lowest quintile of the pay distribution received no training at all. These differences support the proposition that the current British training system is, if anything, a recipe for greater inequality in years to come, rather than something that promotes greater equality of opportunity.

Table 8.2 Training count, 1991–95

Number of years in which training took place	Proportion of workers with training in these years
0	50.4
1	21.0
2	12.3
3	8.2
4	4.7
5	3.4

Source: British Household Panel Study.
Note: Proportion of all those with jobs at time of interview and on at least one occasion in previous five waves.

Table 8.3 Exclusion from training, 1991–95

	Proportion with no training in any of five years (%)
Wage* quintiles in job held at wave 5	
lowest	59.7
2nd	45.0
3rd	38.4
4th	29.4
highest	19.7
Occupation held at wave 5	
professional	20.6
managerial	28.2
skilled non-manual	39.7
skilled manual	51.1
partly skilled	60.1
unskilled	72.0
Highest qualification in wave 1	
degree or above	23.8
teaching	24.0
other higher education	34.0
nursing	33.8
GCE 'A' level	38.8
GCE 'O' level	46.3
commercial	56.0
CSE grades 2–5 or equivalent	51.9
apprenticeship	66.0
no qualifications	71.2

Source: British Household Panel Study.
Note: The base is those in employment at time of interview on at least one occasion during five waves.
* Real gross wages.

Who pays?

One obvious reason for not training is the potentially high cost involved. To train a young school-leaver up to an intermediate skill level in, for example, the construction industry costs employers nearly £10,500 over four years, even after allowing for some productive contributions while training and for government subsidies through Youth Training (Hogarth *et al.*, 1996). Most continuing training, however, lasts only a short time and costs far less on each occasion. Individuals, too, will often have to bear substantive costs – either through forgone leisure time or wage-earning opportunities or directly through fees. The balance of these costs between employers, employees and

Table 8.4 Training sponsorship, 1997

	All who had received training (%)	All in receipt of short training (up to 3 months) (%)	All in receipt of medium training (3 months to 2 years) (%)	All in receipt of long training (more than 2 years) (%)
Only current or previous employer *	42.9	61.5	37.8	35.6
Only self or relatives **	6.2	8.2	10.1	3.2
Partially government subsidised ***	11.5	4.5	14.8	13.5
Both employer and self/relatives	38.5	24.8	36.1	47.0

Source: Skills Survey, 1997, see Green et al. (1998).
Note: The base is all those in employment aged 20 to 60, in Britain.
* Employer pays any fees and incurs all the opportunity cost.
** Worker/family pays any fees and incurs all the opportunity cost.
*** Government pays part or all of fees.

government can therefore be crucial in determining the incentives and hence whether the training takes place.

Precise data on all elements of cost are hard to collect, but even those that could be collected easily are not always utilised. One key issue concerns whether employees undertake their training during normal working hours. To the extent that they do (and do not sacrifice any wages), one can deduce that the employer is bearing the opportunity cost of lost production. If, however, workers have to train outside normal work hours they must bear the opportunity cost of either lost leisure time (with possible implications for families) or lost secondary earning opportunities.

Table 8.4 gives a broad picture of who has actually borne the cost (including the opportunity cost) of the training that workers report having received for the type of work they are currently doing.[3] While individuals (or their families) alone have funded the training in only a relatively small proportion of cases (6 per cent), they have been involved in the sponsorship in many more cases, sharing the costs with employers or government. A considerable fraction (43 per cent) of workers have obtained their training solely at employers' expenses, and in addition employers have been involved in sharing the cost of training a further 38 per cent of workers. Even where the government has been involved, employers are likely to have borne some cost. Employers have indeed been an indispensable source of sponsorship for current British workers to acquire their skills, whether through formal off-the-job training or through on-the-job training.

[3] Opportunity cost is attributed on the basis of whether the employer pays less wages during training and on whether the training takes place in work hours; however, it does not allow for employees accepting jobs at lower wages if they offer training, which might be important for younger workers.

They are likely to remain so in the future. The ongoing training for those now in employment is also dominated by employers: some 63 per cent of workers who currently receive any training have that training sponsored entirely by employers, while only 10 per cent are entirely self or family sponsored (Felstead *et al.*, 1997).

Employer-sponsored training has been concentrated, however, on workers with relatively short training periods of less than three months (see Table 8.4). In these cases the financial risk of investing in employees may be the lowest, in that the benefits are likely to be enjoyed in the relatively short term. Individuals (or their families) and also the government tend to have been more involved when the training has been of medium length. In the case of very long training, that is, lasting more than two years, it becomes more likely that employers and employees share the cost in some way.

Training outcomes

Beneath all the statistics about the quantity of training which takes place in Britain there is a considerable range not only in the quality but also in the objectives of training. One might ask, what does all this training actually do?

Many employers believe that their training investments pay off. Remarkably there is no solid evidence to justify this belief, and company decisions to spend resources on training remain essentially a matter of faith and judgement. There have been no scientific studies, as yet, assessing whether profitability has been raised by training. One reason is the difficulty of controlling for the many other factors that may be linked to both training and to profits.

Studies to investigate any impact of training on labour productivity in companies are also absent in Britain, though we can draw on studies from abroad. One recent study in the United States is informative (Lynch and Black, 1995). It showed that the skill level of the workforce mattered a great deal for productivity. One extra year of average educational attainment in a company's workforce raised productivity by between 5 per cent and 12 per cent depending on sector. This finding is consistent with qualitative studies in Britain and Europe which have stressed the impact of intermediate skills on productivity. However, finding that skills are related to productivity does not necessarily mean that company training is related to productivity. Companies may acquire skilled workers by recruitment, and any training they do might not be effective in raising skills much. Moreover, workers who have received the training may quit the company – the well-known problem of 'poaching'. The US study also looked for a direct impact of training on productivity but was unable to find much of an effect, except insofar as the type and sector of the training did make a difference. Computer skills training was positively linked with labour productivity in the non-manufacturing sector though not elsewhere. However, lack of any firm findings does not mean that training has no impact, since it is often hard to measure the quantity and quality of training very accurately.

What is clear from many British studies is that companies put on training courses for lots of different reasons, each of which is only indirectly related to profitability in the long term. For example, among a sample of CBI-affiliated small to medium-sized firms (SMEs) in 1996, some three-fifths of companies inaugurated training for manual workers to meet health and safety regulations (see Table 8.5). Such courses would normally be evaluated in terms of their immediate outcomes. Another three-fifths of companies cited the objective of improving manual employee skills in their current jobs (including new technology training). Also important for manual workers was training about external standards and training for multi-skilling. For non-manual workers health and safety training was not so important but skills improvement was cited by 84 per cent of SMEs. For non-manual workers a second important function was to 'foster a culture of identification or commitment to the business's objectives'. Similar patterns to this range of training objectives can be found in larger firms, and analysis suggests that these objectives are well understood by employees.

It would therefore be wrong to imagine that the sole purpose of company training is to raise technical skills in the workforce. Also important is the aim of changing behaviour and attitudes – that is, raising the 'social skills' of the workforce. The ultimate objective of this part of training is to align workers' interests and values more with those of firms and their shareholders, with

Table 8.5 The objectives of training in small and medium-sized enterprises, by occupation

	Percentage of firms training:	
	manual workers	non-manual workers
Meet health and safety requirements	60.7	26.6
Improve the skills of employees in their current jobs	60.7	84.4
Foster a culture of identification with or commitment to the firm's objectives	27.7	48.1
Implement multi-skilling, i.e. bringing skills from two or more jobs into a single job	37.0	16.6
Prepare employees for different jobs in order to enable them to progress in the business	16.2	26.3
Implement change in employee relations or in the management and supervision structure	8.1	16.3
Meet quality standards or to obtain 'Investors in People' status	41.0	41.9
Attract good recruits	4.0	8.3

Source: Felstead et al. (1997).

consequent favourable implications for long-term profitability. Whether this objective is ever achievable, and if so whether it is desirable from society's perspective, is a debatable issue.

Individuals and society

Despite the lack of studies linking company profits to training, many profit-maximising businesses do continue to invest in training. But what do their employees gain, if anything? If all they get is an increment to their company-specific skills, and a change in their commitment to their company, one could question whether the training is of any real benefit to them or to the wider society. Recent British research is, however, reassuring on this point (Felstead *et al.*, 1997). Most employees (90 per cent) experience an increase in skills resulting from their training. Only about one in ten of these find that their new skills would only be useful for their current employer. In other words, the vast majority, around 82 per cent, of employees receiving training are gaining some transferable skills. Most of the purely firm-specific training is solely employer-sponsored, as one might expect. These findings do not mean that firm-specific skills are unimportant, since other skills derived from informal learning at work, but not from training as such, may be firm-specific (e.g. knowledge of an organisation).

Another indirect way of gauging the quality of training is whether it is leading to any form of qualification. Whether or not that qualification is rewarded in the market with an increment of pay, it at least provides an external stamp. One tenet of British training and education policy over the last decade has been to make the British system of qualifications more transparent, and to provide for external certification of job competences through the NVQ system. The importance of certification has slightly increased. In 1990, 39.2 per cent of non-student employees doing work-related training were aiming directly or indirectly for some sort of qualification; by 1997 this proportion had risen to 43.2 per cent. However, it is doubtful that any greater transparency has been achieved. Moreover, the NVQ system, which has come in for a considerable amount of criticism, has not directly made any large mark on training outcomes. As Table 8.6 indicates, only about one in a dozen trainees are aiming at NVQs. With less than 120,000 employees in training each quarter aiming for an NVQ at level 3 or above, it is unlikely to be making much of a dent in the five million or so net new qualifications at these levels needed to meet the official Lifetime Target One by the year 2000. As for other trainees, the largest number are going for relatively low level qualifications or none at all, while some 8 per cent are aiming at degree-level qualifications.

The acid test for individuals, however, is whether the training they receive actually leads them to getting more pay. Although there are some moderately

Table 8.6 Certification of work-based training, Spring 1997

Whether certified	Proportion of training employees (%)	
Not certified	56.7	
Certified,	43.2	
of which:		
Qualification level aimed at:		
degree or above	7.7	
teaching, nursing or other medical	2.3	
at least 'A' level, below degree	4.6	
academic, below 'A' level	0.8	
NVQ/SVQ, of which:	8.7	
Levels 1 & 2		2.9
Level 3		3.1
Levels 4 & 5		0.7
Don't know level		2.0
RSA or City and Guilds	3.8	
other professional, vocational or foreign qualification	12.6	

Source: LFS, Spring 1997.

Note: The base is all employees doing work-related education or training in last 4 weeks in Great Britain, excluding full-time students. A small proportion (1.8 per cent) did not know whether the training led to a qualification, while another 2.2 per cent did not know or say which qualification.

tricky problems of disentangling cause and effect, the strong balance of evidence suggests that experiencing employer-provided training does indeed pay off. For example, in the cohort of people who were 23 in 1981 (the National Child Development Study (NCDS)), men who had one or more training courses provided between 1981 and 1991 are estimated to have gained between 5 per cent and 15 per cent extra wages compared to those who received no training; for women the gains were found to be less but still positive (Blundell *et al.*, 1996). For another cohort survey of non-college bound school-leavers in 1986, those who had company training were receiving some 7.5 per cent more wages by age twenty-one, compared to others getting no training, and were some 20 per cent better off than those obliged to take the government's Youth Training Scheme route (Green *et al.*, 1996). These sorts of findings are now quite believable because they are mirrored in a range of studies using different data and methods.

An additional key finding from the NCDS analysis is that it hardly mattered whether the training was provided by an individual's current or previous employer – the positive effect on the 1991 wage was the same. This finding is consistent with the above-mentioned evidence that the vast majority of training in Britain provides transferable skills. It suggests that the benefits of investment in training are not lost to society as a whole in the event of job mobility, even though the firm which has sponsored the training forgoes some of the benefit.

Conclusion

In order to avoid, as far as possible, the tendency towards overstatement and false generalisation that bedevils many studies of skills, I have endeavoured in this chapter to give an accurate picture of the training of those in employment in Britain in the late 1990s.

How important is training employed people as a mechanism for upgrading the skills of the British workforce? Its role needs to be put into perspective. In terms of sheer volume, prior education is more important: using the figure of one hour per week per employee (see above), one can deduce that overall, there takes place around a billion hours of on-the-job or off-the-job training each year for employees in Britain. This contrasts with some twelve billion hours' education each year for those in compulsory schooling. The costs of continuing employer training were put at around £10.6 billion in 1993 (DfEE, 1998) for all firms with more than ten workers. This sum compares with some £35 billion worth of net public spending alone on education, leaving aside private education. The deficiencies that the British economy carries in relation to other advanced nations are primarily in terms of educational qualifications and outputs, and in apprenticeships. These deficiencies are only likely to be remedied in the long term if the education system is successfully upgraded to address the poor outcomes in the lower half of the spectrum.

The role of training in the process of learning at work also needs to be seen for what it is, and undoubtedly merits more extended research. One recent study, covering several organisations in the engineering, business services and health care sectors, has shown that formal education and training contribute a relatively limited proportion of learning at work (Eraut *et al.*, 1998). Other important channels of learning (depending on what type of knowledge is being acquired) include organised learning support (e.g. mentoring schemes), consultation and collaboration with a working group, the challenge of the work itself, external consultation (e.g. with clients or customers) and even life outside work. Apart from prior education, perhaps the most important factor determining learning at work is the micro-culture of the organisation. Within this perspective, formal training has a necessary role as a way for certain kinds of knowledge and skill to be acquired for the organisation's workforce, but this role is only one part of the story. Unfortunately, other features associated with learning at work do not always lend themselves easily to statistical measurement.

The most obvious policy conclusion we may draw from the existing picture of training in Britain is to focus policy on improving the distribution of training. In this respect the philosophy underlying the Government's lifelong learning policy proposals is broadly correct (DfEE, 1998). ILAs if properly backed could be aimed at those most in need. The UfI is designed to capture efficiencies in the delivery of learning, thereby opening up training for small firms. In addition, the philosophy is to continue to supply infrastructural support, through the qualifications systems, Industry Training Organisations, TECs and through Investors in People. The big issue remains the question of the demand for skills. Unless, at the same time as lower skilled workers are being equipped with new skills, their jobs are also upgraded to use those new skills, there are two serious dangers. First, companies will not pay for the training of lower skilled workers (unless subsidised and regulated). The UfI could then be poorly used by industry, while ILAs would not be supported other than by government. Second, individuals will become disillusioned with training as any skills they do acquire are under-used. It therefore becomes important to question how firms' product strategies are also going to be changed by the potential renaissance of British workers. Amongst all the policies up for discussion in the government's proposed policies, only the suggestion to encourage more union involvement combines the potential to spread training down the workforce and simultaneously impact on firms' product and process strategies. With unions now limited in their coverage of the workforce, more is needed to move firms' labour demands onto the high skills road.

References

Arulampalam, W., Booth, A. and Elias, P. (1995), 'Count Data Models of Work-Related Training: A Study of Young Men in Britain', Working Papers of the ESRC Research Centre on Micro-social Change, Colchester, Essex.

Blundell, R., Dearden, L. and Meghir, C. (1996), 'The Determinants and Effects of Work-Related Training in Britain', Institute For Fiscal Studies, London.

Booth, A. L., Francesconi, M. and Garcia-Serrano, C. (1997), 'Job Tenure: Does History Matter?', Discussion Paper No. 1531, Centre for Economic Policy Research, London.

Deloitte Haskins and Sells (1989), 'Training in Britain. A Study of Funding, Activity and Attitudes. Employers' Activities', Her Majesty's Stationery Office (HMSO), London.

Department for Employment and Education (DfEE) (1998), 'The Learning Age. A Renaissance for a New Britain', HMSO, London.

DfEE and Cabinet Office (1996), 'The Skills Audit: A Report from an Interdepartmental Group', London.

Eraut, M., Alderton, J., Cole, G. and Senker, P. (1998), 'Development of Knowledge and Skills in Employment', Research Report No. 5, Institute of Education, University of Sussex.

European Commission (1996), 'Key Data on Vocational Training in the European Union', Brussels.

Felstead, A., Green, F. and Mayhew, K. (1997), 'Getting the Measure of Training', Centre for Industrial Policy and Performance, University of Leeds.

Government Statistical Service (1977), 'Education and Training Statistics for the United Kingdom', HMSO, London.

Green, F., Hoskins, M. and Montgomery, S. (1996), 'The effects of training, further education and YTS on the earnings of young employees', *Oxford Bulletin of Economics and Statistics*, 58, 471–88.

Green, F., Machin, S. and Wilkinson, D. (1999), 'Trade unions and training practices in British workplaces', *Industrial and Labor Relations Review*.

Hogarth, T., Siora G., Briscoe, G. and Hasluck, C. (1996), 'The Net Costs of Training to Employers', HMSO, London.

Keep, E. and Mayhew, K. (1996), 'Evaluating the assumptions that underlie training policy', in A. Booth and D. Snower (eds), *Acquiring Skills. Market Failures, Their Symptoms and Policy Responses*, Cambridge University Press, Cambridge.

Lynch, L. M. and Black, S. E. (1995), 'Beyond the Incidence of Training: Evidence from a National Employers Survey', Working Paper No. 5231, National Bureau of Economic Research, Cambridge, Mass.

Westhead, P. and Storey, D. J. (1997), 'Training Provision and the Development of Small and Medium-Sized Enterprises', DfEE, Sudbury.

Further reading

Green, F., Ashton, D., Burchell, B., Davies, B. and Felstead, A. (1998), 'Are workers getting more skilled?', in A. B. Atkinson and J. Hills (eds), *Exclusion, Employment and Opportunity*, Centre for Analysis of Social Exclusion, LSE, London.

9 Peter Robinson

Education, training and the youth labour market

Keypoints

- In 1987 less than half the age cohort stayed on after 16. By 1993 over 70 per cent were staying on. High attainers stay on to do 'A' levels. Those with more modest attainment stay on to do vocational courses.

- The proportion of 18-year-olds entering higher education doubled to over 30 per cent between 1987 and 1993.

- The other consequence of these changes is that the proportion of the age cohort entering the regular labour market at the end of compulsory schooling has fallen significantly.

- Youth unemployment has proved especially sensitive to the economic cycle, rising quickly in recessions but also falling sharply during periods of recovery. Increases in unemployment make it marginally more likely that young people will stay on in education after age 16.

- The introduction of the GCSE has been the most successful education policy of recent years. Improved levels of educational attainment at age 16, brought about by the GCSE, have played a dominant role in the increase in numbers staying on in full-time education after age 16.

- The changes in employer recruitment practices and the occupational structure of employment have also meant fewer immediate employment prospects for 16-year-olds.

- There seems to be no labour market justification for a further expansion in higher education, and the case for an expansion in the proportion of the cohort obtaining level 3 qualifications is also weak. A greater focus on entry and training requirements for jobs in the intermediate and lower reaches of the labour market is needed.

First, this chapter summarises the main trends in the labour market and educational experiences of young people over recent years. It then seeks to flesh out these trends and offer an explanation for them, utilising available data and research. In particular, it tries to understand why enrolment rates in full-time education have increased so sharply and why early entry into the labour market has declined.

The chapter highlights the importance of distinguishing between the 16–18 age group and the 18–24 age group. For both groups the end goal of all policy is to facilitate transition into the regular labour market. For the majority of young people this now involves some period of education and structured training beyond age 16, whether this takes place in full-time education or in a work environment. There is some general agreement that society should aim to maximise the proportion of each cohort that experiences some form of post-compulsory education and training. However, there is possibly an uncomfortable trade-off in public policy between meeting targets to ratchet up the qualifications held by the labour force as a whole, and ensuring that all young people are catered for by the system. There are concerns that the rush to increase the overall stock of qualifications could be marginalising a residual but significant group of young people.

Trends in education, training and employment of young people

The key trends in the pattern of education, training and employment experienced by young people in the United Kingdom are easy to summarise but less straightforward to explain.

Table 9.1 synthesises a range of national data on the education, training and employment of young people in their first year after compulsory schooling.

Table 9.1 Education, training and employment for 16 to 17-year-olds in the first year after compulsory schooling (England, 1979–97)

	% of age cohort							
	end 1979	end 1982	end 1985	end 1988	end 1990	end 1993	end 1995	end 1997
Full-time education	42	50	47	51	59	72	71	69
Government-supported training	5	16	24	21	17	12	10	9
Employment	47	21	19	23	16	9	10	13
Non-participants	6	13	10	5	8	7	8	8

Sources: DFEE and Payne (1995 and 1998).
Notes: Employment refers to those in full- and part-time employment as main activity and excludes students in part-time jobs. Non-participants are those not in education, employment or training. All estimates within + or − 1 per cent. Estimates of employment and non-participants for 1997 subject to wider margin of error.

We can identify five clear trends for this age group. The most important is the sharp increase in the proportion of the cohort staying on in full-time education. In 1979 just over two-fifths of 16 to 17-year-olds were enrolled in full-time education in the first year after the end of compulsory schooling. Enrolment rates rose modestly in the early 1980s before falling back slightly in the middle of the decade. Enrolment began to rise strongly again after 1987–8 and this continued into the early 1990s, peaking in 1993, since when staying-on rates have fallen back modestly.

Some of these trends in enrolment rates over time seem to coincide with trends in unemployment. Enrolment rates rose in the early 1980s and again in the early 1990s during periods of recession. On the other hand the most significant period of expansion in educational enrolment began in 1987–8, at a time when the aggregate labour market was improving strongly. There has clearly been a large secular increase in the staying-on rate that has nothing to do with fluctuations in unemployment. For example, at the end of 1985 and at the end of 1993 aggregate unemployment rates were broadly similar, but enrolment rates had increased by over 25 percentage points between these two dates.

The reverse side of increased rates of participation in full-time education is the sharp reduction in the proportion of young people entering the regular labour market at the end of compulsory schooling. In 1979 nearly half of those aged 16–17 were in regular, almost wholly full-time, employment. By the mid-1990s this had fallen to just one-in-ten of the age group.

Not surprisingly, employment rates fell very sharply in the early 1980s recession, before recovering a little in the middle of the decade. The early 1990s saw a further sharp fall in employment rates for all 16 to 18-year-olds. More recent trends are harder to discern because of limitations in the data, but the proportion of 16 to 18-year-olds in regular employment has probably increased somewhat in the labour market recovery of the mid-1990s. For those 16 to 17-year-olds in full-time jobs in 1996 for whom data were available, only about one-quarter reported receiving apprenticeship or other off-the-job training, two-fifths were receiving on-the-job training only, and about one-third reported receiving no training (Payne, 1998). Only one in five was reported as studying for a recognised qualification.

In the early 1980s government-supported training programmes were expanded rapidly as an urgent political response to the surge in youth unemployment. Youth training programmes were initially expanded in the early 1980s for 16 to 17 year-olds (Table 9.1), and then again in the second half of the 1980s for 17 to 18-year-olds, when the 'youth training guarantee' was extended for a second year. This expansion for 17 to 18-year-olds displaced a large proportion of the regular employment opportunities for this age group. From the late 1980s, however, the proportion of the age cohort taking the government-sponsored training route declined significantly. This decline continued into the second half of the 1990s, despite the launch of the

Modern Apprenticeships programme in Autumn 1995 designed to give the work-based training route more status.

The original rationale for government-sponsored training programmes was clearly to ameliorate youth unemployment. Over time, however, the emphasis has shifted to getting more young people a vocational qualification. This was the rationale behind the Modern Apprenticeship. The Modern Apprenticeship offered a three-year subsidy instead of the two-year Youth Training subsidy in order to increase the proportion of those on the work-based route who obtained an advanced or level 3 vocational qualification, as opposed to the level 2 qualifications aimed for by those on the National Traineeships, which replaced Youth Training in Autumn 1997. At the same time there was increasing concern about the small proportion of each cohort not in any education, training or employment and for whom Modern Apprenticeships or National Traineeships might not be appropriate.

This neatly illustrates the tension in much provision for the over-16s. How far is this provision to be geared toward increasing the aggregate qualifications held by the labour force, and how far is it to be geared toward more immediate employment and social objectives?

Youth unemployment is one of the most emotive political issues. It is also especially sensitive to the economic cycle, rising quickly in recessions but also falling sharply during periods of recovery. This is a pattern common across all the Organisation for Economic Co-operation and Development (OECD) countries, but is especially strong in the United Kingdom. Blanchflower and Freeman (1996) find no other explanation for trends in youth unemployment other than it being a function of trends in aggregate unemployment. The reduction in the size of the youth cohort in most countries, shifts in the structure of employment toward industries which employ many young people, and sharp declines in relative youth wages should all have improved the labour market position of young people. Each cohort entering the labour market has been significantly better qualified than the group before. However, none of these factors seems to have prevented sharp increases in youth unemployment when aggregate unemployment rises. The corollary to this is that improvements in the aggregate labour market are quickly reflected in the youth labour market.

As a proportion of the cohort, youth non-employment in Britain peaked in 1982–3 when one-in-eight 16 to 17-year-olds were not in education, training or employment (Table 9.1), along with nearly one-in-five 17 to 18-year-olds. The expansion of government-supported training programmes, and the labour market recovery of the second half of the 1980s saw the size of this 'non-participant' group fall sharply. In fact, by the end of the decade only 5–6 per cent of 16 to 18-year-olds were not in education, training or employment, a figure which was if anything lower than in 1979.

The early 1990s recession saw this total increase again, though the peaks in youth non-employment rates, expressed as a proportion of the cohort, were significantly lower than in the early 1980s. However, worryingly, non-employment rates amongst 16 to 18-year-olds do not appear to have fallen much in the labour market recovery of the mid-1990s.

An important point to register about Table 9.1 is that it represents a *snap-shot* of the youth labour market and enrolment rates at a number of points in time. The Youth Cohort Study (YCS) allows us to track young people over time. For example, of those who left compulsory schooling in Summer 1991, in Spring 1992 8 per cent were not in education, training or employment (Payne, 1995). By Spring 1993 just under half of this group were now in education, training and employment, though an equivalent number of those who had been in education, training or employment had left these states and joined the ranks of the 'non-participants'.

This makes the point that young people are constantly moving between states. It also makes the point that even the most disadvantaged are not totally disconnected from the labour market. It is more helpful to see young people along a continuum, from those with the highest GCSE scores mostly enrolled on 'A' level courses, all the way down to those who are in unskilled jobs or on non-apprentice government-supported training places, or indeed enrolled on lower level vocational courses in full-time education. These latter groups in turn share some of the characteristics of those young people who we observe at any one point in time not in education, training or employment. Those who might be regarded as truly 'excluded' – for example, young people coming out of local authority care, young offenders, the young homeless – are a further small part of this portion of the age cohort.

There has been much concern expressed about the problems faced by young men in the contemporary labour market. Table 9.2 looks at the routes taken by 16 to 17-year-old men and women in the late 1980s and mid-1990s, drawn from the YCS. In the Spring of 1989, 5 per cent of men aged 16–17 and 7 per cent of women were not in education, training or full-time employment. In the Spring of 1996, 9 per cent of young men and 10 per cent of young women aged 16–17 were not in education, training or full-time

Table 9.2 Education, training and employment for 16 to 17-year-old men and women (England) (percentages)

	Spring 1989		Spring 1996	
	men 16–17	women 16–17	men 16–17	women 16–17
Full-time education	43	53	68	75
Government scheme	27	20	19	9
Full-time job	25	20	9	6
None of the above*	5	7	9	10

Source: YCS, Payne (1995 and 1998).
Note: * includes the unemployed and inactive and a small number in part-time employment.

employment. The proportion of 'excluded' young women broadly matches the proportion of 'excluded' young men. The lack of gender differences in the numbers of 'excluded' young men and women is discussed further in Pearce and Hillman (1998).

The major gender differences in young people's experiences in the first two years after post-compulsory education are not then in the size of the 'excluded' group. A much higher proportion of young women stay on in full-time education, while a much higher proportion of young men enter employment or enrol on government-sponsored training programmes (Table 9.2). As attainment in examinations at age 16 is the most powerful predictor of staying on in full-time education, these patterns in part reflect the higher levels of attainment of young women in GCSE examinations. It also reflects the structure of entry routes into the intermediate reaches of the labour market. The male-dominated skilled manual occupations still undertake some recruitment at age 16, onto apprenticeships and other formal training programmes. The female-dominated clerical and secretarial occupations have traditionally recruited a larger proportion of young people at age 17 or 18 after one (and increasingly two) years of post-compulsory education.

Table 9.3 looks at trends in employment and enrolment rates for the 18–24 age group. The same broad trends identified for 16 to 18-year-olds can also be seen amongst young adults. First the proportion of the age group in full-time education at any one point in time more than trebled between 1984 and 1998, from around 8 to 28 per cent. Enrolment data from the Department for Education and Employment (DfEE) show that in 1988, 15 per cent of the age group were enrolling in higher education by the age of 21,

Table 9.3 Education and employment for 18 to 24-year-olds

	% of age cohort				
	Spring 1984	Spring 1987	Spring 1990	Spring 1993	Spring 1998
Full-time education	7.9	10.3	11.8	18.1	27.8
Employed (inc. schemes)	64.1	67.7	70.7	58.1	55.2
Unemployed	15.1	11.8	7.7	12.7	7.2
Inactive	12.9	10.2	9.8	11.1	9.7
ILO unemployment rate (18–24)*	19.0	14.8	9.8	17.4	11.3
ILO unemployment rate (all ages)*	11.7	10.7	6.7	10.3	6.1

Source: Labour Force Survey, Spring quarter.

Note: * The International Labour Organisation (ILO) unemployment rate measures the proportion of all the economically active (excluding all those who are not in the labour market, including non-working students) who are unemployed and looking for work (including students looking for part-time jobs). It is not the same as the proportion of the whole age cohort who are unemployed. One consequence of this is that, all other things being equal, a rise in the enrolment rate in full-time education will tend to raise the ILO unemployment rate because it shrinks the denominator for calculating the unemployment rate.

and that this had increased sharply to 31 per cent by 1993, at which point the expansion in higher education was brought to a halt by the government. This expansion was very much driven by public policy. The proportion of the age group eligible for entry into higher education had been increasing since the late 1980s due to the rise in staying-on rates amongst over-16s and the proportion of the age group getting 'A' levels or notionally equivalent vocational qualifications. But, translating this into an expansion in higher education required a specific policy decision.

Once again the flip side of this expansion in enrolment in full-time education has been the decline in employment rates, which rose strongly in the late 1980s, before falling back again in the early 1990s. Unemployment (and inactivity) for this age group is very cyclical. Unemployment halved as a proportion of the cohort in the period 1984–90, before rising sharply again in the early 1990s recession, though to levels much lower than were seen in the early 1980s. Between Spring 1993 and 1998 unemployment as a proportion of the cohort fell by nearly half, and by 1998 was slightly lower than the trough reached in Spring 1990. Inactivity rates are also cyclical, but around a modestly downward trend.

The gender differences are interesting. There is little difference in enrolment rates in full-time education. Employment rates for men are much higher, as is the proportion of the male cohort that is unemployed. However, this is balanced by a much higher proportion of young female adults who are inactive. Unemployment and inactivity rates for women are both cyclical and declining over time. Unemployment and inactivity rates for men are also cyclical. Comparing 1998 with 1990 the combined unemployment/inactivity rate for young men had risen by 1 percentage point and for women had fallen by 2 percentage points, though significantly more young women were still not in education or employment when compared with men. There has been a modest shift over this period in favour of women, but again the overall gender differences do not suggest that a focus solely on the problems faced by young men is warranted.

The new Labour Government, elected in 1997, pledged action to reduce the number of 18 to 24-year-olds registered unemployed for over six months by 250,000. In July 1997 there were 150,000 18 to 24-year-olds who had been registered unemployed for more than six months. This was down from 248,000 in July 1996 and 400,000 in July 1993. This rapid fall in youth long-term unemployment proved once again how sensitive the youth jobless rate is to the overall state of the labour market.

Why have enrolment rates in post-compulsory full-time education increased?

The sharp rise in enrolment rates in full-time education and the decline in entry rates into full-time employment are the most clearly identified trends for young people. They are of course two sides of the same coin. However, one question is whether they are linked causally, with the trends in employment and unemployment in themselves helping to drive the changes in enrolment rates?

To assess this, researchers have in the past tried to see how trends over time in staying-on rates are related to various social, educational and labour market variables. These *time-series* studies have a variable record of success. However, the existence of the YCS since 1984 has resulted in more careful *cross-section* work looking at the factors which influence the individual decision to stay on. This has also been supplemented by *longitudinal* work exploiting the National Child Development Study.

The factors influencing staying-on rates after age 16 can be classified into four groups. First, social and economic background factors, such as parental education and social class, parental employment status, family poverty or household composition. Secondly, individual variables such as innate ability (if this can be measured), gender and ethnic background, and, critically, performance in school-leaving examinations at age 16. Some of these individual variables are, of course, also influenced by the social and economic background variables. Thirdly, educational and other policies, such as the introduction of the GCSE examination in the mid-1980s, the expansion of higher education in the late 1980s, the availability of education and training options after age 16 and the availability of benefits; and finally labour market variables such as the overall structure of employment by industry and occupation, the returns to educational qualifications, unemployment rates and the availability of part-time jobs for students.

What do the different kinds of studies – time-series, cross-section and longitudinal – tell us about the relative importance of these different sets of variables?

Time-series work

Time-series studies face several serious problems. In modelling what has happened to enrolment rates in the period after the Second World War, studies are limited to around forty annual observations of the national staying-on rate. This severely restricts the number of variables which researchers can use to try and explain the trends. For any chosen variable it is often difficult to obtain data on a consistent basis over forty years. In practice many time-series studies have themselves not passed the test of time, in that they have failed to successfully forecast the trend in the staying-on rate past their original sample period.

The most thorough and up-to-date work has been conducted by Rice and McVicar (1996), who model the staying-on rate for young men and young women separately. One thing they try to explain is the rise in the staying-on rate between 1988 and 1993, when it rose by 20 percentage points for both young men and young women.

The proportion of households where the head of household belongs to a managerial, professional or related occupation, and the average real income of all households, were used to proxy social and economic background factors, but perhaps surprisingly, neither in fact were found to play a significant role.

The performance of young people in school-leaving examinations at age 16 was found to be the most significant explanatory variable. This is measured by the proportion of the cohort obtaining five or more 'O' levels, or higher grade GCSEs. Over the period 1988–93 half of the increase in the male staying-on rate and fully two-thirds of the increase in the female staying-on rate are explained by this one variable. The other dominant variable is the expansion in higher education, estimated to explain about a third of the increase in the staying-on rate for both genders. In other words, two *educational* policies, the introduction of the GCSE examination with the first full cohort sitting the examination in 1988, and the expansion of higher education after 1988, are seen as the dominant variables in explaining the sharp increase in the staying-on rate between 1988 and 1993.

How do these educational variables compare with any influences from the labour market? Rice and McVicar (1996) use three labour market variables. First, the rising ratio of the average earnings of managerial and professional workers to manual workers was found to have a significant but very small direct impact on the staying-on rate for young men, but not for young women. The decline in the proportion of the cohort entering government-supported training since the late 1980s was marginally associated with the increase in the staying-on rate.

Most importantly the youth unemployment rate was found to be significantly, positively related to the staying-on rate. The sharp increases in youth unemployment in the early 1980s and again in the early 1990s helped boost staying-on rates, while the fall in youth unemployment in the late 1980s would have led to a fall in staying-on rates, other things being equal. However, the size of this impact from youth unemployment needs to be kept in context. Over the whole period 1988–93, when the overall staying-on rate surged by around 20 percentage points, the combination of the *fall* in unemployment between 1988 and 1990 and the subsequent rise between 1990 and 1993 would, other things being equal, have added just 2 percentage points to the staying-on rate for young men and 1 percentage point for young women. Clearly then, this time-series evidence suggests that fluctuations in youth unemployment have had only a modest influence on the overall trend in the staying-on rate.

Put another way, this time-series model would predict that a fall in the overall claimant count, to 5 per cent from its 1993 peak of over 10 per cent, would chop about 4 percentage points off the staying-on rate, other things being equal. This closely mirrors what has actually happened (Table 9.1).

Overall then, this time-series evidence seems to give overwhelming backing to the importance of educational variables, and particularly examination attainment at age 16, in determining the staying-on rate after age 16, with a modest supporting role played by labour market variables and in particular youth unemployment. But the secular rise in the staying-on rate after 1987 cannot be explained by any secular rise in youth unemployment, for the simple reason that youth unemployment in 1993 was similar to its rate in 1987.

Cross-section evidence

A great deal of work has exploited the YCS to look at the factors influencing the decision of individuals to stay on or not. One virtue of the YCS is the large sample size (typically over 15,000 individuals) which allows for a much greater range of variables to be tested. Gray *et al.* (1994) use the third, fourth and fifth youth cohorts, who finished their compulsory schooling in the Summers of 1986, 1988 and 1990 respectively. A great deal of work has compared the third and fourth cohorts, because pupils in the third cohort took 'O' levels and CSEs while the fourth cohort were the first to sit GCSEs, so that a comparison can tell us a great deal about the 'GCSE effect' on staying-on rates.

Table 9.4 shows the trend in the staying-on rate as recorded in the YCS between 1986 and 1995. The top half of the table shows the proportion

Table 9.4   Qualifications achieved and enrolment in full-time education post-16

	Year left compulsory schooling					
	1986	1988	1990	1991	1993	1995
% of 16-year-olds whose main activity was full-time education, by highest qualifications achieved						
5+ GCSEs A–C	84	86	91	92	93	92
1–4 GCSEs A–C	45	46	56	66	69	68
5+ GCSEs D–G	26	28	36	46	55	49
1–4 GCSEs D–G	10	14	22	28	35	34
None reported	4	11	12	19	23	26
Total (% of 16-year-olds)	41	48	58	66	72	71
% of all 16-year-olds, by highest qualifications achieved						
5+ GCSEs A–C	24	30	34	37	41	44
1–4 GCSEs A–C	30	31	33	31	29	28
5+ GCSEs D–G	30	19	16	17	17	18
1–4 GCSEs D–G	11	10	9	7	6	4
None reported	14	10	9	7	6	5
Total (% of 16-year-olds)	100	100	100	100	100	100

Source: YCS all cohorts, sweep 1.

staying on in each cohort, given different levels of educational attainment, and the bottom half of the table shows the highest qualifications obtained by each cohort. Over this time the overall staying on rate rose by 30 percentage points. We can see the sharp rise in the proportion of the cohort obtaining five or more 'O' level/GCSE grades A–C, from 24 per cent of the cohort in 1986 to 44 per cent in 1995. We can also see that the vast majority of this group of high achievers have always stayed on, 84 per cent in 1986, rising to 92 per cent in 1995.

However, there has also been an increase in the propensity to stay on for those with more modest or even quite low attainment in examinations at 16. In 1986 less than half of those with 1–4 'O' levels stayed on, but by 1995 this had risen to two-thirds. In 1986 hardly anyone without qualifications stayed on, but by 1995 a quarter of the unqualified were staying on.

A simple 'shift-share' analysis shows that half of the 30-percentage-point increase in the staying-on rate between 1986 and 1995 can be explained simply by the increase in the proportion of the cohort getting five or more 'O' levels/higher grade GCSEs, with the propensity of these high achievers to stay on fixed at its 1986 value. This then is the 'GCSE effect' in its simplest form. The introduction of this new examination in 1988 has, by significantly raising examination attainment at age 16, raised the staying-on rate after age 16. It is interesting that this simple calculation suggesting that the increase in the proportion of the cohort obtaining five or more 'O' levels/higher grade GCSEs accounts for half the increase in the staying-on rate closely matches the estimate from the time-series work.

Table 9.4 also shows that the dip in the staying-on rate between 1993 and 1995 occurred primarily for those young people with five or more GCSE passes but at lower grades. It is possible that the marginal influence of youth unemployment on the staying-on rate identified by time-series work might impact on these young people with modest GCSE attainment, but not on those with higher levels of attainment, or indeed those with the lowest levels.

Gray et al. (1994) used multi-level modelling to look at the full range of factors influencing the individual propensity to stay on. They confirmed that qualifications attained at age 16 are the most powerful predictor of whether an individual stayed on. They also found that parental social class was important, with an intermediate or manual background leading to a significantly lower propensity to stay on when compared with a professional background, even after controlling for exam achievement. If the father or mother possessed a degree this was associated with a higher propensity to stay on, but this variable was not always independently significant. However, parental social class and parental education are highly correlated so that it is sometimes hard to disentangle their separate effects. Gray et al. (1994) found that if the father or mother was currently unemployed, this had no significant impact on the propensity to stay on. Young people from larger families were less likely to stay on. Conversely, controlling for all other factors, young women were more likely to stay on as were young people from black or Asian back-grounds. Other work using the YCS has found no evidence that young people coming from a lone-parent household were less likely to stay on, controlling for other factors (Rice, 1996).

Most importantly, Gray *et al.* (1994) in their cross-section work found that the local unemployment rate, or changes in local unemployment, had *no* impact on the staying-on rate. This finding thus conflicts with the time-series evidence that variations in youth unemployment over time do have an impact. They also found that the local industrial structure of employment had no significant impact, so that a higher proportion of employment in man-ufacturing, for example, did not seem to significantly reduce the staying-on rate. Thus the labour market variables were generally not found to be of much significance by these authors. However, other work using the YCS (Rice, 1996) did find that the unemployment rate in the local labour market had some impact, but only for those with modest GCSE results, with the find-ings being more robust for young men than for young women.

Staying-on rates vary significantly across schools. However, Cheng (1995), using the YCS, found that most of the variation between schools was accounted for by differences in individual variables such as examination results at age 16 and social and economic background factors such as parental social class. About 10 per cent of the variation in staying-on rates across schools could be explained by the characteristics of schools. However, the school characteristics that seem to matter were associated with economic and cultural deprivation. Staying-on rates were lower in schools with higher rates of teacher turnover and with a high percentage of students taking free school meals. On the other hand the length of experience of teaching staff and the pupil–teacher ratio were not found to be significantly related to staying-on rates.

Gray *et al.* (1994) suggest that part of the increase in the propensity to stay on for those with modest or low GCSE attainment could reflect what some have named the 'peer-group' effect. A young person with given characteris-tics was significantly more likely to stay on in a local labour market with a larger number of better qualified young people than in a similar local labour market with a lower number of better qualified young people. This might suggest that the rising proportion of the cohort staying on because of good exam results further encourages students of modest attainment to stay on as they follow the majority of their peer group into post-compulsory education.

Longitudinal studies

A final source of evidence on the background factors which determine the propensity to stay on in full-time education after age 16 comes from longi-tudinal studies, such as the National Child Development Study (NCDS) which attempts to follow all people born in one week in March 1958.

Gregg and Machin (1998) looked at the determinants of staying-on rates for young men and young women who would have reached school-leaving age in 1974. They confirm the finding from cross-section studies that parental education is an important influence: young men and young women with parents who left school at age 15 or less were themselves significantly less likely to stay on after age 16. On the other hand whether the father had been unemployed when the child was 7, 11 or 16 generally did not show up as significant. Whether the mother was a lone parent when the child was 7, 11 or 16 generally did not show up as significant either. These results are confirmed by recent cross-section work using the YCS (Rice, 1996).

However, if the family had experienced financial difficulties when the child was 7, 11 or 16 this had a significant negative effect on whether the young person stayed on at 16. If a young man had been in care this significantly reduced his chances of staying on, but the impact for young women was not significant. Overall then, coming from a disadvantaged family background had a significant negative impact on the chances of staying on after age 16. However, it was experience of poverty, along with indicators of severe disadvantage such as being in care, which were the significant variables, rather than factors such as unemployment or lone parenthood.

Amongst the most significant variables predicting the staying-on rate were the scores on reading and maths tests undertaken at age 7. Some authors take this as an indicator of underlying ability, but of course by age 7 the social and economic background of a child and indeed their early educational experiences could already be exerting a powerful influence.

There remains much work to be done using the 1958 NCDS and the more recent 1970 British Cohort Study (BCS) in order to understand how different factors interact in determining success in education and how success in education determines subsequent performance in the labour market. So far, however, research using longitudinal data has tended to confirm the role of some of the background variables identified in the cross-section studies.

Summary

It would be no exaggeration to say that the introduction of the GCSE has been the most successful education policy of recent years. GCSEs have brought about a significant improvement in educational attainment, at age 16. This improvement, when supported by the expansion in higher education, has played a dominant role in the increase in the numbers staying on in full-time education after age 16.

Social and economic background factors are also very important in explaining the individual propensity to stay on. These not only include variables such as parental education and social class, about which public policy can do very little, but also variables such as family financial circumstances, which can be influenced by public policy. However, some family variables such as lone parenthood or parental unemployment do not in themselves seem to play a significant role in influencing enrolment.

The influence of labour market variables, and most particularly unemployment, is more contentious. Unemployment may play a role in explaining variations in the staying-on rate over time, though it plays only a marginal role in explaining the trend rise in the staying-on rate. Unemployment may impact especially on young people with modest examination attainment, for whom the decision to enrol on a lower level vocational course in full-time education, or to leave and enter a less skilled job, is a marginal one.

The structure of employment and earnings and its impact on the routes through education, training and employment

The previous section looked at the factors that led to a significant increase in the enrolment rate in full-time education after age 16 between 1987 and 1993. It emphasised the importance of policy decisions such as the introduction of the GCSE in 1988 and the expansion of opportunities in higher education. Over the long run we would anticipate that changes in the *structure of employment* and in the *returns to qualifications* would impact on the choices which young people make with respect to the different routes through full-time education, training and employment.

By the late 1990s the majority of young people in Britain were continuing in full-time education after age 16. In the mid-1990s over 90 per cent of those with five or more higher grade GCSEs stayed on (Table 9.4) and amongst these highest attainers, nearly four out of five of those in full-time education enrolled on 'A' level courses. This means that fully three-quarters of the highest attaining 44 per cent of the cohort took the 'A' level route in 1995. Around 15 per cent of those with five or more higher grade GCSEs were enrolled on other courses in full-time education leading mainly to advanced or level 3 vocational courses. A small proportion of the highest attainers had left full-time education and many will have been recruited to higher status apprenticeships and full-time jobs in, for example, the craft occupations.

In 1995, of the 28 per cent of the cohort with 1–4 higher grade GCSEs, two-thirds stayed on (Table 9.4), with some taking 'A' levels, but with the majority enrolling on courses leading to a range of vocational qualifications. This then is the clear pattern: the highest attainers at 16 mostly stay on and opt for the 'A' level route; a majority of those with a few higher grade GCSEs stay on but enrol mainly on vocational courses. The one-third with 1–4 higher grade GCSEs who left full-time education in 1995 were largely successful in entering employment and government-sponsored training programmes covering the intermediate ranges of the labour market, such as the craft and clerical and secretarial occupations and the personal services.

In 1995 half of those with five or more low grade GCSEs also stayed on

(Table 9.4), mainly enrolling on lower level vocational courses. It has been suggested earlier that it is this group, at the margins, which may be most affected by fluctuations in unemployment. During labour market recoveries more of this group may search for and obtain jobs in the occupations at the lower end of the labour market, rather than enrolling on lower level vocational courses. These courses may indeed eventually lead to some of the same labour market outcomes.

For those with 1–4 lower grade GCSEs about one-third stayed on in 1995 (Table 9.4), to enrol mainly on lower level vocational courses, while one-third went into jobs or training placements. However, fully one-fifth were unemployed. For those with no reported grades only one-quarter stayed on, one-third entered jobs or training placements and a fifth were unemployed.

For those who successfully complete the 'A' level route, and for a high proportion of those who successfully complete the advanced vocational route, the end goal is higher education. For those taking lower level vocational qualifications, the majority will join the labour market at 17/18 to enter the intermediate and less skilled occupations, as clerical and secretarial workers, as craft workers, in the sales and personal service occupations, and in semi-skilled and unskilled manual jobs.

To what extent do these routes reflect the changing structure of employment and the returns to qualifications?

Changes in the structure of employment

Over time the UK labour market has seen a significant decline in the proportion of the workforce employed in manufacturing and a shift primarily toward the business and financial services and the sheltered public and social service sectors. In occupational terms this has been matched by a steady fall in the share of employment of both skilled and less skilled manual occupations and a rise in the share of employment of the managerial, professional and technical occupations, and also of the personal service occupations (see Table 9.5).

These occupational shifts allow one to make some sense of the choices made by young people at age 16. The growing managerial, professional and technical occupations generally require further and higher educational qualifications. The 'A' level route still offers the best chance of getting into higher education and most of those taking this route will be doing so in the hope of entering higher education, and eventually the managerial, professional and technical occupations. This will also be true of many on the advanced vocational route.

The jobs traditionally accessed through lengthy periods of work-based training, notably the craft occupations, have seen the sharpest decline in their share of employment. It is not surprising then to see far fewer young people taking this route. The clerical and secretarial occupations recruit some school

Table 9.5 Changes in the occupational structure of employment

	% of total employment			
	1984	1990	1993	1998
Managers/administrators	12.5	13.8	15.7	16.1
Professional	8.9	9.2	10.1	10.5
Associate professional and technical	7.7	8.8	9.3	10.0
Managerial/professional/technical (total)	*29.1*	*31.8*	*35.1*	*36.6*
Clerical/secretarial	16.1	17.0	15.5	15.0
Craft and related	17.7	16.0	13.3	12.2
Intermediate (total)	*33.8*	*33.0*	*28.8*	*27.2*
Personal/protective services	7.3	7.5	10.0	10.9
Sales	7.0	7.5	7.9	7.9
Plant and machine operatives	11.6	10.7	9.5	9.4
Other occupations	11.3	9.6	8.7	8.0
Other occupations (total)	*37.2*	*35.3*	*36.1*	*36.2*

Source: Labour Force Survey, Spring quarters. Standard occupational classification.

leavers, but a higher proportion of their trainees are now recruited from amongst those aged 17 or 18 who have spent some time in further education (for example on 'business' courses). The growing personal service occupations comprise an important part of the work-based training route (hairdressing, for example) and the vocational route in full-time education (courses, for example, in health and child-care).

In Spring 1996 nearly nine out of ten students aged 16–19 working part-time were employed in just three of the nine major groups of the Standard Occupational Classification – sales, personal services and the other occupations, with sales jobs alone accounting for over two-fifths of the total. In Spring 1996 students accounted for over one-quarter of all part-time employment in the sales occupations. There is some evidence that major retailers use part-time work as a screening mechanism, hiring their full-time workers from their part-time workforce. This seems to indicate that working part-time while studying for a qualification might offer the best of both worlds to a young person wanting to enter some of the jobs on offer in the intermediate or lower reaches of the labour market.

At the bottom end of the labour market some jobs in the semi-skilled and unskilled manual occupations are still available for those young people with few or no qualifications who do not stay on in education and do not enter government-sponsored training programmes.

So it is possible to rationalise some of the choices which young people make in order to access different parts of the labour market. However, employers in turn have had to change their recruitment practices in response to the rising staying-on rate, increasingly recruiting at age 17 or 18 rather than age 16. Although the shifts in the structure of employment over time may help explain some of the trends we see in terms of young people's choices, it is worth emphasising that such ongoing changes cannot in themselves explain the rapid increase in enrolment rates from 1987 onward.

Educational initiatives have resulted in a significant increase in the proportion of the workforce holding higher qualifications. Between 1984 and 1994 the proportion of the employed workforce with some form of higher education rose by 8 percentage points from 15 to 23 per cent. Even with the enrolment rate in higher education pegged at one-third of the cohort, the proportion of the workforce with higher education will continue to rise for many years as younger, better educated cohorts replace older, less well educated cohorts. Work undertaken by the DfEE has suggested that until the second decade of the next century the growth in the proportion of the workforce with higher education should more than keep pace with any likely increase in the demand for graduates (Steel and Sausman, 1997).

Changes in the returns to qualifications

Trying to establish patterns of change over time in the earnings associated with different qualifications is very difficult. The Labour Force Survey now provides the best source of earnings data for people with different qualifications; however, because earnings information is only available from the end of 1992 it cannot be used to construct a time series. The General Household Survey has traditionally been used to establish a time series on the earnings associated with different qualifications.

Figure 9.1 reports results for the earnings of full-time men with different

Figure 9.1 Male earnings by qualification, full-time employees evaluated after 20 years

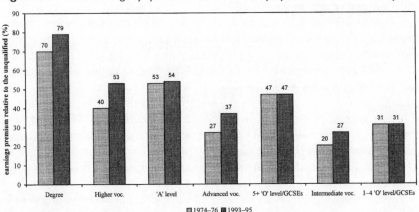

Sources: General Household Survey and Labour Force Survey.

qualifications evaluated after 20 years' experience, compared with men with no qualifications, over the period from the mid-1970s to the mid-1990s. It suggests that, for men in the mid-1990s, the relative earnings associated with having higher academic qualifications (higher, first or other degrees) were slightly higher than in the mid-1970s. The estimates also suggest a modest increase in the relative earnings associated with level 4 vocational qualifications such as the HND/HNC. The results for those holding 'A' levels or their equivalent or in possession of five or more 'O' levels or higher grade GCSEs and 1–4 'O' levels or higher grade GCSEs, would suggest little change in relative earnings. The earnings associated with having level 3 or level 2 vocational qualifications may have risen modestly.

Overall this evidence suggests less change for men in the relative earnings associated with holding various qualifications, when comparing the mid-1970s with the mid-1990s, than might be expected. Earnings differentials by qualification are wider for women, but also have not changed dramatically over time. This relative stability in the earnings associated with qualifications at different levels may appear to be at odds with the well-documented evidence showing a dramatic increase in overall earnings inequality since the late 1970s. However, much of this increase in inequality has occurred *within* groups defined by educational background. Only a small part of it seems associated with any major change in the earnings associated with holding different qualifications.

It is very hard then to explain the sharp increase in enrolment in full-time further and higher education as a response to a sharp increase in the returns to qualifications, for the simple reason that there has *not* been a sharp increase in the returns to qualifications. One of the most striking features of the results presented in Figure 9.1 is that the earnings associated with holding academic qualifications are significantly higher than for notionally equivalent vocational qualifications. There is no parity of esteem between academic and vocational qualifications in the labour market. On average men and women working full-time with academic qualifications at one level in the national qualifications framework earn about the same as men and women with vocational qualifications set notionally one level higher. So, those with 'A' levels have earnings similar to those with higher or level 4 vocational qualifications, those with five or more 'O' levels or higher grade GCSEs have earnings similar to those with level 3 vocational qualifications, and so on.

These higher earnings occur first because academic qualifications at a given level are more successful in buying access to more highly paid occupations. Second, *within* the most highly paid managerial, professional and technical occupations, academic qualifications are associated with higher earnings (Robinson, 1996).

These results do help us make sense of the choices made by young people with respect to the different routes through education and training. Not only does the 'A' level route in full-time education offer the best chance of access to higher education, those with 'A' levels who enter the labour market also have relatively good earnings prospects. It is no surprise therefore to see the vast majority of young people with good GCSE results at age 16 opting for the 'A' level route. So, although changes over time in the returns to qualifications may explain little of the increase in enrolment in full-time education, the higher returns to academic as opposed to vocational qualifications do help to explain the course options of those who do stay on in full-time education.

Conclusions: equilibrium or further systemic change?

By the mid-1990s, the patterns of young people's enrolment and entry into employment had reached some kind of equilibrium. The significant increase in staying-on rates after age 16 appeared to come to a halt in 1993, with enrolment rates falling back modestly in subsequent years. The labour market route, including government-supported training, was still favoured by a substantial minority of the cohort at age 16, and was still of relevance, especially for access to occupations in the intermediate and less-skilled reaches of the labour market. However, a residual group was still facing an uncertain transition from compulsory education into the world of work.

Research into the determinants of the staying-on rate seems to predict relative stability in enrolment rates in the late 1990s. Further falls in aggregate and therefore youth unemployment may be expected to marginally reduce enrolment, as some young people with modest GCSE results enter the labour market rather than taking lower level vocational courses in full-time education. On the other hand, the effects of rising GCSE results will partially offset this. A further expansion in higher education enrolment could also increase the staying-on rate after age 16, though the DfEE's own analysis shows that there is little labour market justification for such an expansion. Of course, if the economy went back into recession then this would tend to increase enrolment rates.

While the impact of the introduction of the GCSE examination is now well documented, the impact of other policy initiatives has yet to be established. The introduction of a new set of General National Vocational Qualifications (GNVQs) in 1994 was meant to reinvigorate the full-time vocational route. However, these new qualifications could not have played a role in boosting staying-on rates for the obvious reason that enrolment rates after age 16 peaked in 1993. GNVQs have mainly replaced other vocational qualifications, at the same time having much lower successful completion rates than the qualifications they have displaced (Robinson, 1996).

Indeed if one goal of policy was to further increase the qualifications held by each age cohort, tackling low successful completion rates across a range of qualifications could be at least as important as increasing enrolment in full-time education.

Meanwhile, the work-based route in the mid-1990s was meant to be re-invigorated by the Modern Apprenticeships programme launched in Autumn 1995. As the proportion of 16 to 18-year-olds on the government-sponsored training route has continued to fall gradually, enrolments on Modern Apprenticeships seem to have largely displaced enrolments on Youth Training (renamed National Traineeships in Autumn 1997). This may enhance the quality of the work-based route but not the quantity of young people under-taking it.

If it is correct that further major shifts in the balance between the full-time education and work-based routes are unlikely, then this part of the public policy debate might usefully fall into abeyance. It is right that a range of choices should be on offer to young people and few could argue that the Eng-lish post-compulsory education and training system lacks choices at present. Policy makers should try harder to understand the choices which young people make, and to recognise that those choices do seem to reflect a ratio-nal appreciation of labour market opportunities and constraints.

The plethora of inquiries into both the education and work-based routes, and the range of policy initiatives on offer in the late 1990s, suggest that many policy makers remain dissatisfied with the nature of the equilibrium which seems to have been established. A useful way to assess these initiatives is to examine the possible public policy trade-off between meeting targets to increase qualifications held by the labour force and ensuring that all young people are offered something by the system.

There seems to be no labour market justification for a further expansion in higher education, and the case for an expansion in the proportion of the cohort obtaining level 3 qualifications is also weak. A greater focus on entry and training requirements for jobs in the intermediate and lower reaches of the labour market is needed, in the clerical and secretarial, sales and personal service occupations, and in the semi-skilled and unskilled manual occupa-tions. A reasonable level of basic literacy and numeracy and of personal and social skills is likely to be a requirement for most of these jobs, though in some cases they may require modest formal qualifications.

Quite rightly there remains some concern about the proportion of the cohort leaving full-time education with few or no qualifications and a limited grasp of basic skills. As was emphasised in Chapter 8, those without qualifi-cations are significantly less likely to receive further work-based training as adults. Narrowing the dispersion of educational attainment at the end of compulsory schooling may be the most effective way of equalising access to training. GCSE scores have risen strongly across cohorts, but the bottom quarter registered much less improvement in the 1990s. On the other hand the targets which schools in England faced in the late 1990s to improve per-formance at GCSE and in statutory tests in literacy and numeracy at age 11, could be met without doing much for the lowest attaining 10–20 per cent of the cohort.

Within the state education and training system the key issues facing the United Kingdom in the late 1990s are, first, whether public resources are going to be used to finance a further expansion in higher education enrolment and chase National Targets for raising the proportion of the workforce with higher qualifications, for which there is little labour market justification. Second, whether any additional resources are to be used to help the bottom of the attainment range with schools given incentives to improve the performance of the lowest attainers, rather than concentrating their attention on the middle and upper reaches of the attainment range.

References

Blanchflower, D. and Freeman, R. (1996), 'Growing into Work', Discussion Paper No. 296, Centre for Economic Performance, LSE, London.

Cheng, Y. (1995), 'Staying On in Full-Time Education After 16: Do Schools Make a Difference?', Youth Cohort Report No. 37, DfEE, London.

Gray, J., Jesson, D. and Tranmer, M. (1994), 'Local Labour Market Variations in Post-16 Participation: Evidence from the End of the Eighties', Youth Cohort Report No. 26, DfEE, London.

Gregg, P. and Machin, S. (1998), 'Child Development and Success or Failure in the Youth Labour Market', Discussion Paper No. 397, Centre for Economic Performance, LSE, London.

Payne, J. (1995), 'Routes Beyond Compulsory Schooling', Youth Cohort Report No. 31, DfEE, London.

Payne, J. (1998), 'Routes at Sixteen: Trends and Choices in the Nineties', Research Report RR55, DfEE, London.

Pearce, N. and Hillman, J. (1998), 'Wasted Youth: Disaffection and Non-Participation Amongst 14 to 19 Year Olds in Education', Institute for Public Policy Research, London.

Rice, P. (1996), 'Further Education or The Job Queue?', mimeo, University of Southampton.

Rice, P. and McVicar, D. (1996), 'Participation in Full-Time Further Education in England and Wales: An Analysis of Post-War Trends', mimeo, University of Southampton.

Robinson, P. (1996), 'Rhetoric and Reality: Britain's New Vocational Qualifications', Centre for Economic Performance/Gatsby Foundation Special Report, LSE, London.

Steel, J. and Sausman, C. (1997), 'The Contribution of Graduates to the Economy: Rates of Return', Report 7, National Committee of Inquiry into Higher Education, DfEE, London.

10 Tanvi Desai, Paul Gregg, Julian Steer and Jonathan Wadsworth

Gender and the labour market

Keypoints

- Over the last 20 years men's employment rates have fallen while women's have risen. In 1975 more than 92 per cent of working age men had a job, and only 81 per cent by 1998. For women the figure rose from 59.4 per cent to 69.3 per cent over the same period. The gender gap in employment rates fell from almost 33 per cent to 12 per cent in just 23 years.

- Maternity Rights legislation now enables nearly two-thirds of women to return to the same employer after child-birth. This is an important factor increasing job tenure for women, particularly for women aged between 25 and 34, for whom it has risen from under two years to three years since 1985.

- The improvement in employment rates for women has come almost entirely from amongst women with working partners. Employment rates for these women have risen from 53 to 73 per cent. There has been no change for single women, lone parents and women with unemployed partners.

- The gender pay gap is also narrowing; in 1998, women earned, on average, 75 per cent of the average male hourly wage compared to only 62 per cent in 1974. However all this gain comes from amongst women in full-time jobs; in part-time jobs the pay gap is actually increasing.

- One in five women now earn more than their working partners, compared with one in fourteen in the 1970s.

- One reason for the narrowing of the gender pay gap may be the increase in women's educational attainments. 60 per cent of people in further education and 51 per cent of undergraduates are now women.

One of the most profound labour market developments of the past twenty years has been the continual improvement made by women relative to men. Whether changes are measured by the level of earnings, or by the rate of employment, it is clear that there has been a relative shift in labour market fortunes across gender. Gender gaps in pay, job tenure and employment have all narrowed appreciably over time. Women have substantially lower unemployment rates than men and are now achieving consistently better examination results than men. Policy intervention has taken place in almost all industrialised countries over the last quarter-century to promote equal opportunities for women. So, the advances made by women in the labour market could be seen as a sign of the success of these interventions. At the same time it is clear that certain groups of men have fared badly over the past twenty years (see Chapters 3 and 4 on inactivity and older men). Yet it must be emphasised that in most areas women have still not attained parity with men. The progress made by women and the reasons why this has happened are the subject of this chapter.

Employment gains for women

We begin with an analysis of the pattern of employment since 1975. Over the last two decades the proportion of the working age population in work (the employment rate) in Britain has moved in line with the economic cycle, but has shown no sign of a trend rise or fall (see Figure 10.1 and Table 10.1). The aggregate employment rate in 1975 was 76.6 per cent. In 1998 it was 75.4 per cent. However, a rather neutral performance at the aggregate level masks

Figure 10.1   Employment rates by gender

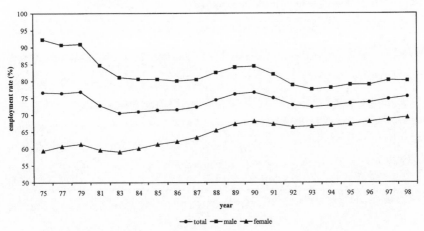

Source: LFS.

Table 10.1　Employment rates by gender

Year	Total	Men	Women	Difference, men–women
1975	76.6	92.3	59.4	32.9
1981	72.7	84.7	59.6	25.1
1984	70.9	80.6	60.1	20.5
1987	72.3	80.4	63.3	17.1
1990	76.6	84.4	68.1	16.3
1993	72.3	77.5	66.6	10.9
1998	75.4	81.0	69.3	11.7

Source: Labour Force Survey, Spring quarter.
Note: Employment rates = percentage of all working age adults in work.

large changes in employment fortunes across gender. In 1975 more than 92 per cent of working age men had a job. By 1998 only 81 per cent were in work. In contrast, the employment rate of women has grown from 59.4 per cent to 69.3 per cent over the same period. As a consequence, the gender gap in employment rates fell from more than 32 per cent in 1975 to just 11 per cent at the end of the last recession in 1993, and has remained constant since then, with the latest economic recovery benefiting both sexes equally. It is, as yet, too early to be sure if this is a new flatter trend or a pause.

Child-rearing no longer a barrier to work

While the above figures are striking, the changes in female participation rates are not the same for all women. Female rates of employment over the life-

Figure 10.2　Female employment rates by age

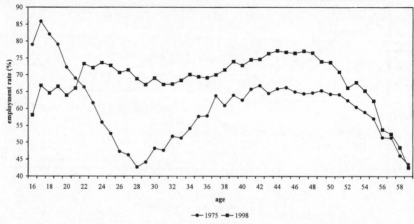

Source: LFS.

Table 10.2   Employment rates by age

Year	Women's employment rate				
	Age 16–24	Age 25–34	Age 35–49	Age 50–59	Total
1979	72.8	52.1	65.5	56.7	61.4
1990	74.0	65.0	72.5	58.5	68.1
1998	69.1	69.2	73.8	61.7	69.3

Source: Labour Force Survey, Spring quarter.

cycle have altered dramatically. Traditionally, life-cycle patterns of labour force participation have been quite different for men and women. The pattern for women reflected the timing of child-birth and child-rearing, and subsequent return to the labour force. Figure 10.2 plots female employment rates by age in 1975 and 1998. In 1975 the pattern had a characteristic double hump shape. High employment in the late teens and early 20s, a peak of around 80 per cent, falling to around 40 per cent for 30-year-olds, rising thereafter to a lower peak of 60 per cent in the late 40s. By 1998 however, this pattern had almost completely disappeared, replaced by a near-flat age–employment rate of around 70 per cent that only begins to fall after the age of 50. The employment life-cycle pattern for women now resembles that of men but about 10 percentage points lower, up to about the age of 55. Hence the largest increases are found amongst women of child-rearing age. The employment rate for 28-year-old women has increased from 42 per cent to 69 per cent over the period.

Women with young children

Women are postponing the age at which they marry and are waiting longer to start a family: between 1975 and 1993 the average age of first marriage for women rose from 23 years to 26 years, across the European Union. The average age of first birth rose from 26.4 to 28.6 between 1976 and 1996. However, the biggest change has been that women are combining work with rearing young children in far greater numbers. Figure 10.3 tracks the change in employment of women conditional on the presence and age of the youngest dependent child. The child penalty on employment rates is falling. However, employment rates for women with no dependent children have barely changed over the last three decades. Figure 10.3 illustrates that, for women with children at secondary or junior school age, employment rates rose in the 1980s, but have changed little over the past seven years. The largest gains in employment have come from women with young children.

Figure 10.3   Employment rates by age of youngest child

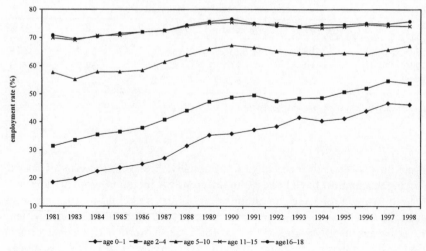

◆ age 0–1 ■ age 2–4 ▲ age 5–10 ✕ age 11–15 ● age16–18

Source: LFS.

Maternity rights and tenure

The evidence suggests that not only are women returning to work more quickly after child-birth, but that maternity leave means they return to the same employer. Maternity Rights legislation passed in 1978 and enhanced in 1993 has enabled around two-thirds of women to return to the same employer after child-birth (see Table 10.3). Waldfogel *et al.* (1998) find this relationship between maternity coverage and job retention after child-birth holds across a number of countries.

Table 10.3   Percentage of women returning to work after pregnancy

Status during pregnancy	1979	1988	1996
Full-time	18	43	69
Part-time	37	50	64

Source: McRae (1997).

The increase in scope and availability of Maternity Rights is also responsible for profound changes in job tenure (see Chapter 7 for more detail). While job tenure for men and women without dependent children is falling, for women with children it is rising, especially for women aged between 25 and 34, where it rose by 87 per cent between 1985 and 1998 (see Table 10.4). Amongst women without children, tenure has been falling, especially for the young. This is akin to the pattern for men.

Table 10.4   Job tenure by age of mother and presence of children

	All women	Women with dependent children	Women with no dependent children
1985			
All ages	3 years 11 months	2 years 8 months	5 years 2 months
Age 16–24	1 year 5 months	11 months	1 year 10 months
Age 25–34	3 years 3 months	1 year 11 months	4 years 10 months
Age 35–49	5 years 1 month	4 years 2 months	7 years 11 months
Age 50 +	10 years 1 month	7 years 11 months	10 years 8 months
1998			
All ages	4 years 5 months	3 years 10 months	4 years 11 months
Age 16–24	1 year 3 months	11 months	1 year 1 month
Age 25–34	3 years 3 months	3 years	3 years 6 months
Age 35–49	5 years 7 months	4 years 10 months	7 years 2 months
Age 50 +	9 years 1 month	7 years 4 months	9 years 5 months
% change 1985/98			
All ages	12.7	43.7	−4.8
Age 16–24	−11.7	0.0	−40.9
Age 25–34	0.0	86.5	−27.5
Age 35–49	9.8	16.0	−9.4
Age 50 +	−9.9	−7.3	−11.7

Source: Labour Force Survey, Spring quarter.

Those left behind

It is essential to note however, that improvement in employment rates for women is almost entirely limited to women with working partners. Employment rates have risen from 53 per cent to 73 per cent where a working man is also present. For those with young children the rise is quite dramatic. Rates of employment have risen from 19 per cent to nearly 56 per cent for women with a youngest child under the age of 2 and from 33 per cent to 64 per cent for women whose youngest child is aged between 3 and 5 years. For single mothers or those with an unemployed partner there has been practically no change. The modest rises for single parents, and women with non-working partners and young children are minuscule when compared to those for women with working partners. These trends lie at the heart of the rise in the number of workless households discussed in Chapter 5. Table 10.6 explores how much characteristics, such as age of children or educational attainment, can explain the differences in employment chances. It compares employment rates of lone mothers and mothers with an out-of-work partner with those with a working partner. It then introduces controls to see by how much they

Table 10.5   Female employment rates by age of youngest child (percentages)

	1981	1986	1990	1993	1998
Single women					
Children	47.2	40.7	42.5	39.4	44.5
No children	69.5	67.6	72.4	67.7	72.1
Age of youngest child					
Age 0–1	18.2	12.9	18.0	17.3	20.2
Age 2–4	27.3	23.8	28.4	26.9	32.8
Age 5–10	50.5	43.0	49.7	44.3	49.3
Age 11–15	58.6	60.4	61.8	58.6	59.3
Age 16–18	64.8	63.5	74.6	70.2	73.4
Total	61.9	56.9	60.0	56.2	59.3
Women with working partner					
Children	52.8	59.6	65.3	69.0	72.5
No children	72.9	78.3	82.4	82.5	83.6
Age of youngest child					
Age 0–1	19.2	29.8	41.6	52.0	55.7
Age 2–4	33.2	44.7	55.4	58.9	64.3
Age 5–10	60.9	65.2	74.0	75.4	78.1
Age 11–15	73.1	78.4	80.6	81.7	83.6
Age 16–18	76.3	80.6	82.3	80.8	85.1
Total	60.7	67.4	73.1	75.2	77.5
Women with non-working partner					
Children	33.6	28.9	35.9	33.5	35.3
No children	51.5	45.0	49.9	49.7	46.7
Age of youngest child					
Age 0–1	12.6	10.9	15.0	19.6	26.0
Age 2–4	17.6	15.3	30.1	28.9	27.9
Age 5–10	40.3	30.9	41.0	36.5	34.3
Age 11–15	54.8	44.5	51.0	47.3	42.3
Age 16–18	57.0	59.9	59.7	51.7	58.5
Total	41.1	36.8	44.2	42.1	42.1

Source: Labour Force Survey, Spring quarter.

cause the gap to diminish. In 1998, unadjusted employment rates were 27 points lower for lone mothers and 35 points lower for mothers with out-of-work partners compared with mothers with working partners. Controlling for differences in age of youngest child has no effect in explaining the gap, nor does region or the age of the mother. The fact that lone parents and those

Table 10.6 Effects of family status on female employment rates

	No controls	Age of youngest child	Age of mother	Qualification	Region
1981: Mean rate of employment: 47.7%					
Lone parent	−7.6	−9.2	−9.6	−9.1	−9.5
Non-working partner	−20.8	−18.0	−19.0	−17.2	−17.2
1990: Mean rate of employment: 58.1%					
Lone parent	−24.2	−24.2	−24.2	−22.0	−21.5
Non-working partner	−31.9	−32.8	−34.2	−30.1	−29.3
1998: Mean rate of employment: 62.0%					
Lone parent	−27.4	−27.6	−27.7	−24.1	−23.8
Non-working partner	−35.3	−35.6	−37.8	−31.9	−31.9

Source: Labour Force Survey, Spring quarter.

with out-of-work partners are, on average, less qualified does have some limited power in explaining these gaps, but still leaves a large unexplained residual. We are left needing other explanations, such as the way that the tax and
benefit system is currently skewed in favour of participation of women with
partners in work (see Chapter 5). Couples who are both in work can claim
separate tax allowances, with the extra married person's allowance going to
one of the couple. Whereas for workless couples or single parents, when a
member of the household goes into low-paid work, means-tested benefits are
likely to leave them little better off than if they were not working. Together
with the greater ability to buy child-care that a dual income brings, this may
help explain the trends which we observe. The best image we can give is that
children, in themselves, are a declining barrier to work. This means weighing
the problems of financing child-care and other work costs (such as inconve-
nience) against income gains from working. Women with working partners
have fewer constraints and are choosing to work.

The glass ceiling

If women are more likely to be in work than ever before, is there any evidence that they are moving up the occupational hierarchy as well? Table 10.7
gives data from the Institute of Management National Management Salary
Survey on the share of women in senior management positions (as reported
by the company). There is a suggestion from these numbers that women are
making some progress in management. The share of women in all senior
positions has risen from 7 per cent in 1989 to 14 per cent in 1998. At each

Table 10.7 Percentage of women in management positions

Position	1989	1990	1991	1992	1993	1994	1995	1996	1997	1998
Chief/deputy chief executive	1.1	1.5	1.7	2.5	2.9	3.0	2.9	3.1	3.0	3.4
Other directors	2.5	3.6	4.3	4.4	6.5	5.6	5.6	5.8	6.9	7.0
Senior function head	3.4	4.3	5.5	6.5	7.5	6.3	6.5	6.9	7.4	8.3
Function head	6.4	7.4	8.2	8.9	9.6	9.3	9.1	10.3	10.7	12.5
Department manager	7.3	7.7	8.3	8.7	10.0	11.4	13.0	17.7	19.3	18.7
Section manager	10.6	12.1	12.7	11.6	13.5	14.4	16.3	17.4	13.4	16.1
Section leader	13.6	15.9	17.0	17.4	19.1	20.8	22.2	18.2	18.8	22.2
Total	6.9	8.0	8.9	9.1	10.5	10.7	11.2	12.4	12.6	14.0

Source: Institute of Management National Management Salary Survey.

management level women are making gains, with the proportion of women directors growing from 2 per cent in 1989 to 7 per cent in 1998. Women have raised their representation by roughly two tiers of the hierarchy within a decade. So, 3.5 per cent of chief executives are now women which was the share of women who were senior function head ten years ago. Likewise senior function heads are now 8 per cent female, which was approximately the share of women amongst department managers a decade ago. At this rate of change, it will take women thirty years to achieve parity with men in top management. The scarcity of women in very senior positions also extends to public bodies, according to data from the Equal Opportunities Commission. Just 10 per cent of judges and magistrates were women in 1996 and only 5 per cent of circuit or high court judges, 22 per cent of barristers and 29 per cent of solicitors are women. 14 per cent of the police force is female but only 4 per cent at the rank of Inspector or higher, while only 18 per cent of Members of Parliament are women.

The gender pay gap

In 1998, a woman could expect to earn, on average, around £200 a week. The average man could expect to earn around £370 a week. Since many more women work part-time than men, a more reliable measure of the gender pay gap is given by the difference in hourly rates of pay. In 1998, women earned, on average, £6.67 an hour, some 75 per cent of the average male hourly wage of £8.94. There has been a steady narrowing of this gender pay gap since the early 1970s (see Figure 10.4). In 1974, women earned only 62 per cent of average male pay.

However, as Figure 10.4 also demonstrates, the pattern of change in women's pay relative to men's depends heavily on whether women work full-time or part-time. Back in the 1970s, women in part-time work earned more,

Figure 10.4 Changes in the gender earnings gap

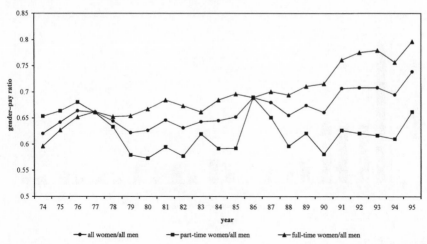

Source: LFS.

on an hourly basis, than women working full-time. At the end of the 1990s, part-time work now carries a pay penalty. All the relative gain in pay made by women has come from those who work full-time (see Harkness (1996) and Blau and Kahn (1993) for more details). The ratio of earnings of women in part-time work to the earnings of men is little different now than in the mid-1970s. In contrast, the ratio of the pay of women who work full-time relative to men has grown from 60 per cent to 80 per cent over the same period. The net effect of these two trends has been to lower the overall gender pay gap by around 11 percentage points.

Rising wage inequality (see Chapter 11) could mean that simple comparisons of average wages of men and women give a misleading impression of the change in the labour market status of women. For example, if wage inequality rewards experience more than before, then women will lose out because they typically have less experience in work, due to taking time off for child-care. Figure 10.5 graphs the ranking of all women in the distribution of male hourly earnings. The horizontal axis ranks men's pay from the bottom 10 per cent to the top 10 per cent. The graph then shows how many women are paid in each of these ten male pay deciles. The horizontal line shows the share of women we would expect to find in each pay decile if women were paid the same as men. There would be 10 per cent of women in each of the ten male pay bands. The graph shows however, that in 1974, over half of all women in work were earning a wage that paid less than or equal to that earned by the bottom 10 per cent of men. Nearly 90 per cent of women earned less than the typical man (the middle of the male pay distribution). Over time, the position of women has improved. The distribution of women's pay is much less concentrated at the bottom end of the male pay

Figure 10.5   Women's ranking in the male pay distribution

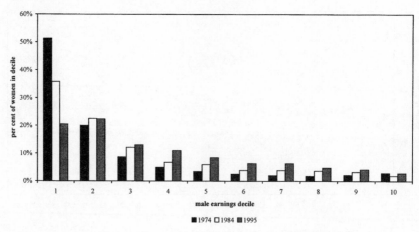

Source: LFS.

scale. By 1995, only 20 per cent of women earned less than or equal the pay of the bottom 10 per cent of men. However, in 1995 still only 3 per cent of women earned as much as the top 10 per cent of men, and around 75 per cent of working women fell into the bottom half of the male pay distribution. Nevertheless, despite rising wage inequality, it appears that some women are making steady improvements in their relative earnings.

Figure 10.6 shows that the proportion of women of working age whose hourly wages are higher than their working partners' has increased from 7.4

Figure 10.6   Proportion of women earning higher hourly wages than their working partner

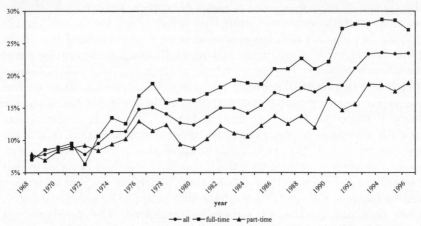

Source: LFS.

per cent in 1968 to 23.4 per cent in 1996. Amongst women who work full-time the increase is even more significant, from 7 per cent to 27.1 per cent. Even amongst women who work part-time the proportion has increased by 11 percentage points. This last figure may be somewhat surprising given that women who work part-time are amongst the lowest earners in the labour market, and as mentioned above, pay for part-time workers has declined in relative terms since 1975. However, women who work part-time tend to be less qualified than the average and thus more likely to have low-skilled partners, and as low-skilled men are also amongst the lowest paid this may go toward explaining the increases in the proportion of part-time working women earning more than their working partners.

Why has the gap closed?

The narrowing of the gap was helped, initially, by the implementation of the Equal Pay Act of 1970 (finally ratified in 1975) which outlawed different wages for the same work on the grounds of sex, required that the lowest paid woman in a firm received no less than the lowest paid man at the firm and that the firm comply with the recommendations of existing comparable worth studies. Since the labour market was, and remains, highly segregated by gender across industries and occupations, significant wage gaps remained between so-called 'female jobs' done mainly by women and occupations dominated by men. This led to the 1983 amendment of the Equal Pay Act which obliged firms to comply with 'equal pay for work of equal value' studies, if requested by the workforce. After the gains of the early 1970s there was a pause, followed by large gains in female relative pay from the mid-1980s onward.

In the past, economists studying male–female wage differentials have justified a significant part of the pay gap through differences in the levels of training, education and experience between men and women. Pay, it is said, will be higher the more of these attributes a worker possesses. If women have less education, for example, then this will be reflected in lower pay. Table 10.8 outlines the changing levels of educational attainment of those in work by gender and age. The table also makes a distinction between the qualifications held by women who work full-time and by those who work part-time. In the mid-1970s, women as a group were less qualified than men. Nearly 60 per cent had no qualifications compared to 50 per cent of men. The difference in educational attainment across gender was, however, much greater for older age cohorts. Since then, as older cohorts have dropped out of the labour force and younger cohorts, with less differences in educational attainment by sex, have entered the labour force, so the overall gender gap in educational attainment has narrowed. By the mid-1990s, the educational attainment of women in work had improved markedly relative to men.

Table 10.8 Employment by education, gender and age

| | 1974–76 | | | | 1993–95 | | | |
| | Men | Women | | | Men | Women | | |
	All	All	Full-time	Part-time	All	All	Full-time	Part-time
Age 16–59								
degree	5.2	1.9	2.1	1.5	15.6	10.1	13.0	6.1
higher intermediate	9.1	9.3	9.1	9.5	20.1	19.1	21.6	15.8
lower intermediate	36.3	29.9	34.4	23.5	44.0	47.2	47.3	47.2
none	49.3	58.9	54.5	65.4	20.4	23.6	18.1	30.9
Age 16–24								
degree	2.6	1.7	1.7	2.0	6.8	6.4	8.3	2.7
higher intermediate	10.6	10.6	9.5	16.1	18.7	19.3	20.8	16.5
lower intermediate	51.0	53.4	54.9	46.1	63.3	65.9	65.9	66.1
none	35.7	34.2	33.9	35.8	11.2	8.4	5.0	14.7
Age 25–34								
degree	7.5	3.9	5.1	2.1	17.6	14.3	18.8	6.7
higher intermediate	12.0	12.0	12.7	11.1	22.5	22.0	24.2	18.3
lower intermediate	40.0	34.3	37.8	31.0	49.1	54.1	50.5	60.0
none	40.5	49.9	44.4	55.8	10.9	9.7	6.4	15.1
Age 35–49								
degree	5.5	1.4	1.4	1.4	18.2	10.3	12.3	7.7
higher intermediate	8.3	9.0	8.6	9.3	21.6	18.9	21.2	16.0
lower intermediate	32.7	21.7	23.1	20.1	38.3	41.9	41.5	42.5
none	53.6	67.9	66.9	69.2	22.0	29.0	25.0	33.8
Age 50–59								
degree	4.0	0.8	0.8	0.8	13.2	6.2	8.5	3.8
higher intermediate	5.4	5.8	5.7	5.8	14.1	15.0	18.1	12.1
lower intermediate	25.3	15.4	16.9	13.1	35.3	33.2	35.0	31.6
none	65.3	78.0	76.6	80.4	37.3	45.6	38.4	52.5

Source: General Household Survey.

Indeed, the level of attainment amongst working women in the youngest age group is now higher than that of men of the same age. Table 10.9 shows that in the 1990s, women are clearly surpassing men in educational attainment. At GCSE level, substantially larger numbers of women are achieving passes in English and foreign languages and equal numbers in mathematics. These gaps are nearly as marked at 'A' level, but more men achieve higher results in mathematics. Nearly 60 per cent of those in further education are women,

Table 10.9   School examination results, 1995/6

	Female (thousands)	Male (thousands)
GCSE – Grades A–C		
English	214.5	162.2
Mathematics	157.3	158.7
French	116.6	75.4
History	76.2	62.9
GCE 'A' level – Grades A–E		
English	21.7	13.1
Mathematics	21.4	33.6
French	13.2	5.5
History	14.6	11.3

Source: Equal Opportunities Commission, 'Facts about Women and Men in Great Britain 1998'.
Note: Figures are for England.

and 51 per cent of university undergraduates are now women. A clear distinction has arisen between the level of qualifications of women in full-time work and those in part-time work at all ages. It may be that some of the narrowing gender pay gap can be explained therefore by a growing share of more qualified women in full-time work.

Education is, of course, not the only factor that can determine the level of earnings. We have already observed rising job tenure amongst women with children. Differences in the amount of labour market experience, variations by industry, occupation and union presence between genders will all influence the pay gap. It is also conceivable that even if women had identical characteristics to men, they would receive lower pay, perhaps because of discrimination.

Table 10.10 assesses how much of the gender pay gap can be attributed to differences in characteristics and differences in rewards to the same characteristics and how this has changed over time. The table shows that in the mid-1970s, differences in age and education (column 1) accounted for just 9 points of the total gap of 43 points (16 per cent), the rest was attributable to the same characteristics, age and qualifications being rewarded at lower rates. Most of this was accounted for by differences in rewards at a given age or experience level. Women in part-time work were actually more qualified and older than the average man. So we might have expected women in part-time work to earn more than the average man by around 3 per cent (bottom panel, column 1). However, the rewards to these characteristics were so much lower for women than men, that the pay of women in part-time work was around 46 per cent below that of men. The addition of other controls for job tenure, industry, region and children (columns 2 to 4) does increase the

Table 10.10 Decomposing the gender pay gap

	1975/7				1993/5			
	Education, age (1)	(1) and Job tenure (2)	(2) and Industry, region (3)	(3) and Children (4)	Education, age (5)	(5) and Job tenure (6)	(6) and Industry, region (7)	(7) and Children (8)
All men/full-time women								
Female pay gap	43%	43%	43%	43%	24%	24%	24%	24%
of which:								
Characteristics	9	10	11	12	2	3	5	5
Rewards	26	29	23	28	9	3	5	12
Unexplained	8	4	9	3	13	18	14	7
All men/part-time women								
Female pay gap	46%	46%	46%	46%	55%	55%	55%	55%
of which:								
Characteristics	-3	1	3	3	8	12	15	15
Rewards	36	30	26	33	52	34	46	53
Unexplained	13	15	17	10	-5	9	-8	-13

Source: General Household Survey.

amount of the gap that can be explained by differences in characteristics, but this never amounts to more than one-quarter of the gap for women in full-time work and 15 per cent for women in part-time work.

So what explains the gains made by women in full-time work over time? Comparing, for example, columns 1 and 5 in Table 10.10, for full-time women it seems that most of the improvement is caused by improved rewards to given characteristics. Education and experience are now rewarded at nearly the same level as for men. There has also been a narrowing of gender differences in workforce characteristics like age, education and job tenure for women in full-time work, which all help to reduce earnings differentials. The unexplained residual now accounts for much of the remaining gap, often interpreted as labour market discrimination.

For women in part-time work the story over time is different, for here the gender pay gap has increased. Why? It is not that women in part-time work lack qualifications or experience, since differences in characteristics, principally across age, education, tenure and industry no longer account for as much of the gap as in the 1970s. Rather, there is now a large pay penalty associated with part-time jobs. In the 1970s, part-timers received lower returns for the same amounts of experience and education. In the 1990s these differential rewards have increased. In part-time work there is no reward for increased age and experience unlike in full-time jobs. The problem of low pay in part-time work is more a problem of the jobs themselves.

Conclusion

The labour market has undergone a profound transformation over the past twenty years. There are more women and fewer men in work than ever before. Most of the rise in female participation has been amongst women with infant children who, rather than drop out of the workforce after giving birth, are returning to employment in ever increasing numbers. By staying with the same employer tenure is rising for women with young children. Whether this trend can continue at the same rate is uncertain, but it looks likely that women may soon become a majority of the workforce. At the same time, the gender pay gap has narrowed appreciably, but all the gains have been made by women in full-time work. As women's education and tenure patterns are converging on men's, we may see continued improvements in relative pay at least for full-time women. The relative pay of women in part-time work has declined. In the near future, part-time jobs will be the major beneficiaries of the minimum wage. Why part-time work has become so badly paid is worthy of further investigation.

References

Blau, F. and Kahn, L. (1993), 'The gender pay gap: Some international evidence', *American Economic Review*, 82, 533–8.

Harkness, S. (1996), 'The gender earnings gap: Evidence from the UK', *Fiscal Studies*, 17:2, 1–36.

McRae, S. (1997), 'Maternity Rights in Britain', Policy Studies Institute, London.

Waldfogel, J., Higuchi, Y. and Abe, M. (1998), 'Maternity Leave Policies and Women's Employment after Childbirth: Evidence from the United States, Britain, and Japan', CASE Paper No. 3, ESRC Research Centre for Analysis of Social Exclusion, LSE, London.

11 Stephen Machin

Wage inequality in the 1970s, 1980s and 1990s

Keypoints

- Since the late 1970s wage inequality in Britain has risen faster than in most other developed nations to reach its highest levels this century.

- In the 1990s the pace of rising inequality slowed compared to the 1980s.

- Demand has been shifting in favour of the more highly educated and skilled because, despite the fact that there are many more workers with higher educational qualifications, their wages relative to other groups have not fallen.

- Relative demand shifts in favour of the more educated and skilled are more pronounced in technologically advanced industries. This is in line with the notion that technology underlies much of the change in labour market wage inequality.

- There is much less evidence that increased international trade (measured in terms of observable indices of trade) has been strongly linked to rising labour market inequality.

- Some of the rise in wage inequality can be attributed to the declining role of trade unions in the British labour market.

Wage gaps between the rich and poor have widened dramatically in Britain since the late 1970s, with wage inequality reaching the highest levels experienced this century. At the same time the relative employment rates of the skilled have risen, leading to an overall increase in labour market inequality. This chapter uses several individual and industry-level data sources to examine the issue of rising labour market inequality. Data from the 1990s are used to explore whether the rapid rises of the 1980s have continued into the current decade.[1] Evidence on the validity of the different explanations of what may be behind recent rises in labour market inequality is also surveyed.

The data sources show a similar picture. After the very rapid inequality increases of the 1980s, the 1990s have seen more slowly rising wage inequality. Unless a big acceleration occurs in the next few years, the 1980s will go down as the decade of the twentieth century where wage inequality rose by most.

The 1990s have also seen rapid educational upgrading. The late 1980s reforms to the education system (for example, the introduction of the GCSE system of examinations – also discussed in Chapter 9) appear to have generated an acceleration in the supply of highly educated labour. The increase in the supply of more-skilled labour probably lies behind the slowdown in the rate of increase of wage inequality in the 1990s. However, while the gap between the high and low paid is probably still rising, and certainly not falling, it seems that rising supply is still not enough to meet employers' changing skill requirements and so demand has continued to shift in favour of the more skilled.

What of the underlying explanations? Changes in technology, globalisation and the decline of labour market institutions have all been pinpointed as possible explanations of this increased labour market inequality.[2] The principal cause of shifting demand in favour of the skilled seems to be related to technology, as faster skill upgrading has occurred in more technologically advanced industries. Technological changes that have altered the nature of work, and the way it is rewarded, appear to be central to the changes in labour market inequality observed in recent decades. It proves much harder to find convincing evidence of large changes associated with increased trade with developing countries. But there is some evidence of rising wage inequality being connected to union decline that has occurred in the British labour market since the late 1970s.

Basic facts about changes in wage inequality in the 1970s, 1980s and 1990s[3]

Data sources

There are several sources of data for looking at wage inequality trends in Britain. The main data sources which go back far enough in time are the

[1] See Machin (1996a) and Schmitt (1995) for summaries of the evolution of wage inequality in the 1970s and 1980s.

[2] See Berman, Bound and Machin (1998) for arguments about connections between labour market inequality and technology; Wood (1994) is the leading exponent of the trade view; DiNardo, Fortin and Lemieux (1996) and Freeman (1993) are examples of papers looking at the declining role of labour market institutions.

[3] Much of this section is reproduced from Machin (1998).

household-level Family Expenditure Survey (FES) and General Household Survey (GHS) and the employer-reported individual-level New Earnings Survey (NES). The potential drawbacks with the FES are its relatively small sample size, as it only covers around 10,000 people in work each year, and the fact that it does not contain any data on educational qualifications.[4] The GHS also has a relatively small sample size (of similar order to the FES) and its main drawback is that it does not report hourly wages on a consistent basis through time. But it does have the big advantage of reporting data on the highest educational qualification of individuals. Sample size is not a problem for the NES which, in principle, covers 1 per cent of the working population thereby generating large sample sizes (in what follows, over 100,000 per year). But it should be noted that the NES has its own problems if one wishes to consider inequality trends because it under-samples low-wage part-time workers and contains no data on education.

Because they each have their relative advantages and disadvantages, wage inequality trends from all the data sources have been considered. For trends in wage inequality, the FES and NES have been more heavily focused upon, due to their long time series and because they both report data on hourly wages. For describing the shifts in relative wages across education groups that are explored later in this chapter the GHS[5] has been used.

Trends in Gini coefficients

The Gini coefficient is a simple, single number, summary statistic describing the extent of inequality. As Atkinson (1983) notes, it is often used in official publications as a statistic to summarise the distribution of income or wealth. Here it is used to characterise inequality of the distribution of labour market earnings. It ranges from 0 (complete equality) to 1 (complete inequality). Table 11.1 reports Gini coefficients for male and female earnings based on the GHS, NES and FES between 1975 and 1996. All earnings are expressed in 1996 prices. The patterns in the data are very clear. Irrespective of whether one looks at weekly or hourly earnings, there was a slight fall in inequality in the 1970s, which continued up to around 1977 or 1978 (depending on which data source is looked at), after which inequality rises. The scale of the 1970s' fall (which commentators at the time thought corresponded to a large compression) pales into insignificance compared to the rises that followed.

From the late 1970s and through the 1980s, inequality in earnings rose massively for both sexes. For example, according to the FES, Gini coefficients for male hourly earnings rose from 0.240 in 1979 to 0.312 by 1990,

---

[4] It does contain information on years of schooling since 1978.

[5] The other large-scale microdata source that could be used is the Labour Force Survey (LFS) which, like the GHS, has good education data going back to the 1970s. Unfortunately, wage data have only been collected since 1992 and, as I am interested in longer run changes in wage inequality, it is not used here.

Table 11.1a   Gini coefficients, male wages

Year	Weekly wages			Hourly wages	
	GHS	NES	FES	NES	FES
1975	0.249	0.236	0.244	0.223	0.239
1976	0.242	0.239	0.240	0.229	0.235
1977	0.240	0.233	0.238	0.221	0.236
1978	0.237	0.239	0.244	0.227	0.244
1979	0.231	0.245	0.246	0.228	0.240
1980	0.244	0.245	0.262	0.233	0.256
1981	0.250	0.251	0.266	0.246	0.264
1982	0.277	0.254	0.260	0.248	0.258
1983	0.256	0.260	0.279	0.253	0.276
1984	0.281	0.274	0.276	0.261	0.273
1985	0.283	0.275	0.292	0.261	0.285
1986	0.294	0.279	0.298	0.266	0.287
1987	0.301	0.289	0.319	0.277	0.305
1988	0.298	0.295	0.311	0.284	0.299
1989	0.302	0.298	0.302	0.288	0.291
1990	0.301	0.299	0.324	0.289	0.312
1991	0.313	0.303	0.321	0.294	0.301
1992	0.316	0.306	0.330	0.296	0.309
1993	0.314	0.311	0.338	0.301	0.319
1994	0.324	0.316	0.338	0.308	0.320
1995	0.325	0.322	0.326	0.317	0.358
1996	–	0.325	0.329	0.318	0.335

Sources: GHS, NES, FES.
Note: Wages in 1996 prices.

corresponding to a 30 per cent increase over eleven years. For females, the Gini rose from 0.252 to 0.320, or a 27 per cent increase. In the 1990s the Gini coefficients seem to show inequality continuing to rise, but at a slower rate. For example, the FES Gini for male hourly wages rises from 0.312 in 1990 to 0.335 by 1996, or a rise of just over 7 per cent. For women the slow-down is even more marked: between 1990 and 1996 the FES Gini for hourly wages actually fell, from 0.320 to 0.312. The other data sources show similar patterns. In all cases, the 1979–90 annualised change in the Gini is higher, usually considerably higher, than the 1990–6 annualised change.

Changes at different percentiles of the distribution

The Gini coefficient is a good statistic for describing aggregate inequality trends, but is less useful for identifying shifts that lie behind the overall change. Table 11.2 therefore reports what has happened to male and female

Table 11.1b   Gini coefficients, female wages

Year	Weekly wages			Hourly wages	
	GHS	NES	FES	NES	FES
1975	0.349	0.281	0.356	0.215	0.256
1976	0.350	0.294	0.360	0.225	0.261
1977	0.349	0.288	0.353	0.206	0.244
1978	0.347	0.290	0.353	0.205	0.258
1979	0.342	0.295	0.355	0.203	0.252
1980	0.350	0.300	0.359	0.210	0.253
1981	0.365	0.313	0.377	0.231	0.279
1982	0.371	0.315	0.381	0.227	0.270
1983	0.364	0.323	0.388	0.230	0.281
1984	0.375	0.337	0.381	0.236	0.277
1985	0.390	0.335	0.387	0.236	0.283
1986	0.390	0.340	0.386	0.237	0.298
1987	0.400	0.348	0.397	0.240	0.311
1988	0.392	0.355	0.394	0.250	0.310
1989	0.394	0.362	0.393	0.260	0.295
1990	0.395	0.366	0.401	0.260	0.320
1991	0.401	0.370	0.396	0.268	0.300
1992	0.402	0.377	0.409	0.270	0.306
1993	0.414	0.377	0.403	0.277	0.306
1994	0.403	0.380	0.403	0.278	0.307
1995	0.404	0.386	0.407	0.289	0.300
1996	–	0.388	0.400	0.288	0.312

Sources: GHS, NES, FES.
Note: Wages in 1996 prices.

real hourly earnings at different points in the distribution using data from the FES. Figure 11.1 also plots the evolution of the 10th, 50th and 90th percentiles of the male distribution over time.

Consider the ratio of the earnings of the 90th percentile (the person in each year who is 10 per cent from the top of the earnings distribution) relative to the 10th percentile (the person 10 per cent from the bottom of the distribution). The 90–10 ratios given in Table 11.2 show much the same pattern as the Ginis in Table 11.1. Wage inequality for both men and women rises sharply from the late 1970s to the late 1980s/early 1990s, but slows down in the 1990s. The ratios describing the evolution of the lower end of the distribution (the middle relative to the bottom 10 per cent – the 50–10 ratio) and the upper end (the 90–50 ratio) demonstrate that the 1980s rise in wage inequality was characterised by an opening out at both ends of the distribution with the highest earners doing much better than those in the middle, but in turn the middle doing much better than the bottom.

Table 11.2   Changes in the wage distribution

	Percentiles									Ratios		
	10th	20th	30th	40th	50th	60th	70th	80th	90th	90–10	50–10	90–50
Men												
1975	3.37	4.17	4.68	5.19	5.68	6.19	6.83	7.80	9.63	2.86	1.69	1.70
1980	3.44	4.32	4.96	5.54	6.13	6.83	7.64	8.65	10.65	3.10	1.79	1.74
1985	3.46	4.46	5.25	5.93	6.64	7.43	8.47	9.92	12.26	3.55	1.92	1.85
1990	3.64	4.87	5.75	6.55	7.41	8.44	9.73	11.56	14.43	3.97	2.04	1.95
1995	3.77	4.84	5.79	6.70	7.65	8.65	9.87	11.57	14.52	3.86	2.03	1.90
1996	3.69	4.74	5.67	6.61	7.57	8.65	10.07	11.76	14.62	3.96	2.05	1.93
Women												
1975	2.21	2.60	2.96	3.30	3.61	3.99	4.42	5.08	6.42	2.91	1.64	1.78
1980	2.31	2.85	3.12	3.42	3.73	4.11	4.60	5.35	6.93	3.00	1.62	1.86
1985	2.49	2.91	3.21	3.58	4.01	4.54	5.19	6.14	7.96	3.20	1.61	1.99
1990	2.77	3.31	3.69	4.18	4.76	5.36	6.32	7.63	10.03	3.62	1.72	2.11
1995	2.94	3.41	3.91	4.49	5.16	5.81	6.79	8.13	10.48	3.57	1.76	2.03
1996	3.00	3.52	4.06	4.63	5.29	6.05	7.08	8.37	10.62	3.54	1.76	2.01

Source: FES.

The numbers so far cover the wage distribution for all workers. It may also be interesting if there are any differences when focusing only on full-time workers, particularly given the compositional changes in the nature of employment that happened over the period. Limiting to full-timers shows a

Figure 11.1   Men's hourly wages (indexed to 1975)

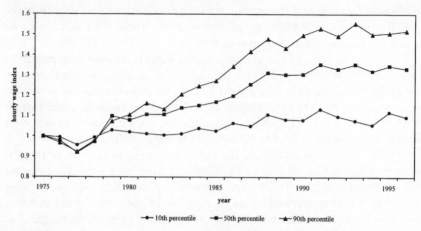

Source: FES.

bigger compression in the 1970s, due to higher wage growth for the bottom tenth than that for all workers (see Machin, 1998, for precise numbers).[6] Nevertheless the overall pattern remains, with wage inequality falling a little in the 1970s, followed by the rapid rise of the 1980s, and then a slowdown in the 1990s.

Table 11.3 reports changes in 90–10 wage ratios for male workers in a number of countries. It shows very starkly that the countries where wage gaps have widened are the United Kingdom, the United States and, more recently, Ireland. In some other countries, especially in Continental Europe, wage inequality has barely altered.

Table 11.3 International changes in wage inequality (male workers)

Country	Late 1970s/early 1980s	Mid-1990s	Annualised change
Australia	2.74 (1979)	2.94 (1995)	0.013
Austria	2.27 (1980)	2.40 (1994)	0.010
Canada	3.46 (1981)	3.77 (1994)	0.024
Finland	2.44 (1980)	2.53 (1994)	0.006
Germany	2.38 (1983)	2.25 (1993)	−0.013
Ireland	4.07 (1987)	4.54 (1994)	0.067
Italy	2.29 (1979)	2.64 (1993)	0.022
Japan	2.59 (1979)	2.77 (1994)	0.001
Sweden	2.11 (1980)	2.20 (1993)	0.007
United Kingdom	2.45 (1979)	3.31 (1995)	0.054
United States	3.18 (1979)	4.35 (1995)	0.073

Source: OECD *Employment Outlook*, July 1996, except for Ireland which is from Barrett, Callan and Nolan (1997).
Note: These are 90–10 wage ratios except for the 80–10 ratio for Austria.

Changes in the wage returns to education

An important part of the 1980s' rise in wage inequality was rising wage gaps between more and less highly educated workers.[7] I now go on to compare and contrast changes in the wage returns to education in the 1970s, 1980s and 1990s. I start by presenting simple estimates of the changing wage returns to different educational qualifications, and then move on to consider

[6] See Harkness (1996) for more details on differences in the evolution over time of the full-time and part-time female earnings distributions.

[7] Of course, while education-based wage differentials are of particular interest as they are likely to pick up skill-related dimensions of changing wage inequality they are not the only 'between-group' wage gap of interest. Another between-group wage comparison, changes in the gender wage gap, is discussed in Chapter 10.

how the structure of employment has altered for workers with different education levels.

Change in relative wages

Table 11.4 presents estimates of differences in log (weekly wages) by education, for full-time men and women in the GHS, for five grouped periods (1974–6, 1979–81, 1984–6, 1989–91 and 1993–5). The table reports the percentage difference in log (wages) for each level of qualification relative to those with no qualifications after controlling for other characteristics (age, age squared, industry and region). According to the second column of Table 11.4, men with a degree in 1974/6, had a 54.5 per cent higher log (wage) than men with no educational qualifications and a 26.7 per cent higher log (wage) than men with two or more 'A' levels as their highest educational qualification.

As it is changes in inequality over time that are of most interest here, it is necessary to look at changes in the estimated wage returns to education as one moves across the table. For the earlier years the estimated wage differ-

Table 11.4 Changes in wage returns to education, full-time workers

| | % Log (weekly wage) difference | | | | |
	1974–76	1979–81	1984–86	1989–91	1993–95
Men					
degree	54.5	48.7	54.7	61.3	65.6
higher vocational	39.4	31.8	39.0	41.4	41.0
teaching/nursing	29.0	29.1	28.8	37.2	34.8
2 or more 'A' levels	27.8	24.3	35.3	40.3	45.2
1 'A' level	19.8		26.6	33.7	38.1
middle vocational	24.2	22.4	27.7	29.2	26.4
some qualifications	11.9	12.3	15.8	18.6	18.1
Women					
degree	70.6	65.2	65.3	77.0	74.6
higher vocational	59.4	45.5	52.3	60.7	52.1
teaching/nursing	52.4	52.9	53.9	64.7	65.6
2 or more 'A' levels	46.9	32.9	40.2	48.0	43.8
1 'A' level	28.6		35.5	44.3	42.8
middle vocational	19.2	25.3	31.1	37.2	27.5
some qualifications	15.0	14.8	20.2	24.0	23.9

Source: GHS.
Note: The reference group = those with no educational qualifications. These are log (weekly wage) differentials holding constant age, age squared, region and industry.

entials show a familiar pattern, with falls in the 1970s and rises in the 1980s (as in Schmitt, 1995), and smaller rises in the 1990s. Looking in a little more detail reveals some small differences in the results for men and women. For example, for men with a degree the return rises in the 1990s, but falls for women. But the overwhelming picture of narrowing differentials in the 1970s, followed by a rapid widening of differentials in the 1980s, is revealed across all comparison groups.

Shifts in relative employment rates

Simple supply and demand analyses of the labour market would predict that if a particular group increases its number relative to another group then the relative wage accruing to that group should fall as employers have a larger pool of potential employees to pick and choose from. Table 11.5 shows that fast educational upgrading has occurred since the mid-1970s as the share of workers with higher qualifications has rapidly increased. The table reports employment shares of the workforce by educational qualifications.

The numbers in the table make it clear that the employment shares of more educated workers increased in the 1970s, 1980s and 1990s. All things

Table 11.5   Changes in employment shares of specific education groups (percentages)

	1974–76	1979–81	1984–86	1989–91	1993–95
Men					
degree	5.77	8.16	12.11	12.48	15.31
higher vocational	4.68	6.78	10.46	11.39	11.88
teaching/nursing	1.17	1.29	1.37	1.19	1.37
2 or more 'A' levels	2.36	3.34	3.24	3.79	4.10
1 'A' level	0.78		1.67	1.62	1.92
middle vocational	4.44	5.95	8.07	8.87	9.92
some qualifications	30.61	31.93	27.73	33.62	33.86
no qualifications	50.18	42.55	35.36	27.06	21.64
Women					
degree	2.21	3.57	6.20	7.53	10.12
higher vocational	0.73	1.34	2.01	2.91	3.82
teaching/nursing	5.77	6.77	8.43	7.88	7.75
2 or more 'A' levels	2.06	3.51	3.44	4.89	4.50
1 'A' level	0.90		2.12	2.17	2.81
middle vocational	0.40	0.97	1.90	3.02	3.88
some qualifications	29.68	35.09	39.08	42.79	43.41
no qualifications	58.25	48.76	36.81	29.61	23.69

Source: GHS.

held constant, one would expect this to reduce the wage returns to education. But this clearly has not happened. While the 1970s sees rising relative supply coupled with falling relative wages this is not true of the periods from 1980 onward, as there is a positive relation between changes in relative supply and changes in relative wages. This suggests that relative demand shifts in favour of the more highly educated must have happened. Employers are still prepared to pay higher wages to more educated workers even though there are more of them in employment.

However, the time-series pattern of relative supply and wage changes across the 1970s, 1980s and 1990s does suggest something of a dampening down of wages in response to supply. Table 11.6 shows relative supply changes in the three decades, for graduates against non-graduates, and graduates against those with no educational qualifications, revealing that relative supply rose fastest in the 1970s and 1990s for both sexes, with the 1980s seeing increased supply but at a slower rate. Because the relative wages of graduates rose in the 1980s and 1990s, these increases in supply were clearly not enough to bring relative wages down, but the decade comparisons seem to suggest that supply did have some moderating influence. However, the evidence presented clearly shows that, while changes in relative supply seem to have contributed to the 1990s' slowdown in rising wage inequality, labour demand has continued to shift in favour of more educated and skilled workers.

Table 11.6 Relative supply changes

	% changes in relative supply		
	1975–80	1980–90	1990–94
Men			
degree vs non-degree	7.46	4.73	5.93
degree vs no qualifications	10.25	8.77	10.69
Women			
degree vs non-degree	9.90	7.87	8.11
degree vs no qualifications	13.18	12.44	12.98

Source: GHS.

Shifts in relative demand and wage inequality: technology, trade and union decline

What lies behind the relative demand shifts in favour of more educated and skilled workers? The literature focuses on two particular explanations. First, the introduction of technology that encourages the increased use of skilled workers and replaces less-skilled workers (skill-biased technological change). Second, increased international competition from low-wage countries for goods traditionally made by less-skilled workers. Here, the merits of these two explanations are examined. Also considered is a further explanation of rising wage inequality, namely that union decline has gone hand-in-hand with rising wage gaps.

Skill upgrading and technology

Recent UK findings on the links between skill upgrading and technology have reported a robust correlation, for various skill upgrading and technology measures. Machin (1996b) reports evidence showing that more R&D (research and development)-intensive and more innovative industries experienced faster increases in non-production wage bill shares in the 1980s. Machin and Van Reenen (1998) show the same to be true of industries with higher computer usage. Finally, Harkness and Machin (1998) report that the graduate wage bill share rose by more in industries with higher computer usage. This industry-based evidence is clearly in line with the idea that technology is still shaping the more recent changes in skill structure that have occurred.

Cross-country evidence on skill upgrading and technology

The fact that technology must be important is also revealed by cross-country evidence. When one considers the relationship between skill upgrading against R&D intensity for the same industries in different countries a positive association always seems to be uncovered. The relationship between skill upgrading and R&D intensity is graphed for six countries in Figure 11.2 (see Machin and Van Reenen (1998) for more details). In all six countries there is a clear upward sloping relationship between skill upgrading and R&D. Such regularities are uncommon and not easy to find in international comparisons and suggest an important link between the extent of demand shifts in favour of the more skilled and observable measures of technology.

Skill upgrading and international competition

International competition with developing countries has risen sharply in recent decades. To illustrate the scale of the increased importance of imports from the developing world in the UK context, the ratio of imports from eleven developing countries[8] to GDP quadrupled between 1970 and 1994,

---

[8] The eleven developing countries are Argentina, Brazil, China, Hong Kong, India, Indonesia, Korea, Malaysia, the Philippines, Singapore and Taiwan.

Figure 11.2 The relationship between industrial skill upgrading and R&D intensity
United Kingdom, slope=0.024

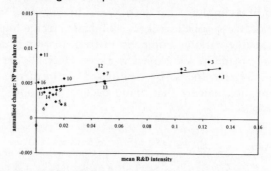

Germany, slope=0.026

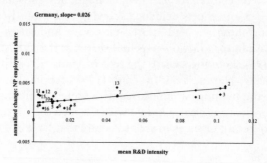

Japan, slope=0.050

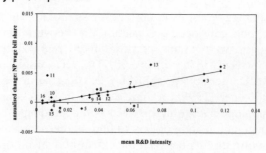

United States, slope=0.021

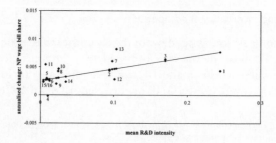

Denmark, slope=0.039

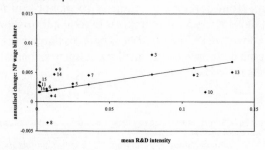

Sweden, slope=0.039

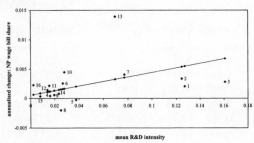

Source: Machin and Van Reenen (1998).

Key

1. Transport
2. Chemical
3. Electrical machinery and communications equipment (inc. computers)
4. Food, beverages and tobacco products
5. Iron and steel
6. Metal products
7. Non-electrical machinery
8. Non-ferrous metal products
9. Non-metallic mineral products
10. Other manufacturing
11. Paper products and printing
12. Petroleum
13. Professional goods
14. Rubber and plastic products
15. Textiles
16. Wood products and furniture

NP=non-production

although the ratio remains small at less than 0.04 in 1994. Table 11.7 reports ratios of imports from developing countries to manufacturing production and the share of developing country imports in total imports for the six countries examined above, in 1970 and 1994. There are large rises in the importance of developing country imports in all six countries, increasing from very low starting levels in 1970.

Table 11.7   Changes in imports with developing countries in manufacturing

	Manufacturing imports from developing countries/ manufacturing GDP			Manufacturing imports from developing countries/total manufacturing imports		
	1970	1994	Percentage change	1970	1994	Percentage change
Denmark	0.015	0.039	160	0.032	0.083	159
Germany	0.004	0.025	525	0.035	0.107	206
Japan	0.005	0.022	340	0.125	0.382	206
Sweden	0.007	0.028	300	0.028	0.069	111
United Kingdom	0.007	0.037	429	0.051	0.108	112
United States	0.005	0.046	820	0.099	0.272	175

Source: OECD Bilateral Trade Database. The developing countries are Argentina, Brazil, China, Hong Kong, India, Indonesia, Korea, Malaysia, the Philippines, Singapore and Taiwan.

Is there any correlation between skill upgrading and rising import competition from developing countries? A clear answer emerges – there is no systematic relation between industrial skill upgrading and these directly observed measures of increased international trade linkages with developing countries. Figure 11.3 plots the relationship for the six countries (derived from data in Machin and Van Reenen, 1998). The slopes are more-or-less flat, display no consistent pattern and reveal much less of a relationship between directly observed measures of increased trade linkages with developing countries and skill upgrading compared to the technology correlations in Figure 11.2.

It should be pointed out that, in terms of actually testing the trade-based explanation of shifts in relative demand, this approach may be much too crude, as it could be the threat of trade that actually matters. So far no one has produced any persuasive evidence that points to important threat of trade effects. Furthermore, other observations cast doubt that trade has had a big impact. First, the trade flows from developing countries are still very small, as most trade in the developed world takes place with other developed countries (see the shares of imports from developing countries in total imports reported in Table 11.7). Second, one sees skill upgrading occurring in non-traded sectors. Both of these make it rather difficult to argue that trade is the key factor behind rising labour market inequalities in the developed world.

Changes in wage inequality and union decline

Trade unions have traditionally been seen as defenders of egalitarian pay structures. This is reflected in 'equal pay for equal work' notions and the standardisation of pay-setting mechanisms, often in the forms of rigid pay scales attached to jobs rather than individuals. Indeed, the majority of the empirical evidence suggests that, for point in time comparisons, higher unionisation is associated with a lower dispersion of wages. As there has been a sharp decline in the unionisation rate since the late 1970s it seems natural to ask whether this is connected to rising wage inequality.

Table 11.8 shows union membership density figures since the Second World War. The numbers are striking: the stability of the post-war period was followed by the 1970s' increases, since when there have been big falls. By 1995 only just over 30 per cent of the workforce were union members, and this number has dropped beneath 30 per cent at the time of writing. Other measures clearly reflect the sharpness of this fall: the number of trade unions fell from 438 in 1980 to 226 by 1996; 13 million people were union members in 1980, but by 1996 this had fallen below 8 million (see Cully and Woodland (1998) for more details).

Of course, the change between 1970 and now provides a nice contrast with that of rising wage inequality, which fell during the 1970s and has rapidly expanded since. Indeed, there is a strong negative correlation between these changes in wage inequality and aggregate union density, as shown in Figure 11.4. However, care must be taken here. Many other macroeconomic shifts took place over this time period and the correct way to consider the distrib-

Table 11.8 Aggregate union density in Britain

Year	Union density (union membership/employment)
1946	0.43
1950	0.41
1960	0.41
1970	0.46
1975	0.51
1980	0.52
1985	0.46
1990	0.38
1995	0.32

Source: Cully and Woodland (1998).

Figure 11.3 The relationship between industrial skill upgrading and import competition from developing countries

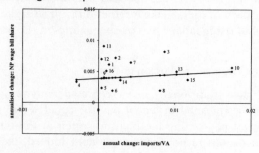

United Kingdom, slope=0.068

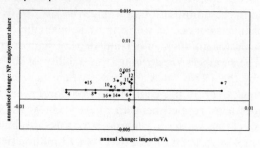

Germany, slope=0.001

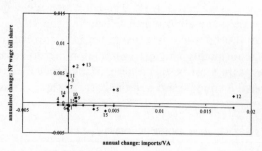

Japan, slope=0.014

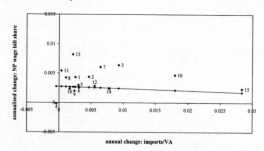

United States, slope=0.35

Denmark, slope=0.003

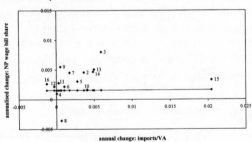

annual change: imports/VA

Sweden, slope=0.024

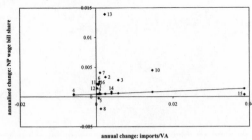

annual change: imports/VA

Source: Machin and Van Reenen (1998).

Key

1. Transport
2. Chemical
3. Electrical machinery and communications equipment (inc. computers)
4. Food, beverages and tobacco products
5. Iron and steel
6. Metal products
7. Non-electrical machinery
8. Non-ferrous metal products
9. Non-metallic mineral products
10. Other manufacturing
11. Paper products and printing
12. Petroleum
13. Professional goods
14. Rubber and plastic products
15. Textiles
16. Wood products and furniture

VA=value added

utional effects of trade unions is not at the aggregate economy-wide level, but at the microeconomic level. This is particularly the case if, as here, one is interested in the link with distributional outcomes like inequality. Clearly, a different picture can then emerge and, when one considers microeconomic evidence on links between union decline and wage inequality using data on individuals and workplaces, it does.

Figure 11.4   Aggregate union density and wage inequality

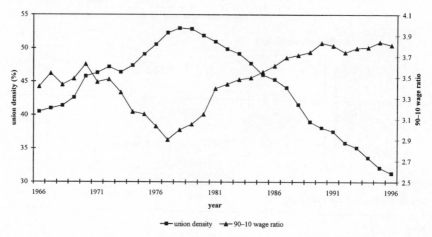

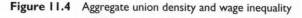

Sources: Cully and Woodland (1998) for union density data and FES for wage inequality data.

Table 11.9 summarises the results from several studies using microdata that have reported calculations of the magnitude of any link between rising wage inequality and union decline in Britain and the United States. All point to an increased wage dispersion associated with union decline. US estimates attribute between 12 per cent and 21 per cent of the rise in wage inequality to falling unionisation. The British results apportion around 17 per cent to 37 per cent of the wage inequality rise to union decline.

These results seem to suggest a clear link between union decline and rising wage inequality, but not a big one. Union decline is clearly part of the story, but it is necessary to look at the wider picture to fully understand rising wage inequality, and labour market inequality in general. To make this point more clearly, the overall dispersion of wages can be thought of as reflecting the dispersion of wages within the union and non-union sectors and wage gaps between them. It is interesting that wage inequality is rising within both the union and the non-union sector. For example, between 1983 and 1991 the variance for male workers grew by 0.011 for individuals in the union sector and by 0.036 in the non-union sector (Machin, 1997). Between 1980 and 1990 the variance of wages of semi-skilled workers grew by 0.024 in union

Table 11.9 Changes in wage inequality and union decline in Britain and the United States

Study	Country/time period	Change in variance	Change due to lower unionisation	Per cent	Notes
Bell and Pitt (1996)	GB: 1982–93	0.113	0.022	20	Individual data,
	GB: 1983–91	0.048	0.012	25	male hourly wages
Card (1998)	US: 1973–93	0.067	0.008	12	Individual data, male hourly wages
DiNardo, Fortin and Lemieux (1996)	US: 1978–88	0.034	0.007	21	Individual data, male hourly wages
Freeman (1993)	US: 1979–88	0.034	0.007	21	Individual data, male hourly wages
Gosling and Machin (1995)	GB: 1980–90	0.018	0.003	17	Workplace data, semi-skilled weekly earnings
Machin (1997)	GB: 1983–91	0.043	0.016	37	Individual data, male hourly wages

sector workplaces and by 0.051 in non-union workplaces (Gosling and Machin, 1995). So, even though the rise is faster in the non-union environment, during the 1980s wage inequality also rose in unionised workplaces.

None of this work considers the employment dimension of skill upgrading with respect to union decline. This is clearly an under-researched area about which we know little. However, it is hard to imagine union decline adding explanatory power here as one would presumably expect to see employment shifts in favour of lower skilled workers if union wage-setting behaviour is weakened. That is, lower skilled workers should become cheaper to employ if unions are no longer present in the workplace. This clearly goes in the wrong direction to explain employment shifts against the low skilled.

Conclusions

This chapter has considered overall shifts in wage inequality in Britain between the mid-1970s and mid-1990s, showing that the key decade of rising wage inequality in Britain was the 1980s. In the 1990s the rising gap between the highest and lowest paid was either stable or rose a little, but by nowhere near as much as in the 1980s. This seems to be, at least partially, due to the fact that faster educational upgrading has dampened down some of the rising wage differentials experienced by the more educated.

Nevertheless, demand still seems to be shifting in favour of the more highly educated and skilled. Despite the fact that there are many more workers with higher educational qualifications, employers' demand for them is still rising, hence their wages relative to other groups have not fallen. These relative demand shifts in favour of the more educated and skilled are more pronounced in more technologically advanced industries in a number of developed countries. This is in line with the notion that technology is key to changes in labour market inequality. There is much less evidence that international trade (in terms of observable measures of trade) has been strongly linked to rising labour market inequality. Finally, at least part of the rise in wage inequality can be attributed to the declining role of trade unions in the labour market.

References

Atkinson, A. (1983), *The Economics of Inequality*, Oxford University Press, Oxford, Second Edition.

Barrett, A. Callan, T. and Nolan, B. (1997), 'The Earnings Distribution and Returns to Education in Ireland, 1987–94', Discussion Paper 1679, Centre for Economic Policy Research, London.

Bell, B. and Pitt, M. (1996), 'Trade Union Decline and the Distribution of Wages in the UK', mimeo, Nuffield College, Oxford.

Berman, E., Bound, J. and Machin, S. (1998), 'Implications of skill biased technological change: international evidence', *Quarterly Journal of Economics*, 113, 1245–79.

Card, D. (1998), 'Falling Union Membership and Rising Wage Inequality', Working Paper No. 6520, NBER, Cambridge, Mass.

Cully, M. and Woodland, S. (1998), 'Trade union membership and recognition 1996–7', *Labour Market Trends*, 106, 353–64.

DiNardo, J., Fortin, N. and Lemieux, T. (1996), 'Labor market institutions and the distribution of wages', *Econometrica*, 64, 1001–44.

Freeman, R. (1993), 'How much has de-unionization contributed to the rise in male wage inequality?', in S. Danziger and P. Gottschalk (eds), *Uneven Tides: Rising Inequality in America*, Russell Sage Foundation, New York.

Gosling, A. and Machin, S. (1995), 'Trade unions and the dispersion of earnings in British establishments 1980–90', *Oxford Bulletin of Economics and Statistics*, 57, 167–84.

Harkness, S. and Machin, S. (1998), 'Changes in the Wage Returns to Education in Britain: Supply Changes and the Evolution of Wage Differentials by Sex and Subject of Study', mimeo, Centre for Economic Performance, LSE, London.

Machin, S. (1996a), 'Wage inequality in the UK', *Oxford Review of Economic Policy*, 7, 49–62.

Machin, S. (1996b), 'Changes in the relative demand for skills in the UK labour market', in A. Booth and D. Snower (eds), *Acquiring Skills: Market Failures, Their Symptoms and Policy Responses*, Cambridge University Press, Cambridge.

Machin, S. (1997), 'The decline of labour market institutions and the rise in wage inequality in Britain', *European Economic Review*, 41, 647–57.

Machin, S. (1998), 'Recent shifts in wage inequality and the wage returns to education in Britain', *National Institute Economic Review*, 166, 87–96.

Machin, S. and Van Reenen, J. (1998), 'Technology and changes in skill structure: evidence from seven countries', *Quarterly Journal of Economics*, 113, 1215–44.

Schmitt, J. (1995), 'The changing structure of male earnings in Britain, 1974–88', in R. Freeman and L. Katz (eds), *Changes and Differences in Wage Structures*, University of Chicago Press.

Wood, A. (1994), *North–South Trade, Employment and Inequality*, Clarendon Press, Oxford.

12 Richard Dickens

Wage mobility in Great Britain

Keypoints

- Mobility in the wage distribution over the course of one year is limited and those individuals that do move tend to experience short-range mobility.

- Earnings mobility is greater when measured over a longer time period (five or fourteen years) but even here there is little long-range movement.

- Much of the mobility observed over this longer time span is a result of the normal life-cycle progression of earnings.

- Workers at the bottom end of the wage distribution are much more likely to exit into unemployment or inactivity. Similarly the unemployed and inactive that do find work tend to enter into low-paying jobs.

- Earnings mobility is pretty constant across Organisation for Economic Co-operation and Development (OECD) countries but there is some evidence that low pay is more persistent in the United States and United Kingdom relative to other countries.

- Individuals with experience of low pay are much more likely to face future spells in low-paying jobs; there is evidence of a Low Pay – No Pay cycle for certain individuals.

- Short-term mobility rates have fallen for men and women since the late 1970s which has exacerbated the rise in cross-section wage inequality.

- At least half of the rise in cross-section inequality can be explained by increasing permanent differences between workers.

One of the most striking developments observed in the UK labour market over the last couple of decades has been a sharp increase in wage inequality.

After declining in the mid-1970s, since the late 1970s wage dispersion has risen at an alarming rate. This increase has been well documented and the potential causes have been extensively researched.[1] However, relatively little attention has been given to the important question of how much workers move within the wage distribution from one period to the next.

Cross-section studies provide a snapshot of the earnings distribution, so they only tell us about the differences between workers at a point in time. We know that the distribution of these snapshots has widened considerably but this tells us nothing about earnings differences between workers over their 'lifetime'. If workers experience a high degree of mobility in the wage distribution from one period to the next then this will act to offset some of the cross-sectional differences; the low paid today could well be the high paid next year and *vice versa*. If mobility had increased over the last couple of decades it would have offset some or all of the rise in cross-sectional dispersion, so that 'lifetime' earnings differences would remain unchanged. In fact, it turns out to be the case that mobility has fallen which has exacerbated the increase in cross-sectional dispersion.

Until recently little was known about these issues. However, with the advent of a number of longitudinal data sources that follow the same individuals over time, evidence on earnings dynamics and mobility is becoming more widespread.[2]

The degree of earnings mobility

The availability of a number of new panel datasets has facilitated the analysis of earnings mobility and labour market transitions. In recent years we have seen the establishment of the British Household Panel Survey (BHPS) and the increased availability of both the New Earnings Survey (NES) and the Lifetime Labour Market Database (LLMDB). These datasets each have their own strengths for examining a particular facet of earnings dynamics. I begin with an examination of short-run mobility in the 1990s.

Short-run mobility

Tables 12.1a and 12.1b (from Dickens, 1997) present information from the NES on transitions of males and females between 1993 and 1994. The tables include information about transitions within the (hourly) wage distribution

---

[1] See Chapter 11 for a review of the evidence.

[2] See Atkinson, Bourguignon and Morrison (1992) for a survey of the earnings dynamics literature at that date. Stewart and Swaffield (1997), Gosling, Johnson, McCrae and Paull (1997) and Ball and Marland (1996) all provide an analysis of earnings mobility in Great Britain.

and transitions into and out of other labour market states.[3] Earnings are split into deciles; ten bands each containing 10 per cent of employees. The first decile contains the lowest paid 10 per cent, the second decile contains the next lowest paid 10 per cent and so on up to the tenth decile, which contains the highest paid 10 per cent of workers. The figures reported are the percentage of individuals in a certain decile or labour market state in 1993 who are in a given decile or labour market state in 1994.

One of the first things to notice about these matrices is the high degree of persistence associated with labour market states and deciles of the wage distribution. The diagonal elements are all much higher than the off-diagonal elements. For example, over 48 per cent of males in the bottom decile in 1993 are still there one year later. It may sound like a substantial proportion (52 per cent) are escaping the bottom of the wage distribution. However, many of these are leaving employment altogether for unemployment or inactivity and some have missing wage details the next year. Consequently, only 20 per cent move up the wage distribution. Most of those who do move up, do not rise very far. Two-thirds only make it to the second decile and very few progress beyond the median.

There is more movement within the middle deciles of the distribution with about 40 per cent remaining in the origin decile. Again, what mobility there is tends to be quite short range with a high concentration around the deciles close to the diagonal. For example, 68 per cent of those starting in the fifth decile either stay there or move to an adjacent decile. Mobility is much lower at the top of the distribution, with 70 per cent of those in the tenth decile retaining their status. Those that do move down from there tend not to move very far.[4]

Looking at those who leave employment for unemployment (or drop out) we see that far more exit from the bottom end of the wage distribution. For example, 6.4 per cent of the first decile are unemployed a year later compared to 2.8 per cent of the fifth decile and 1.8 per cent of the top decile. Males in the bottom decile are twice as likely to become unemployed as those in the fifth decile. Consequently, focusing only on those in employment in two periods will significantly overstate the degree of progression out

[3] The NES is a sample of employees (see Dickens, 1997 for more details). I have merged in data on individuals in claimant unemployment. The missing category contains the inactive, the unemployed who are not claiming benefits and those missing from the survey for various reasons. The NES under-samples those with low weekly wages, those with high job turnover and those in small firms. This is likely to understate the degree of mobility. Dickens (1997) provides a comparison of these one-year transition matrices with the BHPS and finds slightly more mobility.

[4] That there is less mobility at the extremes of the distribution is perhaps unsurprising. First, if an individual is in the top or bottom decile then they can only move in one direction, whereas those in the middle deciles can move up or down. In addition, wages will be more concentrated in the middle of the distribution than at the extremes, so that a given proportional wage change is more likely to result in movement into another decile.

Table 12.1a One-year transition rates for men 1993/4

State in 1993	State in 1994												
	Unemployed	Missing	Missing wage	1st decile	2nd decile	3rd decile	4th decile	5th decile	6th decile	7th decile	8th decile	9th decile	10th decile
Unemployed	54.80	27.17	4.35	4.62	2.45	1.76	1.35	0.90	0.85	0.57	0.39	0.39	0.40
Missing wage	5.27	17.49	36.70	5.16	4.83	4.34	4.39	4.12	3.78	3.30	3.02	3.42	4.18
1st decile	6.44	14.38	11.12	48.23	13.22	3.14	1.34	0.67	0.55	0.30	0.18	0.23	0.18
2nd decile	4.01	10.28	9.49	6.57	43.65	17.45	5.30	1.56	0.97	0.39	0.17	0.10	0.07
3rd decile	3.71	9.16	8.04	1.91	8.81	40.49	19.69	5.12	1.89	0.67	0.30	0.10	0.12
4th decile	3.24	9.36	8.00	0.87	2.55	9.55	38.42	19.20	5.98	1.87	0.63	0.28	0.05
5th decile	2.82	9.57	7.32	0.53	1.05	2.96	9.34	40.52	18.42	5.16	1.55	0.50	0.25
6th decile	3.02	8.73	7.19	0.48	0.50	0.96	2.77	9.75	42.34	18.85	3.94	1.05	0.42
7th decile	2.94	9.36	6.32	0.37	0.45	0.53	0.98	3.29	10.14	45.83	15.92	2.82	1.06
8th decile	2.47	8.99	5.84	0.28	0.17	0.18	0.43	1.04	2.47	9.25	53.68	13.47	1.72
9th decile	1.97	9.61	6.44	0.15	0.18	0.15	0.25	0.55	0.96	1.67	8.15	59.58	10.34
10th decile	1.84	10.75	7.49	0.35	0.12	0.08	0.15	0.18	0.28	0.42	1.13	6.88	70.32

Source: Dickens (1997) (originally from NES data).

Notes: 1. Figures are % of given state in 1993 in given state in 1994.
2. The NES is conducted in April.
3. The unemployed are those claiming unemployment-related benefits.
4. The missing includes the self-employed, retired, inactive and those not captured by the survey.

Table 12.1b One-year transition rates for women 1993/4

State in 1993	State in 1994												
	Unemployed	Missing	Missing wage	1st decile	2nd decile	3rd decile	4th decile	5th decile	6th decile	7th decile	8th decile	9th decile	10th decile
Unemployed	34.87	36.08	7.11	4.05	3.97	3.24	2.73	2.13	1.42	1.44	1.57	0.94	0.46
Missing wage	2.70	22.07	36.62	5.96	4.85	4.78	3.89	3.33	2.70	3.10	2.58	3.14	4.27
1st decile	2.56	19.16	13.79	43.65	11.45	4.16	1.76	1.16	1.00	0.58	0.28	0.26	0.20
2nd decile	2.25	15.73	12.13	8.59	41.31	12.63	3.94	1.55	0.76	0.66	0.30	0.10	0.06
3rd decile	2.15	13.36	10.37	2.57	7.94	39.67	15.61	4.58	1.71	1.02	0.64	0.30	0.10
4th decile	1.67	11.68	9.65	1.47	2.65	7.98	40.90	16.37	4.32	1.63	0.94	0.62	0.14
5th decile	1.59	10.80	8.28	0.85	1.23	2.70	7.37	43.06	17.52	4.28	1.43	0.67	0.22
6th decile	1.37	11.08	7.46	0.76	0.62	1.23	2.84	7.48	46.15	15.95	3.68	1.07	0.32
7th decile	1.68	11.19	7.90	0.51	0.41	0.51	1.26	2.70	7.51	46.61	16.26	2.96	0.49
8th decile	1.66	11.51	7.44	0.22	0.30	0.47	0.71	0.91	1.99	7.70	50.30	15.23	1.56
9th decile	1.30	11.44	8.52	0.28	0.10	0.18	0.26	0.34	0.53	1.66	7.16	55.97	12.27
10th decile	0.81	12.59	13.36	0.16	0.14	0.12	0.20	0.18	0.26	0.45	1.16	4.95	65.62

Source: Dickens (1997).
Notes: See Table 12.1a.

of low-wage jobs. Those who are unemployed face a high degree of persistence, with 55 per cent remaining unemployed a year later. Those that do make it into work are much more likely to do so at low wages (for more information on entry jobs see Chapter 14). Some 4.6 per cent enter at the bottom decile compared to 0.9 per cent in the fifth decile and practically nobody at the top. Notice also that of those employees that do remain in employment more move up the wage distribution than move down. For example, 26 per cent of those in the fifth decile move up the wage distribution compared to 14 per cent that move down. This is because those entering from non-employment do so at lower wages, pushing those already in work further up the distribution.

Table 12.1b presents the same transition matrix for women. A similar pattern emerges, with evidence of immobility in earnings and labour market state. There is some evidence that women face slightly higher levels of mobility than men, with fewer employees remaining in the same decile year on year. For example, 44 per cent of bottom decile women remain there between 1993 and 1994 compared to 48 per cent of men. However, more women drop out of employment (into unemployment and the missing category) so that still only 20 per cent move up the wage distribution. Persistence at the top of the distribution is also very high for women, with 65 per cent remaining in the tenth decile. Again, those that drop out into unemployment and the missing category (which will include the inactive) are more likely to do so from the bottom of the wage distribution. Similarly, those that enter from these states do so into lower paid jobs.

Overall these tables of one-year transitions paint a picture of quite high levels of persistence. Although there is mobility over the course of a year much of it is very short range. However, perhaps looking at movement over just one year is too restrictive. We may expect there to be more mobility over a longer time period. Let us now turn to examine this issue.

Longer-run mobility

Table 12.2 presents the five-year decile transition matrix of hourly earnings for males between 1989 and 1994 from the NES (see Dickens, 1997). Again, I have included transitions into non-employment states. As expected mobility is higher when measured over this longer time span with much less concentration on the diagonals than over one year. For example, only 22 per cent of males remain in the bottom decile after five years, compared to 48 per cent over one year. Nevertheless, many of the employed men in the bottom decile in 1989 have dropped out of employment altogether by 1994 so that only 30 per cent have actually moved up the wage distribution, compared to 20 per cent moving up over one year. Amongst those that do move few progress very far, with two-thirds finding themselves in the next two deciles. There is more mobility from the middle deciles, but most movement is still fairly short

Table 12.2 Five-year transition rates for men 1989/94

State in 1989	State in 1994												
	Unemployed	Missing	Missing wage	1st decile	2nd decile	3rd decile	4th decile	5th decile	6th decile	7th decile	8th decile	9th decile	10th decile
Unemployed	38.34	36.53	5.31	5.98	3.55	2.47	2.23	1.79	1.19	1.00	0.60	0.67	0.33
Missing	6.80	70.32	4.63	2.33	1.98	1.85	1.72	1.63	1.70	1.73	1.65	1.68	1.98
Missing wage	8.34	30.23	20.09	4.09	4.20	4.14	4.47	4.03	4.03	3.61	3.70	4.29	4.77
1st decile	11.54	26.49	8.82	22.25	13.45	7.53	3.76	2.11	1.59	1.10	0.68	0.31	0.38
2nd decile	9.62	23.18	8.32	6.86	18.76	14.25	8.38	4.96	2.52	1.57	0.88	0.50	0.21
3rd decile	7.84	21.57	8.72	3.56	8.50	17.99	13.29	8.66	5.20	2.69	1.18	0.51	0.29
4th decile	7.04	20.81	8.49	2.33	4.11	8.64	16.53	14.47	8.98	4.88	2.35	0.85	0.53
5th decile	6.67	20.04	7.75	1.77	2.56	4.03	9.79	16.47	14.64	9.70	4.43	1.67	0.49
6th decile	5.77	19.81	6.84	1.39	1.74	1.96	4.28	9.53	18.37	16.15	9.76	3.20	1.19
7th decile	5.79	19.23	7.05	1.10	1.13	1.21	2.10	5.01	10.18	19.43	18.35	7.49	1.95
8th decile	4.85	19.84	6.53	0.83	0.64	0.82	1.29	1.97	3.21	10.31	25.69	19.41	4.62
9th decile	4.61	20.69	8.19	0.53	0.51	0.53	0.61	0.87	1.53	2.78	8.84	33.15	17.16
10th decile	3.93	25.51	8.68	0.54	0.29	0.20	0.34	0.45	0.61	0.87	2.15	8.54	47.89

Source: NES.

Notes: 1. Figures are % of given state in 1989 in given state in 1994.
2. The NES is conducted in April.
3. The unemployed are those claiming unemployment-related benefits.
4. The missing includes the self-employed, retired, inactive and those not captured by the survey.

range. Once again those in the top decile seem to retain their status the most, with some 48 per cent of males remaining there after five years and with very few experiencing large wage falls. Looking at those that exit into unemployment one finds that those in the bottom deciles face a higher probability of this; 11.5 per cent fall into unemployment from the first decile compared to 6.7 per cent from the fifth decile and 3.9 per cent from the top. Similarly, those entering into employment are more likely to enter into low-wage jobs; an unemployed man is three times more likely to enter the bottom decile than the fifth decile. The figures for women (see Dickens, 1997) display a very similar pattern to those for men, with some evidence of slightly more mobility.

Let us now turn to what happens when we expand the time period over which we measure mobility further still. Ball and Marland (1996) use the LLMDB, which is constructed from administrative National Insurance records on earnings and employment states, to examine mobility over a fourteen-year period; 1978/9 to 1992/3. Since it is well known that earnings rise over the life-cycle (see for example Gosling, Machin and Meghir, 1996) they concentrate on two age groups of men. Tables 12.3a and 12.3b present the transition matrices from Ball and Marland (1996) for those aged 25–34 in 1978 and those aged 35–44 in 1978 respectively. Earnings are only present for those individuals that are in employment for the full year. The deciles are computed over annual earnings, pooling both age groups together.

Focusing first on the 25–34 age group, notice that far fewer individuals remain on the diagonal over the course of fourteen years. Only 13 per cent of young men in the bottom decile in 1978/9 are there in 1992/3. However, many of these have dropped out of full-year employment into a full- or part-year of benefits (28 per cent) or into self-employment (7.8 per cent). In fact, only 47 per cent of these young workers have moved up the wage distribution after fourteen years and over half of these only make it into the next three deciles. Much of this mobility is related to the life-cycle progression of earnings. When examining the older workers, aged 35–44 years, one finds less mobility. Some 19 per cent of the bottom decile remain after fourteen years with 41 per cent ending up on full- or part-year benefits. Only 30 per cent of this older group move up from the bottom decile, with 70 per cent of these making it no further than the next three deciles.

Both tables show that mobility over fourteen years is significantly higher than that measured over one or five years. However, the same pattern of relatively short range movement within the earnings distribution emerges even over this long time period, with most individuals moving only a couple of deciles. Persistence is higher at the top of the earnings distribution; 43 per cent of young workers and 30 per cent of older workers in the top decile remain there after fourteen years.

There is also strong evidence that lower paid men are more likely to move onto benefits for at least part of the year. Some 28 per cent of young workers in the bottom decile in 1978/9 end up on benefits in 1992/3, compared to 13

Table 12.3a Fourteen-year transition rates for men aged 25–34 in 1978, 1978/9 to 1992/3

State in 1978/9	State in 1992/3													
	Self-employment	Benefits	Partial employment	Other	1st decile	2nd decile	3rd decile	4th decile	5th decile	6th decile	7th decile	8th decile	9th decile	10th decile
Self-employment	57.30	6.40	2.00	19.20	2.00	1.70	1.90	1.60	1.50	1.80	1.10	1.20	0.90	1.70
Benefits	2.40	64.10	7.10	4.00	6.60	4.00	2.90	2.20	1.10	1.70	1.50	1.10	0.70	0.60
Partial employment	5.30	29.60	13.50	4.60	8.40	6.70	5.50	6.20	4.70	4.70	3.90	3.20	2.40	1.50
1st decile	7.80	17.60	10.20	4.40	13.40	12.60	7.50	5.80	4.80	4.40	3.90	2.80	2.60	2.20
2nd decile	7.30	10.80	9.20	4.00	7.90	12.00	11.20	9.40	8.50	6.80	6.10	3.40	2.10	1.00
3rd decile	6.30	6.90	9.50	3.30	5.90	8.50	9.70	9.80	11.20	9.40	7.90	6.20	3.30	2.10
4th decile	6.00	5.80	8.30	4.40	4.60	6.60	9.80	9.90	9.30	10.80	9.20	8.60	4.70	2.40
5th decile	7.90	5.10	7.80	3.50	4.40	4.60	7.20	8.80	10.30	9.80	10.80	9.80	7.40	2.80
6th decile	5.80	5.00	6.80	3.40	3.30	4.10	6.50	8.00	7.80	11.10	10.70	12.50	9.80	5.20
7th decile	6.20	4.00	7.10	3.40	2.90	3.10	4.20	5.00	7.80	9.90	11.50	14.40	12.80	8.00
8th decile	6.40	3.30	6.90	3.10	2.10	1.50	3.20	4.50	5.80	8.80	10.20	14.70	18.00	11.70
9th decile	7.30	3.00	6.40	4.20	1.90	1.60	2.10	2.40	4.40	5.60	7.80	11.60	19.10	22.60
10th decile	7.20	2.90	4.80	4.70	2.20	0.60	1.40	2.20	1.70	2.30	5.40	6.90	14.30	43.50

Source: Ball and Marland (1996), LLMDB.

Notes: Figures are percentage of given state in 1978/9 in given state in 1992/3.

Deciles 1–10: Those in employment throughout the year.

Benefits: Those unemployed or incapable of work throughout the year.

Partial employment: Those with a mixture of employment and unemployment in the year.

Other: Those with other combinations in the year.

Deciles computed for all 25 to 44-year-olds in full-year employment.

Table 12.3b Fourteen-year transition rates for men aged 35–44 in 1978, 1978/9 to 1992/3

State in 1978/9	State in 1992/3													
	Self-employment	Benefits	Partial employment	Other	1st decile	2nd decile	3rd decile	4th decile	5th decile	6th decile	7th decile	8th decile	9th decile	10th decile
Self-employment	53.10	8.30	2.70	22.80	2.40	2.20	1.60	1.20	1.10	1.10	0.80	0.80	0.90	1.00
Benefits	2.00	78.10	6.10	3.00	3.30	2.90	1.10	1.00	0.60	0.60	1.10	0.30	0.00	0.10
Partial employment	4.30	39.40	14.00	4.30	7.90	7.00	6.10	4.10	3.90	3.40	2.60	1.10	1.20	0.80
1st decile	4.70	27.10	13.80	4.50	19.10	11.40	6.60	3.30	2.60	2.20	1.70	0.80	1.10	1.10
2nd decile	5.10	19.40	14.20	3.30	12.30	15.90	11.10	7.50	5.00	3.10	1.90	0.60	0.30	0.20
3rd decile	4.60	16.60	13.50	3.30	8.70	13.40	13.20	10.00	8.20	4.30	2.10	1.30	0.60	0.30
4th decile	4.70	14.00	14.10	3.10	8.50	12.30	11.10	11.70	8.30	5.40	4.50	1.70	0.70	0.10
5th decile	4.50	12.40	15.10	3.00	8.10	8.50	9.90	11.20	9.70	7.80	5.10	3.00	1.30	0.40
6th decile	4.00	11.50	14.00	3.40	6.50	6.60	8.30	9.60	10.40	9.20	7.80	5.40	2.40	0.90
7th decile	5.20	10.00	15.10	4.00	5.50	4.80	6.70	8.00	8.50	9.20	9.70	7.50	4.70	1.10
8th decile	5.00	9.90	13.00	4.30	5.60	4.20	4.90	6.20	6.90	8.50	10.10	11.20	7.50	2.80
9th decile	4.60	7.90	13.40	4.80	5.30	3.20	2.60	4.40	5.70	6.20	8.90	11.50	14.20	7.30
10th decile	5.50	6.40	11.80	6.30	4.40	1.60	1.60	2.00	2.70	2.50	4.30	6.30	14.10	30.30

Source: Ball and Marland (1996). LLMDB.
Notes: As for Table 12.3a.

per cent of those in the fifth decile and 8 per cent of those in the top decile. Persistence is alarmingly high for those on benefits. Over 64 per cent of young men on benefits in 1978/9 are on benefits again in 1992/3. This rises to 78 per cent for older workers. Those that do manage to enter work do so toward the bottom of the earnings distribution.

Ball and Marland (1996) also examine the transitions of individuals in all the years between 1978/9 and 1992/3 and not just those between these two points in time. For example, having found that 13.4 per cent of those young workers in the bottom decile in 1978/9 are still there in 1992/3 they examine how many of these are there for all fourteen years. They find that a striking 25 per cent of these are stuck in the bottom decile for every year between 1978/9 and 1992/3. Likewise, a quarter of the 19.1 per cent of older workers who are in the bottom decile in 1978/9 and 1992/3 are there for every intervening year. Similar patterns of persistence emerge for those on benefits. Of those 64 per cent of younger workers who are on full-year benefits in both 1978/9 and 1992/3, 20 per cent are on benefits in every year. For older workers, of the 78 per cent who are on benefits in both periods, 28 per cent are dependent on benefits in every year. It appears that for some individuals low pay and benefit dependency is a very persistent phenomenon.

The low pay – no pay cycle

A fact that seems to emerge from all of the above analysis it that low-paid workers are both more likely to exit employment (into unemployment or inactivity) and more likely to have entered low pay from non-employment. This suggests that a group of individuals are prone to moving in and out of unemployment and low-paid jobs; i.e. there is a 'low pay – no pay' cycle. This issue has been examined in more detail by Stewart (in Chapter 13).

International comparisons of earnings mobility

The OECD (1997) provide an analysis of earnings mobility between 1986 and 1991 in six OECD countries; the United States, the United Kingdom, Germany, France, Italy and Denmark. They compute inequality indices and examine how much these decline when earnings are averaged over different time periods. The reduction in inequality over the cross-section measure is then an indicator of mobility. They find similar levels of mobility in these countries, suggesting that the differences in cross-sectional earnings dispersion across these countries are probably reflective of differences in 'lifetime' earnings inequality.

They also study the movement of workers out of low-paying jobs and find that of the workers who are in the bottom quintile (the bottom 20 per cent of earners) in 1986, between 60 and 75 per cent move out of low pay some-time over the next five years. However, there is a potential problem in using the bottom quintile since the range and position of this will vary considerably across countries. When low pay is defined as earnings below 0.65 times median pay, larger differences emerge across the countries. Almost all Dan-ish low-paid workers have escaped by 1991, compared to 80 per cent of French, German and Italian workers. The corresponding figures for the United Kingdom and the United States are around 60 per cent, which sug-gests low pay is more persistent in these countries.

Changes in earnings mobility and inequality

One criticism that is often applied to mobility analysis is that we have no idea what constitutes a high or low level of mobility. The concept of mobility, like most measures in economics, is a subjective one. However, a potentially more interesting question is whether there have been any changes in mobility over time. Given that cross-sectional inequality has risen sharply over the last cou-ple of decades, it is of interest to examine whether mobility has also changed. For example, if mobility has risen then this may offset some of the cross-sec-tional rise in inequality, so that the increase in 'lifetime' inequality is less severe.

Changes in transition matrices over time

Table 12.4 presents information from the NES on one-year decile transitions for 1977/8 and 1988/9 for males and females.[5] For each origin decile I have presented the proportion of individuals who stay in that decile, the propor-tion who move one decile and the proportion who move two or more deciles. (For the full transition matrices refer to Dickens, 1997.) Concentrating on males first, we can see that the number that remain on the diagonal of the one-year transition matrix has risen between 1977/8 and 1988/9 across all deciles. For example, the number remaining in the bottom decile has risen slightly from 40 per cent in 1977/8 to 42 per cent in 1988/9. The number staying in their origin decile has risen by more for those in the middle deciles of the distribution; e.g. the proportion remaining in the fifth decile has risen from 22 per cent to 31 per cent. The corresponding proportion has also increased for the top decile from 61 per cent to 66 per cent. In addition, there is a fall in the proportion of males moving two or more deciles between 1977/8 and 1988/9. This fall occurs across all origin deciles, except for the

5 Analysis in Dickens (1997) shows that the measure of mobility from the NES can be sensi-tive to the rates of inflation. In times of high inflation the timing of wage settlements will be more important for mobility. Consequently, I have chosen these years since they both have a similar inflation rate.

Table 12.4 One-year transition rates for men and women 1977/8 and 1988/9

State in second period

State in first period	Males						Females					
	1977–8			1988–9			1977–8			1988–9		
	Same decile	Moved 1 decile	Moved 2 or more	Same decile	Moved 1 decile	Moved 2 or more	Same decile	Moved 1 decile	Moved 2 or more	Same decile	Moved 1 decile	Moved 2 or more
1st decile	40.19	11.43	10.28	41.73	12.88	8.65	37.66	9.54	10.02	38.18	10.38	11.29
2nd decile	28.56	25.74	12.38	35.97	26.70	10.13	32.44	20.21	9.98	36.93	20.99	8.23
3rd decile	23.26	28.99	16.14	33.04	29.71	12.72	34.72	19.44	10.83	30.78	25.97	13.50
4th decile	22.56	28.55	18.94	31.20	30.69	15.11	26.85	22.59	15.76	30.69	26.86	14.15
5th decile	21.64	29.09	19.86	31.39	31.82	15.26	27.11	24.50	13.99	32.27	29.27	13.08
6th decile	21.65	29.74	18.73	34.81	32.58	13.29	27.86	26.26	13.57	34.84	29.12	12.76
7th decile	25.00	30.98	16.30	37.99	31.15	11.92	27.42	28.82	12.68	35.17	28.58	11.98
8th decile	30.87	30.98	11.22	44.05	28.00	8.26	33.95	28.80	7.80	39.38	29.33	8.35
9th decile	44.75	24.13	5.72	52.48	22.58	5.33	43.70	22.17	6.15	45.83	27.73	4.18
10th decile	61.14	9.49	2.71	66.30	9.13	2.90	57.27	8.71	2.60	60.41	11.06	2.78

Source: NES.

Notes: 1. Figures are the percentage of given state in first period in given state in second period.
2. The NES is conducted in April.
3. The unemployed are those claiming unemployment-related benefits.
4. The missing includes the self-employed, retired, inactive and those not captured by the survey.

top decile. These figures provide pretty strong evidence that mobility has fallen for males over this time period, particularly in the middle deciles of the wage distribution.[6]

Turning to the figures for women we also observe an increase in the number of individuals remaining on the diagonal, albeit less marked than that for males. The number remaining in the bottom decile is practically unchanged from 1977/8 to 1988/9. However, the proportions remaining in the middle and top deciles increase. For example, the proportion remaining in the fifth decile increases from 27.1 per cent to 32.3 per cent and from 57.3 per cent to 60.4 per cent for the top decile.[7]

Changes in the longer span transition matrices can also be examined, to see if longer run mobility has changed over this time period. In Dickens (1997) I provide an analysis of changes in five-year mobility rates for males and females. I find some evidence that mobility has fallen for males between 1975/80 and 1989/94. However, there is evidence that five-year mobility may have risen slightly for females over this time period.

A ranking measure of mobility

There are some potential problems with the above analysis of mobility using transition matrices. First, whether an individual crosses a decile threshold depends on their starting position within the decile. Analysis of movements across deciles takes no account of mobility within these deciles. It could be the case that one individual has a larger wage change than another who changes decile, but does not actually cross a decile threshold themselves. In addition, this problem is compounded when we are examining changes in mobility rates over a time period when cross-sectional inequality has risen. This results in an increase in the wage range within each decile so that movements across deciles are not comparable.[8] That I find more people staying in each decile is, perhaps, unsurprising since to move from one decile to another an individual needs a proportionately larger wage change in later periods.

In order to resolve this problem I employ an alternative measure of mobility based on the individual's actual position within the wage distribution, and examine changes in this between two time periods. I do this by computing each individual's percentile ranking based on their wage in a given year. This gives a measure from 0 to 1 for each individual, depending on where they fall

---

[6] Care needs to be taken in coming to this conclusion since the rate of attrition from the NES has changed over this time period. In Dickens (1997) I provide adjustments to account for this and conclude that mobility has fallen for males, particularly in the middle deciles of the distribution.

[7] If one carries out the same sort of adjustment for attrition for females (Dickens, 1997) then there is some evidence that mobility may have increased between 1977/8 and 1988/9.

[8] For example, the difference between the wage at the second decile and the first decile is 12 per cent in 1975. By 1994 this had risen to 18 per cent.

Figure 12.1a Earnings ranking in 1977 and 1978: men

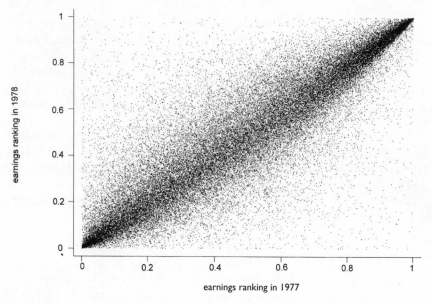

Source: NES.

Figure 12.1b Earnings ranking in 1988 and 1989: men

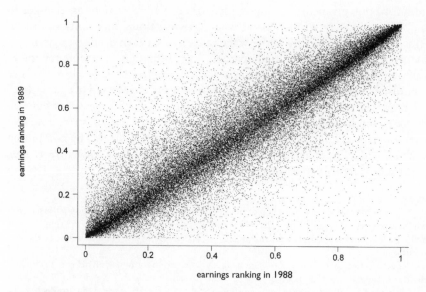

Source: NES.

in the wage distribution. This ranking can then be compared to their ranking in another year to give a measure of the degree of movement amongst individuals within the wage distribution. This can be thought of as a transition matrix where the number of earnings classes is set equal to the number of individuals in the distribution.

Figure 12.1a plots the percentile ranking of individuals in 1978 against that in 1977. If there is no mobility there will be a diagonal line from the bottom left corner of the figure, since nobody changes position in the wage distribution from one year to the next. If individuals' earnings are uncorrelated between the two years then one would see a random scattering. If individuals' earnings are negatively correlated between the two years, so the lowest paid became the highest paid and vice versa, then we would observe a negatively sloped diagonal line starting from the top left corner of the figure. This case corresponds to the highest level of mobility but the uncorrelated case is generally thought of as the benchmark. In fact we see a concentration of individuals around the positively sloped diagonal. This concentration is much higher at the top and bottom of the distribution, indicating lower levels of mobility at these points. It is evident that we are a long way from the case of uncorrelated earnings. Figure 12.1b presents the same scatter plot for earnings rankings in 1988 and 1989. It is clear that there is a greater concentration around the diagonal in this latter year, providing evidence that mobility has fallen over this time period for males. These ranking plots for females (not presented) provide a similar pattern of changes in mobility over this time period.

These plots provide a good visual representation of mobility, but they do not provide any concrete numbers with which to compare changes in mobility over time. However, I have computed an index of mobility based on these changes in percentile rankings of individuals' earnings (see Dickens, 1997 for more details). The index is plotted for males and females from 1976 to 1994 in Figure 12.2. This index takes a minimum value of 0 when there is no mobility, a maximum value of 1 when earnings are perfectly negatively correlated and a value of two-thirds when earnings are uncorrelated across the two years. The first point to notice is that this mobility index is far below what one would observe if earnings were uncorrelated across years; it never rises above 0.2 for either males or females. The second point to note is that both of these indices have fallen over this time period. In 1976 the index is about 0.19 for males and 0.18 for females. It increases up until 1980, where it peaks at 0.20 for males and females. Thereafter it falls sharply in the early 1980s, recovers somewhat in the late 1980s but continues to fall in the 1990s. By 1994 it has fallen to 0.12, which means it has fallen by 41 per cent for males and females since its peak in 1980.

As mentioned above, mobility measures in the NES are highly correlated with inflation (see Dickens, 1997). Nevertheless, I still find evidence of a 22 per cent fall in this mobility index for males between 1976 and 1994 after

Figure 12.2   One-year mobility index

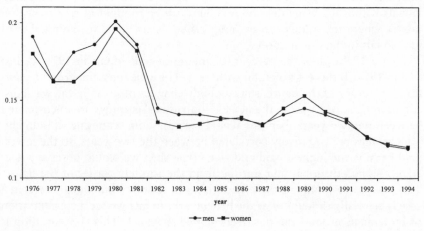

Source: NES.

controlling for the effects of inflation. In addition, there is some weak evidence that mobility has fallen for females by around 11 per cent over this time period.[9]

The evidence presented in this section suggests that short-run mobility has fallen for males and possibly for females since the late 1970s. In addition, there is some weak evidence that longer-run (five-year) mobility has declined for males. Given that the cross-sectional distribution of wages has widened considerably over this time period, this is very worrying from a 'lifetime' inequality perspective. If 'lifetime' inequality were to remain unchanged then we would have to observe an increase in mobility that would offset the rise in cross-sectional dispersion. In fact, we see evidence that mobility has either remained constant or even fallen. This implies that lifetime inequality may have risen even faster than cross-sectional inequality.[10]

[9] This ranking methodology can also be used to examine changes in longer term mobility. In Dickens (1997) I compute this mobility index for males and females over a five-year time span. After controlling for the effects of inflation, I find some weak evidence that mobility has fallen for males but no evidence of any change for females.

[10] Another way of analysing this issue is to decompose earnings differences into that part which is permanent and that part which is transitory and examine how these have changed over this time period. Permanent differences between individuals are those that last forever and may reflect the effects of fixed unobserved ability differences. Transitory differences die out over time and may reflect the effects of job characteristics, bonus payments etc. In Dickens (2000), I find that about half of the rise is accounted for by an increase in permanent differences, with the other half accounted for by a rise in (highly persistent) transitory differences. Consequently, over half of the rise in cross-sectional earnings inequality is explained by increasing differences between individuals that last for a good many years.

Conclusions

The fact that cross-sectional wage dispersion has risen over the last two decades in the United Kingdom has been well documented and is widely accepted amongst academics, politicians and media commentators. However, up until the last couple of years very little information was available on the dynamics of individuals' earnings and the degree of mobility within the earnings distribution. Some politicians claimed that the rise in cross-section inequality was unimportant since we live in a mobile society with a high degree of movement within the wage distribution over time; the low paid today could be tomorrow's high flyers and, presumably, *vice versa*.

In this chapter I have reviewed the evidence that has emerged over the last couple of years on the dynamics of earnings. This has shown that the picture that has sometimes been painted of a mobile society is far from the truth. In fact, the evidence shows a high degree of immobility with little long-range wage movements. A group of individuals appear to be stuck in a cycle of low-paid work followed by unemployment and then further low-paid work. In addition to this, and perhaps most worrying, is the evidence showing that earnings mobility has fallen since the late 1970s. Given that we have also seen a sharp rise in cross sectional wage inequality over this time period, this tells us that not only has the gap between the rich and poor increased but that the ability of the low paid to close this gap has fallen considerably. Far from offsetting the increase in cross-section wage inequality, changes in mobility appear to have exacerbated this rise.

References

Atkinson, A., Bourguignon, F. and Morrisson, C. (1992), *Empirical Studies of Earnings Mobility*, Harwood Academic Publishers, Reading.

Ball, J. and Marland, M. (1996), 'Male Earnings Mobility in the Lifetime Labour Market Database', Working Paper No. 1, Analytical Services Division, Department of Social Security, London.

Dickens, R. (1997), 'Caught in a Trap? Wage Mobility in Great Britain: 1975–94', Discussion Paper No. 365, Centre for Economic Performance, LSE, London.

Dickens, R. (2000), 'The Evolution of Individual Male Wages in Great Britain: 1975–95', *Economic Journal*, forthcoming, January 2000.

Gosling, A., Johnson, P., McCrae, J. and Paull, G. (1997), *The Dynamics of Low Pay and Unemployment in Early 1990s Britain*, Institute for Fiscal Studies, London.

Gosling, A., Machin, S. and Meghir, C. (1996), 'The Changing Distribution of Male Wages in the UK', Discussion Paper No. 271, Centre for Economic Performance, LSE, London.

OECD (1997), 'Earnings Mobility: Taking a Longer Run View', Employment Outlook, Paris, 27–61.

Stewart, M. B. and Swaffield, J. (1997), 'The dynamics of low pay in Britain', in P. Gregg (ed.), *Jobs, Wages and Poverty: Patterns of Persistence and Mobility in the New Flexible Labour Market*, Centre for Economic Performance, LSE, London, 36–51.

13 Mark B. Stewart

Low pay in Britain

Keypoints

- Measuring low pay is not easy. Different datasets give different results. The best available information suggests that (in April 1997) around 1.5 million, one in every fourteen workers, earned below £3 an hour, 3 million earned below £3.50 an hour and 6 million, one in every four, earned below £4.50 an hour.

- Low pay is no longer the preserve of the female and youth labour markets. The incidence of low pay has moved toward older workers and toward men. One in every six male workers over the age of 24 is now low paid, compared with one in thirty in 1968.

- Britain is near the top of the international low pay league of Organisation for Economic Co-operation and Development (OECD) countries. It has a lower incidence than the United States and Canada, where about one in four are low paid, but low pay is higher than in all the other twelve countries considered and much higher than Sweden at the bottom of the league, where only one in twenty is low paid.

- Casual workers, those in small firms, those in non-union firms, ethnic minorities and less-skilled manual workers are all more likely to be low paid.

- The longer an individual remains low paid the lower the probability of moving out of low pay.

- There is strong evidence of a cycle of low pay and no pay. The low paid are more likely to be out of work in the future; those out of work are more likely to be low paid on re-entry. The hypothesis that low-paid jobs act as stepping-stones to higher paid jobs is not supported by the evidence.

- The overlap between low pay and household poverty is not large, although it has grown considerably over the last twenty years. However, around half of those classified as 'permanent' low paid are in household poverty.

As has been documented in Chapter 11, the distribution of earnings in Britain has increased markedly over the last twenty years. In particular the relative earnings of those at the bottom end of the distribution have deteriorated considerably. There has thus been an increase in the number of people classified as 'low paid', if this is measured relative to other workers. The issue of low pay has been further highlighted by the appointment, by the newly-elected Labour Government, of a Low Pay Commission (LPC) to advise on the level at which the minimum wage should be set and the recent publication of their first report (LPC, 1998). Low pay is an important issue. This chapter lays out the basic facts about low pay in Britain today. It examines how many people are low paid, the personal and job characteristics of the low paid, the extent of mobility into and out of low pay, and the relationship between low pay and household poverty.

How many low paid?

Defining low pay

The number of people classified as low paid obviously depends on the level at which we set the low pay 'threshold', but it also depends on how we measure pay and on the data source used. The distinction between low and high pay inevitably involves 'shades of grey' and the selection of a particular threshold is, within limits, an arbitrary one. It is therefore important to examine the sensitivity of any analysis of low pay to the threshold chosen, by using more than one such cut-off. The calculation supporting a particular threshold is often a relative one, for example two-thirds of median earnings. However, the argument to support it should also take account of the implied proportion of low paid. The two need to be evaluated in conjunction.

Different data sets give different answers when asked how many people are paid below a certain threshold. The New Earnings Survey (NES) has many advantages for the analysis of earnings. It provides very accurate earnings information, mainly direct from employers' payroll databases, and it gives a very large sample of employees. However, it also has a serious disadvantage for the analysis of low pay in that it under-samples those in receipt of low pay. There are a number of reasons for this. Most important is that it excludes most of those whose weekly pay falls below the PAYE deduction threshold.[1]

---

[1] For a fuller discussion of the advantages and disadvantages of different datasets for the analysis of low pay and of the reconciliation of the differences between them in the number of low paid, see Stewart (1998a).

The largest of the household-based surveys that one could use as an alternative to the NES to avoid these problems is the Labour Force Survey (LFS), but this is much smaller than the NES. Compared with the NES, the LFS has a better sample design for the analysis of low pay and has the added advantages of being quarterly and providing more information on the characteristics of the individuals sampled. However, it also has a number of disadvantages. First amongst these is measurement error. The earnings information comes from individual questions rather than administrative records and until recently the earnings questions were asked of only one-fifth of the sample, those in the fifth wave of interviews, which are generally conducted by telephone, making inaccurate answers even more likely. This is exacerbated by the fact that about 30 per cent of the interviews are conducted with a proxy respondent, someone other than the person to whom the earnings refer.

The British Household Panel Study (BHPS) is likely to have more accurate earnings information than the LFS. Interviews are conducted in person rather than by phone and wherever possible pay-slips are provided by the respondent and checked by the interviewer. Another advantage of the BHPS over the LFS for later sections of this chapter is that it is a panel. It has earnings and employment information on the same individuals over time and thus permits us to investigate movements into and out of low pay. However, it provides a rather smaller sample than the LFS. All three of these sources have advantages and disadvantages for the study of low pay. Each of them will be used extensively in this chapter. The NES and the LFS (and the comparison between them) are used in this section.

A variety of low-pay thresholds have been proposed. Not surprisingly the discussion of low pay is closely linked with that of the rate for a national minimum wage and typically no clear distinction is made between the definition of a low-pay threshold and the national minimum wage level advocated. However, the national minimum wage to be implemented in 1999 might be argued to cover only the lowest of the low paid and therefore represent a point at the lower end of a range in a broader definition of low pay.

Low pay is defined in this chapter in terms of hourly earnings. The initial examination of the number of low paid uses thresholds of £3, £3.50, £4 and £4.50 per hour (in April 1997 terms).[2] To put these thresholds in perspective it is useful to see how they relate to the distribution of hourly earnings and how they compare to other cut-offs that have been used. Which data source is used to construct the distribution matters a lot. For example, the TUC's advocated formula for a national minimum wage of half male median rising to two-thirds male median would give £4.12 and £5.49 (in April 1997 terms) using the NES and full-timers on adult rates only, but £3.66 and £4.88 using the LFS. Two-thirds of the *overall* median for full-timers is £5.13 using the

---

[2] Throughout this chapter hourly earnings figures are adjusted to April 1997 terms.

NES and £4.57 using the LFS, and this drops to £4.07 if part-timers are included.

How do the thresholds used here compare with distribution-based ones? The £3.50 threshold is roughly half the male median in the LFS, if part-timers are included, and is the lowest decile point for the same distribution. It is also the main cut-off used by the LPC in their report (LPC, 1998: 33) and corresponds roughly to the proposed adult figure for a national minimum wage, adjusted to April 1997 terms. The £4 and £4.50 thresholds are roughly two-thirds the LFS overall median with and without part-timers respectively. The £4.50 threshold leaves nearly 30 per cent of employees low paid (about 6.7 million jobs) and would seem a suitable top threshold to take. At the other end, even with a cut-off as low as £3 an hour, about 1.7 million employees (7.4 per cent) are classified as low paid (on the basis of the LFS).

The measure of earnings used throughout is average hourly earnings. However, there are a number of differences between the constructions in the NES and the LFS. These concern the definition of hours worked, the treatment of bonuses and multiple job holders.[3]

How many low paid?

The different data sources give very different estimates of the number of low paid. However, much of the discrepancy can be explained by the differences in sampling and earnings measurement discussed above. The second column of Table 13.1 gives the percentage beneath each of the thresholds in the NES. Around one in forty jobs in the NES pays less than £3 an hour, around one in five pays less than £4.50. The fourth column gives the estimates from the LFS. The differences are striking. The LFS estimates almost three times as many employees receiving less than £3 an hour and almost one and a half times as many employees receiving less than £4.50. Column 5 gives the number of employees that this represents. Around 1.7 million employees earn less than £3 an hour, another 1.5 million between £3 and £3.50, a further 1.7 million between £3.50 and £4 and in total 6.7 million earn less than £4.50 an hour.

The discrepancies between the two sets of estimates are considerable. Over a million people at the £3 cut-off, rising to over two million at the £4.50 cut-off. The biggest contributor to the difference between the estimates from the NES and LFS is the under-representation in the NES of those below the PAYE threshold.[4] Estimates based on adjusting the NES for this under-representation are given in the third column of Table 13.1. These

---

[3] A fuller discussion of the differences in the measurement of hourly earnings in the different datasets is given in Stewart (1998a).

[4] This threshold was £77.79 per week in April 1997.

Table 13.1   What proportion of employees are low paid? A comparison of different thresholds and data sources, April 1997

Hourly earnings threshold	NES (%)	Adjusted NES (%)	LFS (%)	LFS (millions)	Adjusted LFS (%)	BHPS (%)
£3.00	2.7	4.7	7.4	1.68	6.5	6.6
£3.50	6.8	10.1	14.1	3.20	12.3	12.5
£4.00	13.2	17.7	21.4	4.87	19.3	19.6
£4.50	20.1	24.6	29.5	6.72	26.9	26.9

Sources: NES: % of jobs, UK. April 1997. From D. Wilkinson, 'Towards reconciliation of NES and LFS earnings data', *Labour Market Trends*, May 1998. *Adjusted NES*: Adjusted for under-representation of those below the PAYE threshold. From K. Osborne, 'Official estimates of low pay – bridging the gap', paper presented to Labour Market Statistics User Group, March 1998. *LFS*: % and number of employees, UK. Spring 1997. *Adjusted LFS*: Adjusted as described in the text. From D. Wilkinson *op. cit. BHPS*: % of employees, GB. Excluding full-time students. August 1996 to April 1997. Adjusted to April 1997 using Average Earnings Index ('actual' series). Adjusted on a monthly basis. Own calculations from BHPS wave 6 files.

adjustments use LFS estimates of the numbers of jobs with weekly earnings below the PAYE threshold to re-weight upwards those in the NES below this threshold. It is largely a correction for the numbers of part-time employees. This gives numbers much closer to those from the LFS. Roughly half of the original gap is attributable to the NES's under-representation of those below the PAYE threshold. However, there is still a considerable gap remaining. Indeed, even if one restricts attention to full-time employees with weekly earnings above the PAYE threshold, the NES estimates 11.4 per cent earning less than £4.50 an hour compared with 18.6 per cent in the LFS, a difference of more than a million jobs.

Column 6 gives adjusted LFS estimates. These have been calculated by the Office for National Statistics (ONS) to adjust for some of the differences between the two surveys described above. In particular adjustments are made for proxy response, for multiple job holding and for differences in the hours measures.[5] This column reports their 'central' or 'best' estimate of the incidence of low pay. The estimates imply about 1.5 million people earning less than £3 an hour, 2.8 million less than £3.50, 4.4 million less than £4 and around 6.1 million earning less than £4.50 an hour. The final column of Table 13.1 gives the corresponding estimates from the BHPS for comparison. The estimates are very similar to the adjusted LFS figures. However, this similarity should not be over-stressed as it is partly the result of offsetting definitional differences.

[5] 'Towards reconciliation of NES and LFS earnings data', *Labour Market Trends*, May 1998.

Changes over time

To what extent has the incidence of low pay changed over the last thirty years? Neither the LFS nor the BHPS provides earnings data prior to the 1990s and the NES has problems providing an estimate of total incidence as described above. Webb *et al.* (1996) use data from the Family Expenditure Survey (FES) to track the incidence of low pay over the period 1968–94, defining low pay as below two-thirds of the median for all workers in any year. Including all those between 16 and the state retirement age, about 22 per cent of employees were low paid in 1994 under this definition, very similar to the percentage in 1968. In contrast, restricting attention to those aged over 18 results in a rise in the low pay rate over this period. The composition of the low paid has shifted from women to men and from younger to older workers. In 1994 women were about two and a half times as likely to be low paid as men, whereas in 1968 they were more than six times as likely.

The overall proportion who were low paid was fairly constant between 1968 and 1973. It then fell sharply, reaching a low of 16 per cent in 1977. Since then it has risen steadily, initially fairly rapidly. The sharp fall to 1977 was entirely due to the decline in the rate for women, which fell from 48 per cent in 1970 to 29 per cent in 1977. The subsequent rise was driven largely by the rise in the rate for men, although the extra rapid rise in 1977–81 was also due to women partially reversing the earlier fall. Since 1975 the rate of low pay amongst males has roughly doubled, while for women the rate in 1994 is slightly below that in 1975.

The age composition amongst low-paid men has changed markedly. In 1968 male low pay was predominantly amongst young men. More than half of low-paid men were aged 16–17 and over 85 per cent were aged under 25. By 1994 this had fallen sharply so that about half were under 25 and less than 10 per cent aged 16–17. This is largely due to the large decline in the number of 16 and 17-year-olds in employment. Low-pay rates for those over 25 show a much sharper rise than those for younger men. The number of low-paid men aged 25–49 roughly quadrupled over this period. The age composition amongst women has been much more stable, although for them too there has been a decline (but a less sharp one) in the number of low paid 16 and 17-year-olds.

There has been a marked decline in the extent to which low pay is restricted to women and the young. In 1994 one in six of the low paid were male and 25 or older, compared with one in thirty in 1968.

International comparisons

How do low-pay probabilities in Britain compare with those in other (industrialised) countries? International comparisons of the incidence of low pay are potentially useful to give a wider perspective to the figures for Britain, but suffer from serious limitations and must be treated with great caution. A recent OECD report (OECD, 1996) gives incidence figures for fifteen countries on a fairly consistent basis. Attention is restricted to full-time workers to exclude differences across countries in the incidence of part-time employment. The low-pay threshold is taken as two-thirds of median earnings of all full-time workers. Under this definition, around one in five workers are low paid in the United Kingdom, putting it near the top of the table, a lower incidence than the United States and Canada, where about one in four are low paid, but higher than all the other twelve countries considered and much higher than Sweden at the bottom of the league, where only one in twenty are low paid, Finland (one in seventeen) and Belgium (one in fourteen).

Although there are some definitional differences between the countries, it is unlikely that these differences will alter the ranking between the United States and the United Kingdom on the one hand and the United Kingdom and Sweden on the other. It is also important to note that a relative measure of low pay is being used here. When the thresholds are converted to a common currency (using purchasing power parities), there are considerable differences between the thresholds. For example, converted median earnings is much higher in the United States than in Belgium. Some of those classified as low paid in the United States will earn considerably more (in converted terms) than those just above the threshold in Belgium.

Who are the low paid?

Low pay is more prevalent amongst certain groups than others. This section provides evidence on which personal and job characteristics are associated with an increased chance of being in receipt of low pay. The estimates are based on the LFS for 1997.[6]

For each characteristic, both the raw sample proportion who have hourly earnings below a given threshold, and the differences after controlling for various other characteristics that also influence the probability of being low paid are examined. These low-pay probability differences, both raw and adjusted, are calculated for two thresholds, £3.50 and £4.50. These might be viewed as a fairly low cut-off and a relatively high one. 11 per cent of employees in this sample earn below £3.50 per hour and 26 per cent below £4.50.

Table 13.2 gives raw and adjusted differences for both these thresholds for a range of personal and job characteristics. Column 2 gives the percentage of employees with a specified characteristic who earn less than £3.50 an hour. Column 3 gives the difference between this percentage and that for an

---

[6] The sample is restricted to those aged 18 and over, but below retirement age, who are not full-time students.

Table 13.2 Incidence of low pay (percentage)

	Less than £3.50 an hour			Less than £4.50 an hour		
	Probability	Difference	Adjusted	Probability	Difference	Adjusted
Overall	10.9			25.7		
Gender						
male	6.7			17.1		
female	15.8	9.1	3.5*	35.5	18.3	13.4*
Age						
18–20	46.1	37.6	19.8*	76.1	55.1	39.4*
21–25	14.8	6.3	2.9*	37.4	16.4	9.8*
26–50	8.5			21.0		
51 and over	11.1	2.6	2.0*	26.6	5.6	6.8*
Highest qualification achieved						
degree	2.7	−21.0	−5.7*	7.0	−42.0	−17.3*
'A' level	8.2	−15.5	−4.5*	21.1	−28.0	−11.4*
'O' level	11.8	−11.9	−3.0*	29.2	−19.9	−6.7*
other	15.9	−7.8	−2.0*	36.8	−12.2	−3.5*
none	23.7			49.0		
Apprenticeship						
yes	5.8	−6.3	−0.7	15.9	−11.9	−2.4
no	12.1			27.8		
Marital status						
single	14.4			32.6		
married	9.1	−5.3	−1.4*	22.2	−10.4	−5.4*
separate/widow/ divorced	11.8	−2.6	−1.3	27.2	−5.4	−4.2*
Ethnic origin						
white	10.6			25.5		
black	19.6	9.0	6.1*	34.5	9.1	13.6*
Indian/Pakistani/ Bangladeshi	19.8	9.2	6.9*	30.1	4.7	8.0*
Other groups	10.3	−0.3	−1.7	24.5	−1.0	0.8
Hours						
full-time	7.0			18.8		
part-time	25.5	18.5	6.1*	51.0	32.2	14.1*
Contract type						
permanent	10.6			25.1		
fixed/agency	9.9	−0.7	−0.0	27.2	2.1	2.0
seasonal, casual, other	35.7	25.1	4.4*	56.1	31.0	6.6*
Sector						
private	13.3			29.7		
public	4.5	−8.8	−3.9*	14.7	−15.0	−6.9*

	Less than £3.50 an hour			Less than £4.50 an hour		
	Probability	Difference	Adjusted	Probability	Difference	Adjusted
Number of employees at workplace						
1–10	24.8			44.9		
11–24	14.5	−10.3	−4.0*	33.7	−11.2	−4.9*
25–49	10.1	−14.7	−5.2*	26.6	−18.3	−7.9*
50 or more	5.9	−18.9	−6.3*	17.5	−27.4	−10.3*
Year started with current employer						
1977 or before	2.9			8.6		
1978–87	5.5	2.6	1.3	14.3	5.7	4.2*
1988–93	7.8	4.9	2.0*	22.4	13.8	10.3*
1994	12.6	9.7	3.7*	33.6	25.0	18.8*
1995	16.2	13.3	7.1*	33.8	25.2	19.5*
1996	18.7	15.8	5.0*	39.8	31.2	18.2*
1997	25.6	22.7	7.8*	47.0	38.4	21.3*
Industry						
agriculture etc.	17.6	10.7	0.4	51.7	33.4	23.0*
wholesale/retail trade	16.9	10.0	3.2*	43.5	25.2	17.2*
hotels and restaurants	38.2	31.3	5.4*	65.5	47.1	17.3*
health and social work	13.5	6.6	2.4*	25.7	7.4	1.0
other community services	19.3	12.4	3.7*	37.1	18.8	10.1*
other industries	6.9			18.3		
Socio-economic group						
unskilled manual	37.4	31.0	12.0*	71.4	54.8	38.6*
personal services	34.8	28.4	7.2*	67.1	50.5	25.8*
agricultural worker	25.1	18.7	6.2*	57.7	41.1	10.4
semi-skilled	19.9	13.5	6.8*	43.8	27.2	21.1*
skilled/foreman	7.9	1.5	2.3*	22.8	6.3	9.8*
non-manual	6.4			16.6		
Region of workplace						
Central London	3.0	−9.4	−4.6*	5.7	−23.6	−18.1
London and rest of S.E.	8.7	−3.6	−2.5*	20.1	−9.2	−9.5
other regions	12.3			29.2		
Trade union status						
TU present, member	3.1	−14.1	−3.6*	11.6	−23.6	−9.5*
TU present, non-member	7.8	−9.5	−2.7*	23.9	−11.3	−4.9*
TU not present	17.3			35.2		

Source: LFS, Spring 1997.
Note: * indicates strength or statistical significance. Controls for age completed full-time education, nationality, health, job-related training and shift work are also included in the calculations, but are not shown.

appropriate base group. For example, 15.8 per cent of women earn less than £3.50 an hour compared with 6.7 per cent of men, a difference of 9.1 percentage points.

As can be seen from the table, there are many other characteristics that are also associated with an increased or decreased likelihood of being low paid. Thus part of the difference for a particular characteristic may reflect differences in other characteristics. Column 4 gives the probability difference holding constant the other characteristics in the table. Thus for example holding fixed these other characteristics reduces the percentage low-paid gap between women and men from 9.1 per cent to 3.5 per cent. An asterisk indicates statistical significance. Thus, for example, the gender effect is strongly significant.

Columns 5–7 provide information corresponding to that in columns 2–4, with low pay defined as falling below the £4.50 threshold. Using this definition there is a raw low-pay gap between women and men of 18 per cent, which is reduced to 13 per cent when all the other factors are controlled for.

Both individual and job characteristics matter. The table demonstrates that there are strong age effects on the probability of being low paid. Low-pay probabilities are very high for the 18–20 age group, but decline very quickly. The estimated probability is roughly constant between 26 and 50. Up to the age of 26 the probability of being paid below £3.50 an hour declines 3.5 percentage points a year and the probability of being paid below £4.50 an hour declines 5 percentage points a year, controlling for other factors.

Table 13.2 also shows that educational qualifications matter. Those with higher qualifications, particularly those equivalent to 'A' level or above, are much less likely to be low paid, even after controlling for other factors, including the age at which full-time education was completed. Qualifications obtained matter much more than years of education.

Those who are single are more likely to be low paid than those who are, or have been, married. Of course they are also typically younger. Once age and other factors are controlled for, there is not much difference in the probability of their being paid below £3.50, although there is still a gap of about 5 per cent in the probability of being paid below £4.50. This effect is primarily for men. Estimation separately by gender indicates that marital status effects on the probability of being low paid are insignificant for women.

Ethnic origin seems to influence the probability of being low paid more than nationality. Those with health problems that limit the kind of work that they can do are also more prone to low pay. Low pay is much more prevalent amongst those who work part-time, even controlling for all these other factors. Seasonal and casual workers are more likely to be low paid, although a large part of the raw difference is due to differences in other factors. This effect is primarily for women. For women the differences after controlling for other factors are 10 percentage points at the £3.50 threshold and 14 percentage points at the £4.50 threshold. Apart from this category, there is no difference between those on fixed-term contracts and those on permanent ones.

Those in small workplaces are much more likely to be low paid, as are those not covered by trade unions. There are also significant differences across broad industry groups, across socio-economic groups and across regions. There is not much difference across regions in low-pay probabilities outside London and the South East, but those working in the South East and particularly Central London are less likely to be low paid than the rest of the country.

Low-pay probabilities are also much higher for those who have been with their employer for a relatively short time, than for those who have been there longer. A quarter of those who started only in 1997 are paid below £3.50 an hour compared with only 3 per cent of those who have been with the same employer for twenty years or so. In part this importance of time spent with current employer reflects the fact that those in the youngest age group (who have a high probability of low pay) will tend to have been with their current employer for a relatively short time. However, even when other factors (including age) are held constant, it can be seen from Table 13.2 that there is still a marked gap between those who started with their current employer recently and those who have been there longer. Over the first seven years with an employer the probability of being paid below £3.50 an hour declines 1 percentage point a year and the probability of being paid below £4.50 an hour declines 2 percentage points a year, controlling for other factors.

Among socio-economic groups unskilled manual workers have the highest probability of being low paid. They are about six times as likely to be paid below the £3.50 threshold as non-manual workers and about four times as likely to be paid below the £4.50 threshold. The gap shrinks when other factors are controlled for, but is still 12 percentage points for the lower threshold and almost 40 percentage points for the upper one. Personal service workers, agricultural workers and semi-skilled manual workers are also far more likely to be low paid than non-manual workers.

There is even more variation in low-pay probabilities across more narrowly defined occupations. Stewart (1998a) identifies a group of twelve occupations with very high proportions low paid.[7] They are listed in Table 13.3. Just over half of those earning less than £3.50 an hour work in one of these twelve occupations, compared with about 15 per cent of all employees. They are the basement dozen of the pay league.

Column 2 of Table 13.3 gives the proportion of those in each occupation who are paid less than £3.50 an hour. Column 3 gives the difference in this proportion between the given occupation and that in all other occupations (outside this group of twelve occupations). Adjusted differences (for the factors listed in Table 13.2) are given in column 4. Typically the difference is reduced by about one-third. So even after controlling for the

---

[7] They are 3-digit occupations in the standard Occupational Classification. There are about 370 such occupations in total in the classification system.

Table 13.3 Low-paying occupations

Occupation (3-digit code)	% paid < £3.50 an hour	Raw difference	Adjusted difference
Hairdressers, barbers (660)	58.7	52.3	34.6*
Waiters, waitresses (621)	56.2	49.8	33.6*
Bar staff (622)	48.8	42.5	25.5*
Cleaners, domestics (958)	48.7	42.3	30.9*
Sewing machinists, menders, darners, etc. (553)	47.6	41.3	32.2*
Kitchen porters, hands (952)	43.5	37.1	24.7*
Counterhands, catering assistants (953)	40.2	33.9	25.7*
Childcare and related occupations n.e.c. (659)	37.4	31.1	16.7*
Care assistants and attendants (health) (644)	32.0	25.7	16.9*
Retail cash desk and check-out operators (721)	31.4	25.0	14.8*
Sales assistants (720)	30.9	24.5	11.7*
Security guards and related occupations (615)	24.3	17.9	16.6*
Other occupations	6.4		
All occupations	10.9		

Source: LFS, Spring 1997.
Note: * indicates strength of statistical significance.

other characteristics, there is still a core of a dozen occupations in which low pay is hugely over-represented.

Mobility into and out of low pay

There is movement into and out of low pay. Some of the individuals who are low paid in one period are paid above the threshold the following year. Others are no longer employees. Similarly those not working and those above the pay threshold in the previous period may move into low pay. This section looks at these transitions into and out of low pay using data from the BHPS.[8]

Low pay persistence

I look first at transitions within the earnings distribution, restricting attention

---

[8] The analysis in this section uses the first five waves of the BHPS. Earnings are adjusted to April 1997 terms. See Stewart (1998a) for details of sample and variable construction. Transitions are aggregated over the five waves.

to those who are employees at the start and end of any transition considered. Estimated probabilities are presented in Table 13.4. The degree of persistence is strong. The probability of being low paid in year t is much higher if the individual was low paid the year before (i.e. at t-1). For the £3.50 threshold, the probability of being low paid at t for those low paid at t-1 is 57 per cent compared with 3 per cent for those higher paid at t-1. For the £4 threshold the corresponding probabilities are 68 per cent and 5 per cent and for the £4.50 threshold they are 74 per cent and 6 per cent.

Table 13.4 also indicates that persistence is higher for those who have already been low paid for more than one period. The probability of remaining low paid is higher if the individual was low paid at t-1 *and* t-2 than just t-1, for example, 73 per cent against 57 per cent in the case of the £3.50 threshold. Being low paid additionally at t-3 or t-4 results in much smaller changes in the probability of remaining low paid. The general conclusion here is that the longer an individual remains low paid (at least up to two years) the lower the probability of their moving up the distribution and out of low pay.

Table 13.4   Low-pay transition probabilities

	Low-pay threshold		
	£3.50	*£4.00*	*£4.50*
Probability of being low paid at t given:			
low paid at t–1	0.57	0.68	0.74
high paid at t–1	0.03	0.05	0.06
Probability of being low paid at t given low paid at:			
t–1, t–2	0.73	0.79	0.83
t–1, t–2, t–3	0.72	0.84	0.85
t–1, t–2, t–3, t–4	0.77	0.83	0.85
Probability of being low paid at t given low paid at t–j–1 but higher paid at each of the j years in between:			
j=1	0.27	0.28	0.30
j=2	0.10	0.15	0.19
j=3	0.10	0.11	0.12
Probability of being low paid at t given higher paid at:			
t–1, t–2	0.02	0.03	0.04
t–1, t–2, t–3	0.02	0.02	0.03
t–1, t–2, t–3, t–4	0.01	0.02	0.02

Source: BHPS, waves 1–5.
Note: Earnings adjusted to April 1997.

For those above the low-pay threshold, prior experience of low pay increases the probability of returning to it. Having been low paid at t-2 increases the probability of making the transition from higher paid at t-1 back to low pay at t: about 30 per cent compared with about 3 per cent if the person had also been higher paid at t-2. Looking at this the other way round, for those low paid at t-2, moving up to being higher paid at t-1 reduces the probability of being low paid at t: about 30 per cent compared with about 80 per cent for someone who had remained low paid at t-1.

The longer the period in higher pay, the lower the chance of returning to low pay. For someone low paid at t-4, but higher paid from t-3 to t-1, the probability of returning to low pay at t has fallen to about 10 per cent. For each threshold the probability falls with each additional period of higher pay (going backwards in time).

The conclusion from Table 13.4 is that in aggregate terms there is considerable persistence, particularly for those who have already been low paid for more than one period, and that the probability of becoming low paid declines the longer a person is higher paid.

Might this aggregate persistence be driven by the constancy of certain important characteristics? Might it be driven by certain sub-groups? Evidence in Stewart (1998a) and Stewart and Swaffield (1998) suggests not. Stewart and Swaffield (1998) find that being low paid in one period *in itself* increases the probability of being low paid in the next period. They estimate that this accounts for between three-fifths and three-quarters of the raw aggregate probability difference. Stewart (1998a) shows that there is also strong persistence *within* all the sub-groups examined.

The 'low pay – no pay' cycle

As well as there being transitions between low and higher pay, there are also transitions into and out of employment. The next part of the analysis incorporates those not in the earnings distribution. As well as being more likely to remain low paid, the low paid are also more likely to leave employment. Thus restricting attention to those who remain employees overstates the probability of the low paid moving up the earnings distribution and over the threshold.

Using the £3.50 threshold, 48 per cent of those low paid a year ago (t-1) are still low paid now (t) and 17 per cent are no longer employees. Thus only 35 per cent have moved up the distribution into higher pay. The figures corresponding to this for £4 and £4.50 thresholds are 28 per cent and 23 per cent moving into higher pay respectively. Thus restricting attention to those who remain employees (Table 13.4) overstates this probability by between 3 and 8 percentage points.

The greater propensity of the low paid to move out of employment represents part of a cycle of low pay and no pay, which is illustrated in Table 13.5.

Table 13.5   The 'low pay – no pay' cycle: conditional probabilities

	Low-pay threshold		
	£3.50	£4.00	£4.50
Probability of not working at t given:			
low paid at t–1	0.14	0.12	0.11
higher paid at t–1	0.05	0.05	0.04
Probability of being low paid at t given employee at t and:			
not working at t–1	0.33	0.47	0.60
employee at t–1	0.08	0.15	0.22
Probability of being low paid at t given employee at t, not working at t–1 and:			
low paid at t–2	0.42	0.61	0.68
higher paid at t–2	0.14	0.22	0.32

Source: BHPS, waves 1–5.
Note: Earnings adjusted to April 1997. Not working includes both the unemployed and those out of the labour force.

The low paid are more likely to be out of work in the future; those out of work are more likely to be low paid on re-entry; and are even more likely to be so if they had been low paid prior to being out of work.

First, those who are low paid at t-1 are more likely to not be working at t than those higher paid at t-1: 14 per cent against 5 per cent in the case of the £3.50 threshold with similar differences for the other two thresholds.[9] Second, those not working at t-1 who become employees at t are more likely to be low paid than those who were already in employment at t-1: 33 per cent against 8 per cent for the £3.50 threshold for example. Third, amongst re-entrants who were not working at t-1, those who were low paid at t-2 are more likely to be low paid again at t when they are working again than those who were higher paid at t-2: 42 per cent against 14 per cent for the £3.50 threshold and similar differences for the other two thresholds.

There is a 'low pay – no pay' cycle for men and women, for those aged above and below 25, and for those with and without qualifications. The strength of this cycle is almost identical for men and women and for those with and without qualifications. There is, however, an interesting difference in the age split. The effect of not working on the probability of being low paid in the future is greater for older workers. This is because the higher low-pay probability for younger workers is found amongst those who were employees last period, but not amongst those who were out of work. The

[9] The 'not working' category includes both those unemployed and those out of the labour force.

probability of being low paid at t given not working at t-1 is virtually identical for those above and below 25. So the gap between those working and those not working at t-1 is much less for those who are 25 or under and therefore the effect of not working is greater for the older group. Older workers out of work in the previous period look like younger workers in terms of low-pay probabilities. The usual advantage experienced by older workers is restricted to those working last period.

The impact of not working in the previous period on the likelihood of being low paid on re-entry is the result of both the occupations entered and the pay received within these occupations. Those re-entering after a spell of non-employment are more likely to enter a low-paid occupation and also more likely to be low paid within an occupational group. For example, they are more likely to enter one of the 'basement dozen' of low-paid occupations identified in Table 13.3: 29 per cent of those not working at t-1 are in one of these twelve occupations at t compared with 13 per cent of those who were employees at t-1. In addition, the effects of not working at t-1 on the probability of being low paid at t and of low pay at t-2, identified in Table 13.5, are exhibited both amongst those entering these twelve low-paid occupations and amongst those who do not. Also, those in one of the twelve low-paid occupations at t-1 are more likely to be out of work at t than those in other occupations. So part of the cycle is due to a link with this group of low-paid occupations, but the 'low pay – no pay' cycle is exhibited both for those in this group and those outside it.

Another way to consider movements into and out of low pay is to think in terms of permanent versus temporary low pay. The 'permanent' low pay group is defined here as those who were low paid in at least one wave and higher paid in none, i.e. in the waves when they were not low paid they were not an employee at all. The 'temporary' low paid are those who were low paid in at least one wave and also higher paid in at least one wave. Finally, the never-low-paid group are those who were higher paid in at least one wave and low paid in none.[10]

The frequencies of these three categories are given for each of the three thresholds in the top half of Table 13.6. The proportion of those low paid in at least one wave who are permanently low paid under this definition is 29 per cent for the £3.50 threshold, 39 per cent for the £4 threshold, and 45 per cent for the £4.50 threshold. The permanent low-pay proportion is 64 per cent of the cross-sectional low-pay proportion for the £3.50 threshold, 71 per cent for the £4 threshold, and 74 per cent for the £4.50 threshold. A lot of low pay is permanent. Within sub-groups, low pay when it occurs is more likely to be permanent for women than for men, for older workers than for younger ones, and for those without qualifications than for those with.

Do low-paid jobs act as stepping-stones to higher paid jobs? This question

---

[10] Individuals who were not an employee in any of the five waves are excluded.

Table 13.6 Permanent vs temporary low pay (percentage)

	Low-pay threshold		
	£3.50	£4.00	£4.50
permanent low pay	5.7	11.1	16.9
temporary low pay	13.8	17.5	20.8
never low paid	80.4	71.4	62.3
permanent as % of permanent + temporary	29.4	38.8	44.7
permanent as % of cross-section low paid	63.9	71.1	74.3

Source: BHPS, waves 1–5.
Note: Earnings adjusted to April 1997.
Permanent low pay = low pay in at least one wave, higher in none.
Temporary low pay = low pay in at least one wave, higher in at least one.
Never low paid = higher paid in at least one wave, low paid in none.

is addressed here by looking at those who are not in work at t-2, but are at t. Do those who enter a low paid job at t-1 have a better chance of being paid above the threshold at t than those who remain not employed at t-1 and enter at t? The evidence presented in Table 13.7 indicates that they do not. For all three thresholds those who have a low-paid job at t-1 have a lower probability of being paid above the threshold at t than those not employed at t-1. This finding is also repeated within the main sub-groups. Low-paid jobs are more likely to act as blind alleys than as stepping-stones to positions higher up the pay distribution.

Table 13.7 Low paid jobs as stepping-stones? The probability of being higher paid at t, for those who are employees at t, but not at t–2, by status at t–1 (percentage)

	Low pay threshold		
Status at t–1	£3.50	£4.00	£4.50
low paid	41.9	30.5	22.9
higher paid	87.7	84.9	87.8
not employee	65.5	50.0	38.7

Source: BHPS, waves 1–5.
Note: Earnings adjusted to April 1997.

Low pay and poverty

Many of the low paid live in households with other higher paid workers and hence are not in poverty. Many of those in poor households are not in paid employment and hence have no earnings. Low pay and poverty are very different concepts. It is important to consider the extent of overlap between the two. In addition, this needs to be considered in a dynamic context as well as a purely static one.

Stewart (1998b) uses data from the BHPS to examine this issue. The low-pay thresholds are the same as in the previous section. The poverty thresholds in needs-adjusted, real household net income are (i) half of the wave 1 sample average income, and (ii) the poorest fifth in each wave and (iii) income below £160 a week.[11] The first and third of these is fixed (in real terms) across waves, the second varies across waves. For an individual who is married, with a non-working spouse and no children, the first poverty threshold corresponds roughly to forty hours' work at the first low-pay threshold, the second, forty hours' work at the second low-pay threshold, and similarly with the third. However, for other groups the translation is very different.

Table 13.8 The overlap between low pay and poverty

	Poverty threshold		
	(1)	*(2)*	*(3)*
Per cent of low paid who are in poor households:			
LP threshold = £3.50	14.5	18.2	25.5
£4.00	12.3	15.7	22.5
£4.50	10.5	13.7	19.8
Per cent of higher paid who are in poor households:			
LP threshold = £3.50	1.9	2.8	4.6
£4.00	1.4	2.1	3.7
£4.50	0.9	1.5	2.8
Per cent of pre-retirement adults in poor households who are employees:			
	19.0	21.0	25.5
Per cent of employees in poor households who are low paid:			
LP threshold = £3.50	42.7	38.5	34.6
£4.00	61.2	56.0	51.5
£4.50	76.4	71.6	66.4

Source: BHPS, waves 1–4.
Note: Earnings adjusted to April 1997. Poverty thresholds (in April 1997 terms).
(1) £133.08 a week in all 4 waves: half wave 1 mean.
(2) £139.70 a week in wave 1 to 147.14 a week in wave 4: poorest fifth in each wave.
(3) £160 a week in all 4 waves.

[11] Calculated across full samples, including those not employed and the retired.

The cross-sectional overlap between low pay and poverty is illustrated in Table 13.8. The overlap is not all that large. The first panel shows the percentage of the low paid who are in poor households. One in seven of those paid below the low-pay threshold of £3.50 an hour are in households with equivalent net income below the first poverty threshold, rising to about a quarter for the highest of the three poverty thresholds. Of course these figures (and those for the other thresholds) are all much higher than the corresponding figures for those paid above the threshold – between five and ten times as great in all cases.[12] However, it is still the case that the majority of those who are low paid are not in poor households.

Typically, poor households do not contain earners. The third panel of Table 13.8 indicates that between three-quarters and four-fifths of pre-retirement adults in poor households are not employees. Looking at all those in poor households relatively few are low paid, because relatively few are in employment. If we restrict attention to those in work, the association is much closer. A substantial number of the employees in poor households are low paid, particularly for the higher two low-pay thresholds. For example, over three-quarters of employees in households with income below the first poverty threshold earn below £4.50 an hour.

While the overlap between low pay and poverty for the full sample is not very great, it has increased considerably in the last twenty years or so. The low paid in the 1990s are much more likely to be in poor households than in the 1970s. Webb *et al.* (1996), using FES data and slightly different definitions of the poverty and low-pay thresholds to those used here, find that in the 1970s and early 1980s only around 3 per cent to 4 per cent of the low paid were in poor households, compared with 13 per cent in the early 1990s. The poor in the 1990s are more likely to be working than the poor in the 1970s. This rise in the number of working poor over this period is all the more remarkable because it has occurred despite another of the most important trends of the period: the fall in the proportion of families which have at least one worker.

Some of the reasons for the relatively low overlap are obvious and were highlighted by the Royal Commission on the Distribution of Income and Wealth about two decades ago.[13] On the one hand, as pointed out above, the majority of poor families do not contain anyone in employment, and on the other hand, many of those who are low paid have other earners in the family and/or do not have children to support. Thus family type is important to the association between low pay and poverty. This is shown in Table 13.9, where (for the £4.50 low pay threshold) the overlap is shown by gender of the individual and family type.

[12] In contrast they are much lower than the corresponding figures for those who are not working (includes both unemployed and out of the labour force): 31.8 per cent, 38 per cent and 45.9 per cent.

[13] See Royal Commission on the Distribution of Income and Wealth (1978).

Table 13.9 Family type and the overlap between low pay and poverty (low pay threshold=£4.50)

	Poverty threshold		
	(1)	(2)	(3)
Per cent of low paid who are in poor households			
Male:			
couple, with children	25.7	33.7	49.1
couple, no children	3.6	5.6	8.7
single, no children	4.2	5.4	9.2
Female:			
couple, with children	9.7	13.3	19.8
couple, no children	3.7	4.2	6.9
single, with children	32.7	39.5	47.9
single, no children	9.0	13.0	20.4
Per cent of employees in poor households who are low paid			
Male:			
couple, with children	64.4	55.6	46.2
couple, no children	79.8	59.6	50.5
single, no children	58.5	59.3	63.5
Female:			
couple, with children	81.4	81.2	80.0
couple, no children	63.0	57.2	55.9
single, with children	91.0	85.2	82.7
single, no children	83.8	86.2	88.0

Source: BHPS, waves 1–4.
Note: Earnings adjusted to April 1997. Poverty thresholds, see notes on Table 13.8.

For married men with children the overlap is considerably larger: over a quarter of those below the £4.50 low-pay threshold are below the first poverty threshold and nearly a half are below the third poverty threshold. The figures are around six times as great as those for men without children (whether they are part of a couple or single).

In the case of couples with children the probability of the household being poor is much lower where it is the woman who is low paid than where it is the man – because for women, the probability of the spouse working and their earnings if they do are both likely to be higher. However, for couples without children the probabilities are very similar for men and women. Here it seems that the higher earnings of their spouses are offset by the fact that women in this category work fewer hours than the average. (Nearly half the women in this group work part-time and on average the women work seventeen fewer hours a week than men.)

Single women with children are also more likely to be in poor households, with similar probabilities to men in couples with children: higher for two thresholds and lower for the third. For low-paid singles without children, women are more likely to be in poor households than men, partly because on average they work fewer hours: about nine fewer per week, with about a quarter working part-time.

An important consideration when looking at the overlap between low pay and poverty is transitory variation – both in equivalent net income and in hourly pay rates, but particularly in the latter. As illustrated in the previous section, there are significant differences between those who can be classified as 'permanent' low paid and those who are 'temporary' low paid. The importance of this for the overlap between low pay and poverty is reinforced by the cycle of low pay and no pay, also discussed in the previous section.

To address this issue, 'permanent', 'temporary' and never low paid are defined as in the previous section; those who did not have a job at any of the four waves being analysed are excluded; and the probability of being poor (in household terms) in at least one of the four waves is examined. This seems the appropriate poverty focus here from a welfare perspective, due to the borrowing constraints faced by poor households. The percentages for each of the three low-pay thresholds and each of the three poverty thresholds are given in Table 13.10.

Table 13.10 Permanent and temporary low pay and the overlap with poverty (percentage)

	Poverty threshold		
	(1)	(2)	(3)
LP threshold = £3.50			
'permanent' low paid	49.4	52.5	63.1
'temporary' low paid	29.4	34.7	43.4
never low paid	10.4	12.2	16.0
LP threshold = £4.00			
'permanent' low paid	42.1	46.5	58.6
'temporary' low paid	25.3	29.9	36.6
never low paid	8.8	10.3	13.6
LP threshold = £4.50			
'permanent' low paid	41.7	45.6	56.1
'temporary' low paid	18.1	21.5	29.3
never low paid	7.2	8.7	11.2

Source: BHPS, waves 1–4.
Note: Earnings adjusted to April 1997. Poverty thresholds, see notes on Table 13.8.

246   Mark B. Stewart

Around half of those who were 'permanent' low paid using the £3.50 threshold are in a poor household for at least part of the period, if the lowest poverty threshold is used. In contrast, only one in ten of those who were never low paid using the £3.50 threshold are in poverty in any of the waves if the lowest threshold is used, around one in six if the highest threshold is used. The position for those who were 'temporary' low paid is roughly halfway between the 'permanent' and the never low paid. Clearly from this more longitudinal (although still relatively short-run) perspective, the overlap between low pay and poverty is considerably greater than when viewed in a single snapshot.

This shows the importance of taking a non-static view. It is also informative to look at the degree of association between movements into and out of

Table 13.11 Movements into and out of low pay and poverty (%)

	Poverty threshold		
	(1)	(2)	(3)
LP threshold = £3.50			
Probability of a move into poverty given:			
move from higher to low pay	11.4	13.6	13.5
remain higher paid	1.0	1.2	1.7
Probability of a move out of poverty given:			
move from low to higher pay	85.4	74.4	68.4
remain low paid	60.1	63.4	49.9
LP threshold = £4.00			
Probability of a move into poverty given:			
move from higher to low pay	11.2	11.2	11.5
remain higher paid	0.6	0.8	1.3
Probability of a move out of poverty given:			
move from low to higher pay	88.8	74.2	64.7
remain low paid	61.1	57.8	48.8
LP threshold = £4.50			
Probability of a move into poverty given:			
move from higher to low pay	8.2	8.5	9.3
remain higher paid	0.3	0.5	1.0
Probability of a move out of poverty given:			
move from low to higher pay	87.1	73.2	66.1
remain low paid	63.9	58.6	49.8

Source: BHPS, waves 1–4.
Note: Earnings adjusted to April 1997. Poverty thresholds, see notes on Table 13.8.

poverty and movements into and out of low pay. Statistics on the probability of movements into and out of household poverty are given in Table 13.11. Movements between t-1 and t are considered using data aggregated across waves. First, consider the association between movements into low pay and movements into poverty. In this case the group in focus is those who were paid above the low pay threshold and were not in poor households at t-1. For those who became low paid at t, 11.4 per cent move into poverty, compared with only 1 per cent amongst those who do not become low paid (first poverty threshold and £3.50 low-pay threshold). Thus becoming low paid has a large (relative) impact on the probability of the household becoming poor. The other thresholds show similar differences between the two groups.

Next consider the association between movements out of low pay and movements out of poverty. Now the group in focus is those who were both low paid and in a poor household at t-1. For those who move out of low pay at t, 85.4 per cent move out of poverty, compared with 60.1 per cent amongst those who remain low paid. While this indicates that leaving low pay is not the main determinant of leaving poverty, it is also clear that it is a very important influence.

Conclusions

This chapter has attempted to piece together a picture of low pay in Britain. The main findings are as follows. About 1.5 million people have average hourly earnings of less than £3, 2.8 million less than £3.50, 4.4 million less than £4 and around 6.1 million earn less than £4.50 an hour. Youth, women, those with low educational qualifications, and those in small, non-union workplaces are all more likely to be low paid. The chapter identifies a group of twelve occupations in which the probability of being low paid is extremely high, the 'basement dozen' of the pay league. Just over half of those earning less than £3.50 per hour work in one of these twelve occupations, compared with about 15 per cent of all employees.

There is considerable persistence in low pay, in aggregate terms, particularly for those who have already been low paid for more than one period. In addition, the probability of becoming low paid declines the longer a person is higher paid. There is also strong evidence of a cycle of low pay and no pay. The low paid are more likely to be out of work in the future; those out of work are more likely to be low paid on re-entry; and are even more likely to be so if they had been low paid prior to being out of work. The hypothesis that low-paid jobs act as stepping-stones to higher paid jobs is not supported by the evidence here. Low-paid jobs are more likely to act as blind alleys than as stepping-stones to positions higher up the pay distribution.

The cross-sectional overlap between low pay and household poverty is not large, although it has grown considerably over the last twenty years. However, around half of those classified as 'permanent' low paid are in household poverty. From this perspective, the overlap between low pay and poverty is considerably greater than when viewed in a snapshot context. Movements into and out of low pay exert an important influence on movements into and out of poverty.

References

LPC (1998), 'The National Minimum Wage', Cm. 3976, HMSO, London.

OECD (1996), 'Earnings inequality, low-paid employment and earnings mobility', *Employment Outlook*, Chapter 3, Paris.

Royal Commission on the Distribution of Income and Wealth (1978), 'Lower Incomes', Report No. 6, Cmnd. 7175, HMSO, London.

Stewart, M. (1998a), 'Low Pay in Britain: Piecing Together the Picture', mimeo, University of Warwick.

Stewart, M. (1998b), 'The Dynamics of the Relationship Between Low Pay and Poverty in Britain', mimeo, University of Warwick.

Stewart, M. and Swaffield, J. (1998), 'Low pay dynamics and transition probabilities', *Economica*, forthcoming.

Webb, S., Kemp, M. and Millar, J. (1996), 'The changing face of low pay in Britain', *Policy Studies*, 17, 255–71.

The cost of job loss

Keypoints

- In an average year 1.8 million workers in Britain will suffer involuntary job loss.

- On average a worker re-entering work after involuntary job loss will earn 9 per cent less than in the previous job.

- When compared with an employee in continuous work the average wage loss of someone re-entering the workforce is 14 per cent.

- The cost of job loss is most severe among more experienced workers and those with longer tenure.

- Tenure is the most important single predictor of job loss. There is an 11.7 per cent chance of a worker with tenure less than one year losing a job, this drops to just 4 per cent after five years.

- The longer a person is unemployed the higher the cost of displacement, displaced workers out of work for more than six months experience average wage losses that are twice those of people out of work for less than one month.

Industrial restructuring, changes in technology, industrial location and recession are all associated with worker displacement: the involuntary separation from a job. Workers also leave jobs for personal reasons, but because these are considered voluntary actions and are not always associated with economic hardship, there is less concern over the consequences of this type of movement. The media and, perhaps because of this, the general public in Britain are also preoccupied with the idea of declining job security. While job security is difficult to quantify, public concern seems to arise from a belief that long-term employment is now less likely (see Chapter 7). Greater unease may also be generated by a belief that, if they are unlucky enough to lose their job, any replacement job is likely to be of lower quality, paying lower wages and being less secure.

This chapter focuses on the earnings loss associated with job displacement in Britain. How much lower are wages in a replacement job than in the one lost? Kletzer (1998) provides a useful summary of over ten years of research into the issue in North America. As yet the evidence from Britain is sparse. Gregory and Jukes (1997) supply the first evidence of the wage falls between jobs either side of a spell of unemployment for male benefit claimants. They find that, on average, earnings for men who have been unemployed fall by around 10 per cent compared with men who remain in jobs. We draw on data from the British Household Panel Survey (BHPS) over the period 1991–6 to broaden the scope of inquiry into job displacement by including all unemployment spells (claimant or otherwise) and spells of economic inactivity (allowing for discouraged job seekers), together with information for women and part-time workers. We focus particularly on those suffering involuntary displacement. We highlight the groups that are most likely to experience displacement, those that are most likely to get back into work and the earnings changes associated with re-entry into work.

Involuntary displacement

Involuntary displacement, as discussed here, covers all workers who report that they were dismissed, made redundant or had a temporary contract terminated. In some cases displacement results in redundancy pay.

Employment Protection Legislation, as covered by the Statutory Redundancies Payments Scheme (1965), has operated almost unchanged since its inception. This covers mandatory severance pay, advance notice, legal requirements and procedures for dismissal. The one substantial change has been to the qualifying period for general rights, that is, the period a person must work before they are able to claim redundancy payments and challenge unfair dismissal. This was extended from six months to one year in 1979, and in 1985 to two years for full-time jobs and five years for part-time jobs. From 1995 a European Union anti-discrimination ruling was brought in which equalised the qualification period at two years' tenure for all jobs. The new government has indicated an intention to shorten this to one year. Workers on fixed-term contracts of two years or more may also be excluded from redundancy rights if they agree in writing to renounce their rights to any claim. Such a clause is now common to many fixed-term contract agreements.

Estimation of the cost of job loss utilises information contained within the labour market histories embedded in the BHPS. Our basic strategy is to compare earnings data for current and previous jobs for those with an intervening spell of worklessness with those in continuous employment. Thus we report the earnings changes of three groups: those reporting no change in employer (stayers), those who lost their job either through redundancy, dismissal or the termination of a temporary contract (displaced), and those who left their last job for promotion, a new job, family, health reasons or retirement (leavers). The sum of the displacement and leaver rates gives the total separation rate.

Why a cost to job loss?

Why might job displacement involve reductions in wages? If wages rise with the experience gained within any occupation or skill group, then the job currently held is likely to pay more than any new job gained after displacement. The longer a worker has been in the job, the greater this penalty is likely to be if some or all of the returns to accumulated on-the-job experience are lost in the next job. So the costs of job loss may be higher amongst older and more experienced workers or wherever job loss is a relatively rare event.

This is not the only reason why we might find wage costs to displacement. Those in work seek to secure good job matches through promotion or by moving firms. These matches may be provided by good firms that pay high wages and generally promote good working conditions, or just by positions that suit an individual's talents. If workers with good jobs are unlucky enough to lose their jobs, they are unlikely to get as high-quality matches on re-entry to work. For instance it has long been established that certain industries offer pay premia and that unionised firms generally pay higher wages. Displacement from these industries, and re-employment in the non-union sector, could mean a significant drop in wages.

In addition to earnings losses, new jobs are likely to be less stable. Employer or employee may decide the match is not a good one, and the kind of rules described above mean that firms tend to target recent recruits when shedding labour. With variable or uncertain labour needs, firms often enshrine this practice through the use of temporary contracts. The share of full-time work in entry jobs (those taken by people saying they were out of work previously) is much lower than in the workforce as a whole. Full-time permanent jobs make up just over 42 per cent of entry jobs, down from around 47 per cent in the mid-1980s. Temporary jobs account for almost a fifth of entry jobs, but just 6 per cent of all jobs.

Incidence of displacement

Who is at risk from displacement? Around one in five employees, some 5 million workers, will separate from their jobs during one year (Table 14.1). At

Table 14.1 Annual separation and displacement rates

Year	Separation rate	Displacement rate
90/1	24.7	7.8
91/2	19.8	6.9
92/3	20.5	7.2
93/4	21.9	6.4
94/5	20.6	5.7
95/6	26.8	5.1
Average	22.4	6.5

Source: BHPS.

the beginning of the sample period the economy had just entered recession. Recovery began in 1992. Movements in the separation and displacement rates over time are consistent with the change in the economic cycle: more displacements in bad times, more separations in good times, because of the dominance of job quits. On average, some 6.5 per cent of employees (or 1.8 million people) will lose their jobs as the result of displacement.

The most important single predictor of displacement is job tenure. There is an 11.7 per cent chance that a worker in a job for less than twelve months will lose a job compared with a less than 4 per cent chance of displacement for a worker in a job for five years or more (Table 14.2). Men are almost twice as likely to be displaced as women are, 8.4 per cent compared to 4.5 per cent. The displacement rate for younger workers, under the age of 25, is 11.5 per cent, twice that of other age groups.

There is some evidence that education affects displacement. The lower the level of educational attainment, the higher the displacement rate. However, the difference between the highest and lowest education groups, at around 2 percentage points, is not large when compared with other variables. The industrial sector with the highest displacement rate is construction, at 13.4 per cent. The lowest is the public services at around 2 per cent. There is little variation across other sectors. Most of those displaced get back into the labour market in under six months (about two-thirds), but around 5 per cent take longer than a year to get back and a further 10 per cent were still out of work at the end of the time window in the data.

How much do displaced workers lose?

How much do displaced workers lose? Table 14.3 summarises the mean percentage difference in earnings between the old and new job for displaced workers. As a comparison, we show the annual earnings changes recorded for those workers who remain in the same job over the year.

Table 14.2   Separation and displacement rates by worker and firm characteristics

	Separation rate	Displacement rate
Gender		
female	19.2	4.5
male	23.4	8.4
Age		
youths <25	36.6	11.4
prime 25–49	19.5	5.6
mature 50+	17.0	5.2
Marital status		
single	26.9	8.2
married	18.0	5.4
Qualifications		
none	21.7	7.0
'O' level & equivalent	25.3	7.8
intermediate & 'A' level	29.4	6.4
degree or equivalent	29.6	5.2
Job tenure		
0–1 year	33.2	11.7
1–2 years	23.7	6.0
2–5 years	17.7	4.5
5–10 years	14.1	4.0
10+ years	13.4	3.6
Industry		
agriculture/energy/water/extraction	19.8	5.4
manufacturing	22.1	6.4
construction	32.4	13.4
distribution	24.8	4.5
transport/communications	19.6	4.5
banking	29.7	5.2
public services	29.3	2.0
private services	16.9	4.4

Source: BHPS.

Weekly wages of the average displaced worker are around 9 per cent lower in the new job than in the job lost. If the worker moves from one full-time job to another the penalty is around 2 per cent.[1] Weekly earnings of those who remain with their employer rise by around 5 per cent over the year. So displaced workers not only experience wage losses relative to their previous job but they also forgo general increases in wage levels. The total pay penalty is therefore 14 per cent in weekly earnings, with a 9 per cent overall pay penalty for those working full-time both before and after displacement.

Table 14.3　Real weekly pay change by displacement status

	Displaced	Stayers	Difference
full-time to full-time	−2.1%	7.0%	−9.1%
part-time to part-time	−5.6%	2.9%	−8.5%
full-time to part-time	−60.1%	−53.6%	−6.5%
All	−8.6%	5.6%	−14.2%

Source: BHPS.

There is considerable variation around these averages. Comparison of weekly earnings changes of displaced workers and stayers, by individual characteristics, are given in Table 14.4. Displaced women experience around twice the wage losses of men. Older workers and the least qualified also face higher monthly pay cuts than the average. The wage loss for those over 50 is around 23 per cent. The displaced with more than five years' job tenure suffer losses of around 30 per cent. Displacement tends to be rarer as jobs lengthen but the cost of losing these jobs rises greatly. Even those out of work for very short periods suffer wage losses: including the forgone wage growth the loss is around 12 per cent. Displaced workers out of work for more than six months experience average wage losses that are twice those of people out of work for less than one month.

[1] These numbers are similar to Gregory and Jukes' (1997) findings for unemployed men. On average, there is only a very small hourly wage penalty to being displaced, but this is mainly a selection effect, as the monthly wage gap is much smaller for those where hourly wages are defined.

Table 14.4 Average real weekly percentage pay change by worker characteristics

	Displaced	*Stayers*	*Difference*
Total	−8.6	5.6	−14.2
Gender			
female	−16.1	6.3	−22.4
male	−6.5	4.7	−11.2
Age			
youths <25	1.3	14.1	−12.8
prime 25–49	−12.9	5.4	−18.3
mature 50+	−22.7	1.4	−24.1
Marital status			
single	−1.7	8.2	−9.9
married	−19.8	4.0	−23.8
Qualifications			
'O' level & below	−14.0	5.1	−19.1
intermediate	−10.3	5.7	−15.8
degree/further education	6.7	5.8	0.9
Tenure in previous job			
0–1 year	−6.7	18.2	−24.9
1–2 years	−5.3	7.6	−12.9
2–5 years	−14.4	6.2	−20.6
5+ years	−30.0	2.8	−32.8
Length of time out			
0–1 month	−6.6	−	−
1–3 months	−8.3	−	−
3–6 months	−13.3	−	−
6+ months	−13.6	−	−

Source: BHPS.

Are the costs of job loss increasing?

We do not have data on the cost of job displacement over a long period of time, but we can say something about the changing nature of wages likely to be on offer to those out of work. Table 14.5 gives the typical wages associated with entry jobs. These are wages earned by re-entrants into the

Table 14.5   The changing pattern of real wages in entry jobs

	Median (£)	Entry wage in overall distribution (%)
Weekly wages		
GHS		
1980	104.20	19.1
1984	107.30	19.3
1988	106.70	17.6
1990	107.10	15.7
LFS		
1993	99.80	17.0
1995	93.90	15.3
1997	99.20	16.0
Hourly wages		
GHS		
1980	3.63	22.3
1984	3.73	20.8
1988	3.98	19.2
1990	3.98	16.6
LFS		
1993	4.35	23.2
1995	4.17	20.7
1997	4.02	19.3

Sources: LFS 1993–7, GHS 1980–90. GHS data are three-year averages centred on year shown. LFS data are based on the annual panel, GHS data on a retrospective question on economic status one year ago. Figures in April 1998 pounds.

labour market irrespective of how they left their last job and therefore include jobs taken by those who quit into non-employment as well as those laid off. The table gives wages for workers in the middle of the pay distribution (the median). Entry jobs pay wages that are considerably below the national average. The typical entry job pays just over £100 a week compared with around £260, the average for all jobs. 55 per cent of entry jobs pay below half typical earnings. In part, this is because there are relatively more part-time jobs in the stock of entry jobs than in the workforce as a whole. However, as the bottom half of Table 14.5 shows, there is still a substantial wage gap in hourly wages. The typical job now pays around £6.70 an hour. The typical entry job only pays around £4 an hour. Moreover, the wage gap has risen over time. In the 1980s, according to the General Household Survey, entry wages fell from being equivalent to those received by a worker in the bottom 19 per cent of the aggregate weekly pay distribution to the bottom 16 per cent. More recently, the Labour Force Survey (LFS) suggests a more rapid decline. Some of the sluggish weekly wage growth in entry jobs reflects the growing importance of part-time jobs, but real hourly wages also struggled to rise in the 1980s, falling sharply when compared to the whole wage distribution. LFS data show that hourly entry wages have been declining in the 1990s both in absolute terms and relative to other jobs. This does seem therefore to indicate a shift in the nature of jobs on offer to the jobless toward more part-time and more low-paid work and may help explain why there is a cost to job loss that is greater for older more experienced workers. New jobs on offer are increasingly less like the jobs from which workers are displaced.

Conclusions

Every year around 1.8 million workers in Britain will lose their jobs as a result of layoff, plant closure or the end of their contract. Job loss is most likely to occur within the first year of any job. As already noted in Chapters 12 and 13, employees with job tenure under one year are already amongst the lowest paid. Yet displaced workers will enter jobs that pay weekly wages on average around 10 percentage points less than those they left behind. Compared with those who remain continuously in the same post, the wage gap is around 15 per cent. However, even larger costs are experienced by older, experienced displaced workers with longer seniority, and the less educated. We have already observed falling job tenure amongst older workers in Chapter 7. This is a group for whom voluntary job changes are rare, so the fall in job tenure is most likely to be caused by a greater incidence of displacement amongst this age group. The result is the prospect of a large wage cut for those seeking new work. This rather bleak picture for older, less educated workers may lie behind the dramatic increases in the incidence of economic inactivity amongst this group (see Chapters 3 and 4).

References

Gregory, M. and Jukes, R. (1997), 'The Effects of Unemployment on Subsequent Earnings: A Study of British Men, 1984–94', Working Paper, DfEE, London.
Kletzer, L. (1998), 'Job displacement', *Journal of Economic Perspectives*, Winter, 115–36.
OECD (1997), 'Making Work Pay', *Employment Outlook*, Chapter 2, 25–58, Paris.

Further reading

Farber, H. (1993), 'The Incidence and Cost of Job Loss: 1982–9', Brookings Papers on Economic Activity: Microeconomics, 73–132.

Gregg, P. and Wadsworth, J. (1996), 'Mind the Gap: The Changing Distribution of Entry Wages in Great Britain', Discussion Paper No. 303, Centre for Economic Performance, LSE, London.

15 Simon Burgess and Carol Propper

Poverty in Britain

Keypoints

- Poverty is a major economic and political issue in Britain in the late 1990s. It makes front-page news. The latest official figures show that in 1995/6 about one in five Britons were living in poverty (details and definitions are given below), compared with less than one in ten in 1979.

- All individuals shared economic growth in the 1960s and 1970s, but growth in the 1980s was concentrated in the top half of the income distribution so that poverty increased. In the 1990s poverty has stabilised, with economic growth once again also benefiting the poorest.

- Poverty has risen most amongst households with children. In 1979, one in twelve children lived in households that were poor. By 1995/6 one in three children were living in poor households. Children are replacing pensioners amongst the poorest members of our society.

- Many people will experience some poverty in their lives, but only a minority of people are permanently poor.

- Such income mobility does not mean that poverty should not be a major social concern. While poverty is a transient phenomenon for most of the population, for most of the poor, poverty is a repetitive feature of their lives.

As we shall show, poverty is a complex issue to understand, involving an analysis of the interactions between the labour market, household formation and dissolution, and the welfare state. Britain has seen huge changes in all of these spheres since the mid-1970s. The country as a whole has become much richer. National income has risen by 50 per cent since 1975. On the other hand, the unemployment rate more than trebled between 1975 and 1985, before falling back (see Chapter 1 for more detail). Even today it remains at twice the early 1970s level. The dispersion of earnings has increased rapidly in Britain as in the United States, with those on the lowest earnings faring the worst (see Chapter 11). Marriage rates have fallen and divorce rates have increased. The proportion of households containing just one adult with children has risen substantially. The ethos of the welfare state has been challenged and the real value of benefits eroded.

In this chapter we review evidence of what has happened to poverty amidst all this change. We look at evidence produced from cross-section surveys, giving 'snapshot' pictures of poverty, and more recent evidence from longitudinal surveys that document individuals' experiences of poverty over time. Finally, we argue that poverty is a complex issue to analyse and that some simple views do not fit the facts. To make progress, therefore, we need a framework for analysing poverty, and so we conclude this review by briefly setting out such a framework that we have proposed and implemented elsewhere (Burgess and Propper, 1998).

Defining poverty[1]

The United Kingdom has no official poverty line. There is considerable debate about the appropriate definition of poverty (see, for example, Goodman, Johnson and Webb, 1997: Chapter 1), but one of the most commonly used measures is the number of people whose income is less than half the average income. This is a *relative* measure of poverty, rather than a measure against a *constant* benchmark: it depends on the prosperity of society as a whole, not the income needed to buy a fixed bundle of goods. In the United Kingdom, this measure is defined in two ways: before housing costs and after housing costs. Deducting housing costs – rents, mortgage payments etc. – from income gives a flavour of the relative *disposable* income available to a household. The main advantage is that it allows for correction of one of the most important regional differences in living costs in the United Kingdom. Whether incomes are measured before or after housing costs have been paid makes a considerable difference to the measured level of the number who are poor, though it has less impact on the trends over time. Income measured after housing costs (AHC) is more unequally distributed than income measured before housing costs (BHC) and the number who are recorded as poor AHC is correspondingly higher. In this review we use both the BHC and AHC definitions. We also report results based on the poorest quarter of the population as an alternative definition of poverty. All the measures of household income that we report are adjusted for differences in

---

[1] Much of the evidence reviewed in this section comes from Goodman, Johnson and Webb (1997).

household composition, they use income *equivalised* for family size. All of
these measures assume equal sharing of resources within households.

Poverty rates in Britain, 1961–95

Figure 15.1 (lower line) shows the proportion of the population with equivalised household income below half the average equivalised household
income (BHC) from 1961 to 1994/5. The figure shows that the poor num-
bered about 10 per cent of the population during the 1960s, then fell during
the early 1970s to a low of 6 per cent in 1977. The poverty rate then rose
sharply during the last half of the 1980s to over 20 per cent in the early
1990s, since when it has fallen back to 18 per cent in 1994/5. The after housing cost measure, the upper line, shows a greater rise from 7 per cent to 24
per cent of the population who had below half average income between 1977
and 1991/2, and a fall back to 23 per cent in 1994/5.

Figure 15.1   Poverty rates

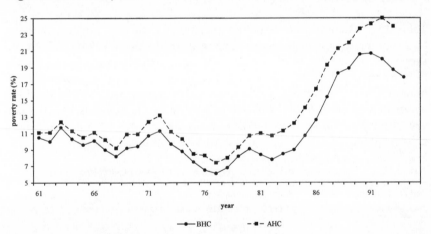

Source: Goodman and Webb (1994).

The change from the gradual decline in poverty up to the early 1980s to
the rapid rise since is very dramatic. While the United States also experienced
an end to the long decline in poverty at the end of the 1970s, the subsequent
rise was nothing like as dramatic: poverty rose from around 11 per cent
through the 1970s to 15 per cent in the early 1980s and rose again in the
early 1990s (see Danziger and Gottschalk, 1995). However, poverty in the
United States is measured against a fixed real value: the real income required
to buy the basket of goods deemed to be necessary for subsistence living. The

United Kingdom numbers quoted above measure the number who are poor against a standard which varies as the prosperity of the population changes. If we take a fixed standard in the United Kingdom (half the average (equivalised) incomes in 1979, adjusted for inflation) then we can define the numbers who are poor when compared with a constant benchmark as the number of individuals whose (equivalised) income fell below this level. Using this measure, absolute poverty fell during the 1960s and 1970s. In 1961, just under 24 per cent of the population were poor in this sense, falling to 8 per cent in 1979. However, between 1979 and 1991 the numbers below this *fixed* standard fell only slightly on a BHC basis (to 7 per cent), despite national income rising by 23 per cent over those twelve years. Since 1991 the number in absolute poverty has fallen to 5 per cent on a BHC basis.[2]

In summary, in the 1960s and 1970s, all individuals shared economic growth, but growth in the 1980s was concentrated in the top half of the distribution. Since the early 1990s it appears that economic growth is once again also benefiting the poorest.

Poverty by demographic (household) group

Table 15.1 examines the family composition of the poor, defined here as those in the lowest fifth of the income distribution in 1994/5. The table shows the percentage of individuals who are poor, according to this definition, by their family type. It shows that 54 per cent of the poorest live in households in which there are children (either couples with children or lone parents), 21.5 per cent of the poor live in pensioner households and 24.6 per cent in non-pensioner households with no children. In 1995/6 one in four children were amongst the poorest 20 per cent of individuals.

Table 15.1   Composition of the bottom quintile by family type, 1994/5

Proportion of the poor who are:	Single	Single parent	Couple no children	Couple with children	Single pensioners	Pensioner couple
	15.4	16.7	9.2	37.2	9.9	11.6

Source: Hills (1998), Figure 7.
Note: Percentage of individuals.

The composition of the poor population has also changed considerably over time. Table 15.2 shows the composition of the bottom quintile of household income by family type. The table shows an increase in those who live in households with children amongst the poorest in our society, particularly in households where there is only one adult. In 1961–3, 48 per cent of the poor were

---

[2] The AHC figures tell a similar story, though the levels are slightly higher.

Table 15.2 Changes in the composition of the bottom quintile by family type

	1961–63	1971–73	1981–83	1991–93
Pensioner couple	17	20	15	13
Single pensioner	17	19	12	10
Couple with children	43	36	43	37
Couple without children	8	9	8	11
Single with children	5	8	9	15
Single without children	10	8	13	14

Source: Goodman, Johnson and Webb (1997), Table 3.5.
Note: Percentage of individuals.

in households with children, and nearly 90 per cent of these were in households that consisted of couples with children. In 1991–3, 52 per cent of the poor were in households with children, and nearly 30 per cent of these were in single adult households. As the poor come increasingly from households where there are children, the proportion of the poor who are in pensioner households has fallen. In 1961–3, 34 per cent of the poorest people were in pensioner households; the comparable figure in 1991–3 was just 23 per cent.

We can also cut the data the other way and look at how many of each type of household are poor. This gives an idea of the relative risk of poverty in each household type. Table 15.3 shows the percentages of various family types that are poor. Well over half of single parent families had incomes below average in 1992–3. The next most over-represented groups are single pensioners and children, over a third of whom were poor (AHC). Comparison of the 1979 with the 1992–3 data again shows the major deterioration in the position of lone parents relative to other groups. In 1979, 16 per cent of single individuals living with children were poor. In 1992–3, 43 per cent of these households were poor. The rise is even more dramatic when measured

Table 15.3 Percentages of family types with incomes below half the contemporary mean

	Before housing costs		After housing costs	
	1979	1992–93	1979	1992–93
Pensioner couple	16	25	21	26
Single pensioner	16	25	12	36
Couple with children	7	20	8	24
Couple without children	4	10	5	12
Single with children	16	43	19	58
Single without children	6	18	7	22
All family types	8	20	9	25

Source: Goodman, Johnson and Webb (1997), Table 8.8.
Note: Percentage of families.

in terms of incomes after housing costs. However, the table also shows that
no family types escaped the rise in poverty in the 1980s. In 1979, only 4 per
cent of couples under pensioner age who were without children were poor.
In 1992–3 this number had risen to 10 per cent.

Poverty by economic (labour market) group

Table 15.4 breaks down poverty by economic status. Apart from the quarter
of the poorest who are in households with the head or spouse over 60,
another 43 per cent have no earnings. These are the workless households that
are the focus of Chapter 5. They consist of the unemployed, the long-term
sick and disabled and lone parents out of work. Hence two-thirds of the
poorest fifth of the population are in a household without a wage. This pattern has also changed over time. Table 15.5 shows that those who were
retired accounted for almost half the poor (defined as the bottom 10 per cent)
in 1961–3, while those who had no work because they were unemployed
accounted for 6 per cent of the poor. By 1991–3 those who had retired
accounted for only a fifth of the poor, while the unemployed accounted for
31 per cent and other workless non-pensioner households (mainly lone parents and the sick) added another 18 per cent. The table also shows that the
self-employed form a significant proportion of the poorest group, a proportion that has doubled since 1961–3.

Table 15.4 Composition of the bottom quintile by economic status of household,
1994/5

One or more self-employed	Single or couple, all full-time work	Other couple with earnings	Part-time work only	Head or spouse aged 60+	Head or spouse unemployed	Other workless
9.9	2.3	10.9	10.1	23.5	19.2	24.1

Source: Hills (1998), Figure 8.
Note: Percentage of individuals.

Table 15.5 Composition of the bottom decile by economic status

	1961–63	1971–73	1981–83	1991–93
working	18	20	19	16
self-employed	8	7	10	15
unemployed	6	13	34	31
other workless	21	17	14	18
over 60	47	48	23	20

Source: Goodman, Johnson and Webb (1997), Table 3.6.
Note: Percentage of individuals. Working includes households where at least one individual is working at least part-time. Other workless mainly includes the sick and disabled and lone parents.

These changes in the composition of the poor do not necessarily imply similar changes in the risk of becoming poor since the composition of the population as a whole has also changed. The number of self-employed has risen, the number aged over 60 has risen, and so has the number of female workers and households headed by single women. Perhaps most dramatically, the number of people in the traditional single earner couple has fallen, from around 35 per cent of families in 1961 to about 15 per cent by 1991 (see Goodman, Johnson and Webb, 1997: Figure 3.8). In fact, Goodman, Johnson and Webb (1997) have shown that as a result the changes in poverty risk are sometimes surprising. While the proportion of the poorest that are unemployed rose substantially, the chance that any particular unemployed person would be amongst the poorest actually fell. There has also been a fall in the chance of any pensioner household being poor. On the other hand, the relative risk of poverty rose amongst those in work, both for the employed and the self-employed. After spending most of the 1960s being slightly under-represented in the poorest decile, the self-employed were 1.5 times more likely to be poor than not poor by the end of the 1980s. This could in part reflect a change in the type of people who are self-employed. Substantial numbers of people became self-employed in response to the high unemployment of the 1980s, and they may as a group have been less suited to this than those choosing self-employment in easier times.

Poverty by gender: the feminisation of poverty?

There have been counteracting trends affecting the representation of women amongst the poor. Demographic trends have worked toward increasing poverty amongst women. The rising numbers of single parent households are predominantly headed by women. Labour market developments have been more positive, with rising female participation rates and rising relative wages, which should help to reduce poverty (see Chapter 10).

The United States has experienced a feminisation of poverty, a rise in the proportion of the poor who are female, particularly women who are single parents (see Fuchs, 1988). The increase in the number of single parent families headed by women, and the increase in the number of poor who are in one parent families (see Table 15.1), might indicate that the same is happening in the United Kingdom. Davies and Joshi (1998) analyse the Family Expenditure Survey for five selected years between 1968 and 1990 and show that well over half the poor individuals and poor adults were female, and over 40 per cent of poor families had a female head of household. However, the overall trend has seen a small decrease in women's poverty. In 1968, around 60 per cent of the bottom fifth were female. In 1990 women accounted for about 55 per cent of the bottom quintile, with most of the fall occurring between 1977 and 1983. The decline in the percentage of poor families headed by women occurred in spite of an increase in the share of female-headed families in the population.

Davies and Joshi (1998) also show that between 1986 and 1990 female-headed households accounted for a larger proportion of the bottom quintile than either couples or single men,[3] but that the bottom quintile has become increasingly composed of unmarried men under 65 years of age. These single men replaced some of the single women in the bottom quintile, particularly between 1977 and 1983. Davies and Joshi also examine the proportion of the poor accounted for by non-elderly families, split into single women, single men and couples. While the absolute importance of households headed by single women rose over the period, the pattern in terms of absolute contribution for single-men-headed households is the same. The *relative* importance of single-male-headed households compared to single-women-headed households actually rose.

Table 15.6 gives the risk of being in the bottom quintile of the income distribution for women relative to men. The overall picture is one in which women are at greater risk of being in poverty than men, with their relative position improving during the late 1970s and early 1980s, and worsening slightly thereafter.

Table 15.6   Risk of being in the lowest quintile of the income distribution: women relative to men

	All women (relative to all men)	Adult women (relative to adult men)	Female heads of families (relative to male heads)
1968	1.45	1.57	3.16
1977	1.35	1.43	2.63
1983	1.09	1.12	1.84
1986	1.11	1.18	1.88
1990	1.22	1.25	2.08

Source: Davies and Joshi (1998), Table 9.

The relationship between poverty, employment and household formation

The evidence discussed above shows that the poverty rate in the United Kingdom has grown dramatically over the past twenty years. In this section we look at the relationship between the aggregate poverty rate and a set of variables that are often included in popular explanations of poverty. The following figures show that in fact these relationships are actually quite complex.

---

[3] See Davies and Joshi (1998: Figure 3a).

First, we consider national income, GDP. It seems straightforward that as the country gets richer, poverty should fall. Growth is often, perhaps implicitly, the core anti-poverty policy. However, this statement applies to poverty measured against a constant benchmark; using a relative standard, the relationship between poverty and GDP depends on the *distribution* of household income. If there is no change in the distribution, relative poverty should not change with growth. In fact, as Figure 15.2a shows, the reality is more complicated. Over

Figure 15.2a   Poverty and GDP

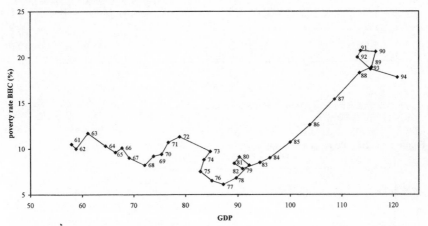

Source: GDP from *Annual Abstract of Statistics*, various issues, Office for National Statistics.

Figure 15.2b   Poverty and unemployment

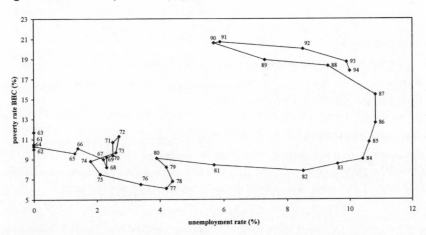

Source: Unemployment rates from *Annual Abstract of Statistics*, various issues, Office for National Statistics.

Figure 15.2c   Poverty and marriage rates

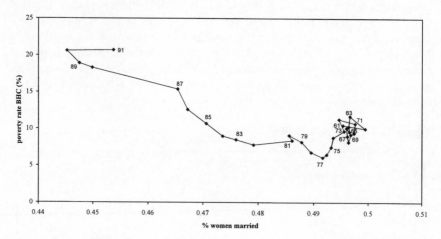

Source: Marriage rates from General Household Survey.

Figure 15.2d   Poverty and male earnings dispersion

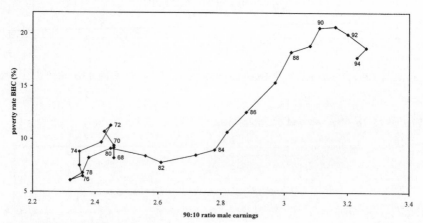

Source: Male earnings dispersion from Hills (1998).

the period 1961–79 there is a negative relationship between GDP and poverty, albeit one with a number of shifts. But thereafter poverty has *risen* with GDP until the negative slope is restored from 1992. This makes the point very clearly that other factors are involved in the determination of poverty rates.[4]

---

[4] Similarly, in the United States it is established that economic growth reduces poverty for whites, but neither change in unemployment nor in real GNP have a significant impact on mobility out of poverty for households headed by blacks (Huff-Stevens, 1994).

Another plausible determinant of poverty rates is unemployment. The aggregate unemployment rate is graphed against the poverty rate in Figure 15.2b. The picture indicates a complex relationship; most noticeably, from 1979 to 1984 unemployment almost triples yet poverty barely changes. Plotting poverty against the proportion of workless individuals or households reveals a similarly complex picture. While joblessness is an important part of the poverty problem at an individual level, this picture suggests caution in linking much of the rise in poverty *rates* to the rise in unemployment.

As we have stressed, demographic factors are as important a part of poverty as labour market factors. Figure 15.2c graphs the poverty rate against the marriage rate (the proportion of women who are married). As we move from the 1960s and 1970s data in the bottom right hand corner of the picture through the 1980s the marriage rate falls and poverty rises. While there is no automatic link between the percentage of women who are married and poverty, increasing divorce and separation has meant a rise in the number of households headed by single adults. Given that these households tend to have access to less resources, a negative relationship between the marriage rate and poverty might be expected. Indeed the rising importance of single parents amongst the poor was noted above. We return to the importance of modelling demographic change as part of an understanding of poverty below.

Finally, Figure 15.2d plots the well-documented rise in the dispersion of earnings against poverty. These figures show that as earnings dispersion has increased, so has poverty. This factor explains the perverse relationship of poverty to GDP in the 1980s. The rise in national income was highly concentrated amongst the rich. This concentration, plus the use of half mean earnings as the poverty line, ensures that poverty so defined will rise. The rise in earnings dispersion in the 1980s seems likely to be one of the factors in explaining the rise in poverty over that period in the United Kingdom and the United States. But although this is a popular explanation for the rise in poverty and similar trends are observed in the United States, detailed analysis by Burtless (1998) has shown that, at least for the United States, it has actually played only a minor role.

Poverty dynamics[5]

Much of the popular and policy debate on poverty understandably focuses on those people who are poor at the time. This would be appropriate if poverty (and non-poverty) was essentially a permanent state of affairs. But taking a wider view, the stock of people in poverty at any point in time is clearly driven by two processes: the chance of falling into poverty and the chance of

[5] Much of the UK evidence reviewed here comes from Jarvis and Jenkins (1996).

subsequently escaping. An analysis from this dynamic perspective reveals much about the nature of poverty, and more fundamentally, about its causes.

The statistics above show that around a fifth of individuals in Britain are currently in poverty. At one extreme a mean poverty rate of 20 per cent may mean that those same 20 per cent of individuals are always poor, at the other every individual may have a one-in-five chance of being poor at any time. The extent to which poverty is a problem is clearly dependent on which of these is closer to the truth. To answer this question requires longitudinal data: that is, a survey that follows individuals over time and determines their poverty status. Figures for the United States indicate considerable differences between the stock of individuals who are poor at any one time and the number who are frequently in poverty over a 'lifetime'. Bane and Ellwood (1986) found most poverty spells in the 1970s (1971–81) in the United States were short: 45 per cent of spells ended within a year and 70 per cent of the spells were over within three years. Using US data on individuals aged between 14 and 30 in the 1980s, Burgess and Propper (1997) found that an average poverty rate of 13 per cent masked considerable differences between individuals: 40 per cent of individuals were poor at least once during thirteen years, but 4 per cent were poor for at least ten years out of thirteen.

Poverty dynamics in the United Kingdom

Until recently, lack of data meant that relatively little has been known about poverty dynamics in the United Kingdom, but the advent of the British Household Panel Survey (BHPS) has meant that we are beginning to establish facts about poverty dynamics in the United Kingdom. First, it is clear that any snapshot picture masks mobility. For the period 1990–4 Jarvis and Jenkins (1998) have analysed movements in and out of poverty. If an individual in poverty is defined as having an income (BHC) of less than half the average income in the BHPS at the first interview (wave 1), then almost a third of individuals were poor at least once during the four-year period. For those starting a low income spell, the exit rate within one year is around 54 per cent. Those who leave poverty have a 30 per cent chance of returning within another year. If persistent poverty is defined as being poor in all four of the years 1991–5, then 4.3 per cent of the sample were in persistent poverty.

Second, while there is mobility out of poverty it is generally to a not much higher income level. Table 15.7 gives Jarvis and Jenkins' comparison of the income group of individuals in 1991/2 and 1993/4.[6] The income distribution

---

[6] This table refers to individuals in the BHPS sample with income reported in each year. Income is net of tax, summed over all household members and over all sources of income. It relates to the month prior to the interview. The averaging is intended to reduce measurement error.

Table 15.7 Income mobility

Quintile income group 'W12'	Quintile income group 'W34'					
	Bottom	2	3	4	Top	All
Bottom	64	24	9	2	0	100
2	22	48	22	5	3	100
3	10	20	46	20	4	100
4	3	5	19	53	19	100
Top	1	2	5	20	74	100
All	100	100	100	100	100	

Source: Jarvis and Jenkins (1998), Table 2. BHPS.
Note: The table gives the percentage of individuals in each quintile in averaged waves 1 and 2 moving to the column quintile in averaged waves 3 and 4. Quintile income group 'W34' means quintile income group of the averaged wave 3 and wave 4 income.

is divided into fifths. If there were complete immobility, individuals would never change income group. If movements were random, 20 per cent of each starting group would fall into each ending group. If we define being poor as being in the lowest quintile of the income distribution, the table shows that 64 per cent of those who are poor in 1991/2 are also poor in 1993/4. The table also shows that 88 per cent either remain poor or have moved up only one quintile of the income distribution.

Third, movements in and out of poverty are not random. Low income observations are linked over time. From the four waves of the BHPS, Hills (1998) has compared Jarvis and Jenkins' findings on how often individuals are found in poverty (defined as half average BHPS incomes) with what would be expected if income movements were uncorrelated over time. He shows that in the BHPS 64 per cent of individuals were never in poverty, compared to 41 per cent if poverty inflows and outflows were uncorrelated. Similarly, 14 per cent of individuals are poor three or four times in four years, compared to 2.7 per cent if movements in and out were uncorrelated. These results show how poverty and non-poverty are concentrated in the population. Another way of seeing this is to compare entry and exit rates, into and out of poverty, for all individuals with those for individuals that have been poor (or not poor) for a certain time. Jarvis and Jenkins found that the exit rate from low income after a year on low income is 54 per cent (the figure given above), but for those who are poor for two years this falls slightly to 51 per cent. Amongst those leaving poverty, the poverty re-entry rate after one year out of poverty is 29 per cent, but the re-entry rate after two years out is considerably lower at 11 per cent. There are insufficient data to determine whether this declining exit probability is due to 'duration dependence' (the fact of being poor changes behaviour in such a way as to reduce the chances of escaping) or 'heterogeneity' (those most able to escape do so first, leaving behind those individuals most susceptible to poverty).

Fourth, movements into and out of poverty are associated with employment and family status. Jarvis and Jenkins examine the characteristics of
those who are poor (defined as in the bottom quintile of the income distribution) in all four years for which they were interviewed and compare
these to those who are only poor in the first year of the survey.[7] The 'poor at
wave 1 only' population mostly comprises elderly persons and non-working
families with children. In the 'persistently poor' population there are more
people belonging to lone parent families (26 per cent compared to 17 per
cent) and to non-working families with children (25 per cent compared to 13
per cent). As a result, persistent poverty is more associated with being unemployed or retired than once-off poverty, and there are more dependent children amongst families with persistently low incomes than amongst those
observed as being poor only once.

Income trajectories

Information on income at two points in time can be used to discuss flows into
and out of poverty. But with data on many periods, the number of possible
poverty 'histories' becomes unmanageably large. Transition matrices of the
sort discussed in Table 15.7 provide a compact way of summarising such
information about income dynamics. However, they do not provide a very
intuitive view of the process, nor do they allow for heterogeneity. The transitions are averages over the whole population. An alternative presentation
of the data has been developed by Gardiner and Hills (1998), and involves
classifying individuals into a set of income trajectory types depending on the
evolution of household income over time. Using the BHPS data, the following types were defined on the basis of the number of boundaries crossed and
the general direction of income change: flat, rising, falling, blips and others
(for details, see the original paper). The results are shown in Table 15.8. They
reinforce the idea of substantial income mobility in general: only 40 per cent
of the population have an income profile over four years that is 'flat'. Indeed,
only 60 per cent have what could be described as 'straightforward' income
profiles (flat, rising or falling) – the remaining 40 per cent experiencing substantial and erratic changes in their income. The authors show, however, that
this mobility does not mean that all poverty is transient and therefore of little concern to policy makers. They show that 43 per cent of poverty-years are
spent in the context of 'poor flat' income trajectories. A further 24 per cent
are spent in trajectories characterised as blipping out of poverty or as
repeated poverty. All of these income histories indicate that poverty is a persistent fact of life for most of the poor.

[7] Given that some individuals who were poor only at wave 1 may have been poor before wave
1, and that the analysis uses only four years of data, we might not expect large differences in the
two groups.

Table 15.8 Types of income trajectory

Trajectory type		Percentage of cases	Percentage of low-income observations
Flat	Poor	9.2	43.0
	Non-poor	30.6	1.0
Rising	Out of poverty	4.0	8.8
	Non-poor	6.4	–
Falling	Into poverty	3.3	8.5
	Non-poor	5.3	–
Blips	Out of poverty	3.7	13.3
	Into poverty	4.6	6.7
	Non-poor	15.2	–
Other	Repeated poverty	4.4	11.2
	One-off poverty	5.9	7.6
	Non-poor	7.6	–

Source: Gardiner and Hills (1998).
Note: Income paths or trajectories are categorised on the basis of the number of crossings allowed of income decile boundaries. Details are provided in the source paper.

In summary, the emerging British evidence suggests that, rather than there being a mass of permanently poor, there is considerable movement both in and out of the population in poverty. There is also evidence that poverty persists for a small but not insignificant group. Most of the people who are poor at any point in time will experience a lot of poverty. While no direct comparisons are possible, Jarvis and Jenkins find that persistence in the United Kingdom in the early 1990s may be less than the United States, but more than other northern European countries.[8]

Interpreting these findings

How are we to interpret these facts? At its simplest, poverty depends on the income individuals have. If they are in work this will be determined by their earnings, if not, it will depend upon the level of benefits. Therefore, changes in poverty rates will depend on earnings, the probability of working and income when out of work. As these have changed over the last thirty years, so have those who are poor.

The probability of being poor is, however, about more than lack of earnings. Individuals live in households and poverty is calculated as a function of

[8] Evidence for the international comparisons is from Duncan *et al.* (1993).

household income, since it is assumed that individuals who live in households have access (implicitly equal) to the total income of that household. Therefore, the probability that an individual will be poor will depend not only on her own earnings or benefits, but also on those of others in the household. Household income will depend on the size of the household, the work-related earnings of each member of the household and other sources of income, such as benefits or pensions.

If households were fixed through time, then analysis of the probability of being poor would be relatively easy. The key issue would be the determination of the household labour supply and the level of human capital available to the household. To understand how poverty evolved, we would need to model dynamic processes, such as the labour supply responses of one partner to the other losing a job. Even in this simple case, individual decisions and events have an impact on the poverty status of all household members. So for example, if an individual loses her job, the nature of the benefit system may mean that if her partner has low earnings, it is not worth her partner continuing to work. Modelling the income dynamics of the household (and so poverty dynamics) requires, amongst other things, modelling labour supply in the presence of job loss risk, and the interaction of the benefit system and earned income at a household level.

However, households are not fixed through time. Individuals form, dissolve and then re-form households. For example, young adults leave the parental home, form partnerships, have children, split up and see their own children leave home. These events may occur more than once in an individual's life and in varying sequences. The individuals who make the economic decisions on employment and earnings are being continually sorted into different household groups. These household transitions are influenced by the behaviour of individuals. Thus an economic model of household income (and so of poverty) is a mix of individual decisions taken in a household context, and decisions on household formation. The probability of a single identified individual being poor depends on the income flows into the household in which the individual lives and the household's needs. The aggregate poverty rate for a group of individuals depends on the earnings available to the group, and how the group organises into households. The central components are labour market factors such as labour supply and earnings generation, household formation and dissolution processes such as marriage, divorce and fertility (see Burgess and Propper, 1998). These are the economic processes that constitute the poverty transition process, and on which future research will need to focus.

References

Bane, M. J. and Ellwood, D. T. (1986), 'Slipping into and out of poverty: The dynamics of spells', *Journal of Human Resources*, 21, 1–23.

Burgess, S. and Propper, C. (1997), 'Young Americans and poverty 1979–91', in P. Gregg (ed.), *Jobs, Wages and Poverty: Patterns of Persistence and Mobility in the New Flexible Labour Market*, Centre for Economic Performance, LSE, London.

Burgess, S. and Propper, C. (1998), 'An Economic Model of Household Income Dynamics, with an Application to Poverty Dynamics among American Women', Discussion Paper No. 1830, Centre for Economic Policy Research, London.

Burtless, G. (1998), 'Effect of Growing Wage Disparities and Family Composition Shifts on the Distribution of US Income', mimeo: paper delivered to European Economic Association Conference, Berlin.

Danziger, S. and Gottschalk, P. (1995), *America Unequal*, Harvard University Press, Cambridge, Mass.

Davies, H. and Joshi, H. (1998), 'Gender and income inequality in the UK 1968–1990: The feminization of earnings or of poverty?', *Journal of the Royal Statistical Society*, Series A, 161:1, 33–61.

Further reading

Duncan, G. J. (1984), *Years of Poverty, Years of Plenty*, University of Michigan, Ann Arbor.

Duncan, G. J., Gustafsson, B., Hauser, R., Schmauss, G., Messinger, H., Muffels, R., Nolan, B. and Ray, J. C. (1993), 'Poverty dynamics in eight countries', *Journal of Population Economics*, 6:3, 215–34.

Fuchs, V. R. (1988), *Women's Quest for Economic Equality*, Harvard University Press, Cambridge, Mass.

Gardiner, K. and Hills, J. (1998), 'Policy Implication of New Data on Income Mobility', mimeo, Centre for Analysis of Social Exclusion, LSE, London.

Goodman, A. and Webb, S. (1994), 'For richer, for poorer: The changing distribution of income in the United Kingdom, 1961–1991', IFS Commentary No. 42, Institute of Fiscal Studies.

Goodman, A., Johnson, P. and Webb, S. (1997), *Inequality in the UK*, Oxford University Press, Oxford.

Hills, J. (1998), 'Does income mobility mean that we do not need to worry about poverty?', in A. B. Atkinson and J. Hills (eds), *Exclusion, Employment and Opportunity*, Case Paper 4, Centre for Analysis of Social Exclusion, LSE, London.

Huff-Stevens, A. (1994), 'Persistence in poverty and welfare: the dynamics of poverty spells, updating Bane and Ellwood', *American Economic Review Papers and Proceedings*, 84, 34–7.

Jarvis, S. and Jenkins, S. (1996), 'Marital Splits and Income Changes: Evidence from the British Household Panel Survey', mimeo, ESRC Centre on Micro-Social Change, University of Essex.

Jarvis, S. and Jenkins, S. (1998), 'How much income mobility is there in Britain?', *Economic Journal*, 108, 428–43.

Jenkins and Cowell, F. (1993), 'Dwarfs and Giants in the 1980s: The UK Income Distribution and How it Changed', Discussion Paper 93-03, University College of Swansea.

Index

Note: 'n' after a page reference indicates a note on that page.